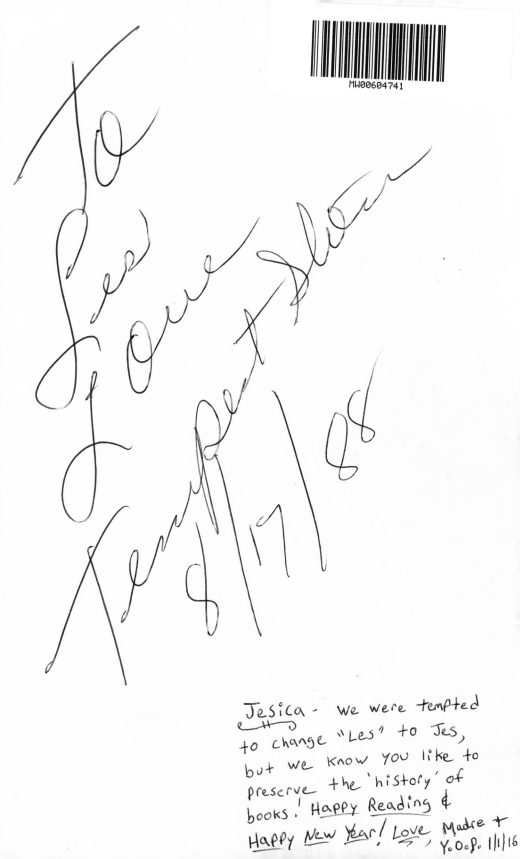

To
Les
Love Sharon
Tempest
8/17/88

Jesica — We were tempted
to change "Les" to Jes,
but we know you like to
preserve the 'history' of
books! Happy Reading &
Happy New Year! Love, Madre +
Y.O.O.P. 1/1/16

# TEMPEST STORM

# TEMPEST STORM

## The Lady Is A Vamp

**TEMPEST STORM with BILL BOYD**

PEACHTREE PUBLISHERS, LTD.

Published by
PEACHTREE PUBLISHERS, LTD.
494 Armour Circle, N.E.
Atlanta, GA 30324

Manufactured in the United States of America

10 9 8 7 6 5 4 3 2 1

Library of Congress Catalog Card Number 87-80974

ISBN 0-934601-25-9

*To burlesque,*
*which made me a star*

*To the wonderful audiences,*
*who, I hope, will finally get to see the real woman*
*behind the naked image*

*For my mother,*
*who knew in her heart I'd make it*

*and*

*For Patty,*
*the best thing*

# The Lady Is A Vamp

# *Prologue*

There are moments in every life when things come completely clear. They don't necessarily stay that way. Complications are bound to happen, even after we experience that wonderful clarity. But those moments are unforgettable. A lifetime of triumph and sorrow, of struggle and reward, takes on meaning, finds a context, that had been missing until that moment.

For me, such a moment came in the spring of 1985. That season found me in the midst of one of my life's greatest battles. I was losing Marty Caplan, the man I loved, to cancer, and as is always the case when we sense somewhere inside ourselves that the battle we are fighting is one that we can't win, my struggle had taken on a desperate quality that was draining me of all energy and hope. It was hard for me to remember that there could be a lower point, a harder struggle, than the one I faced.

To make matters worse, I was not used to losing. My entire life to that point had been a struggle against the poverty and abuse of my childhood, against the insecurities and

i

prejudices that come with being a woman who is on her own and working to make her life better, against the treacheries of love and the pitfalls of romance, against the stigma of being a stripper. In every case, I had prevailed. I had not let the obstacles prevent my becoming what I wanted to be—a class act, a lady who entertained, who made her performances an art, a woman who loved the man she loved with an almost naive faith and trust, who put her all into the relationships in her life. I was a star. I had worked my way to the top of the burlesque world, and I had managed to stay at the top, despite the rise of porno movies and theaters. I had remained successful despite show business's seemingly unstoppable trend toward a brat-pack mentality, a marketing strategy that wrote the performing obituary of artists, especially female artists, who had the misfortune to enter adulthood.

I was a survivor. So why, in April of 1985, did I feel that none of this mattered, that life was bleak and meaningless, the future shorter than yesterday afternoon? Now I think those feelings of defeat and resignation came partly from the terrifying prospect of losing someone I loved very much. It is especially difficult to watch someone die a slow and agonizing death from a debilitating disease. It is almost as if you are forced to watch the death in increments. Piece by piece, your loved one disappears before your eyes. Day by day, the person you have lived for becomes less yours, less present, and there is nothing you can do to reclaim him. He is going, and he will be gone. Those are hard facts to face; they are also inescapable when you are looking into the blank, cold face of cancer.

But, along with the horrors of Marty's death, I was forced to face my own life, to reevaluate, to reconsider my decisions, my choices, my priorities. That kind of examination is not always easy. It was, for me, in fact quite painful. But the reward has been enormous. I have come to know myself and those closest to me better, more wholly, and that knowledge, the reinforcement of that closeness, is the most important thing a person can have. I have come back from that nadir, that terrible valley of 1985, and I now face life with the renewed faith and courage, with the revitalized energy, of a woman reborn.

Appropriately enough, the beginnings of my climb back from the depths of despair came on Easter Sunday of that year. I was alone, under a doctor's care for the nervous tension and stress I had experienced during Marty's illness, and my dying lover was miles away in the fierce grip of his family. The last thing on my mind was the new life this day of the year symbolizes. Then my phone rang.

When I picked up the receiver, a voice said, "Happy Easter, Tempest!"

My response was automatic. I said, "Why, thank you, and happy Easter to you, too." But I was also puzzled. The voice sounded familiar, but I couldn't place it. Finally, I had to ask who it was.

It was my ex-husband, Herb Jeffries. I hadn't spoken with him in several years, and his was the last voice I would have expected to call me with that cheerful greeting.

We chatted briefly, talking about nothing really, the sort of small talk people who have a rich and sometimes difficult past make when they are reaching out, tentatively but hopefully. Then he got around to the real purpose of his call. He put my daughter on the phone.

When she spoke, my entire body went limp. I had not heard her for ten years. Ten years of her life I had spent in silence, not hearing about the school work, the friendships, the dates. I didn't know what color her prom dress had been. I didn't know how she wore her hair. And now she was there, at the other end of the line, and I was hearing her voice.

This may not seem like much to the person who has spent years nagging about homework that doesn't get done, worrying about curfews and driving habits, washing three outfits a day. But to a mother who has not had her child with her, who has lost a decade of those wonderful growing-up years that can never be recaptured, the mere sound of her child's voice is almost too much joy to bear.

Patty, I thought, my baby girl. But I couldn't speak. I was crying, and after she got out a shaky "Hello, Mother," she too was in tears. We struggled to say anything at all. She told me that she and her dad had been talking about the holiday, about families, and she had begun to wonder about her mother, as she often had. Then, without her knowing, her dad was on the phone with me, and the next thing she knew the receiver was in her hand. She didn't have to wonder anymore. Her mother was right there.

Herb told me later that he just figured that it was time, that the two of us had spent too long being afraid to reach out, too long lost to each other, when it was obvious to anybody that we loved each other and wanted to be a part of each other's lives. We needed each other.

That phone call is the greatest gift any man ever gave me. Diamonds, furs, cars—none of them compare to the sound of my daughter's voice. Patty didn't really say much, and neither did I. But words weren't the point. The important thing was that connection. Hard as it was for each of us, we did not let that beginning fade into all the other memories, good and bad, that marked the years of our relationship. We built on it.

Several months later, Patty came to see me, a beautiful, mature woman of twenty-one. She was with me when my lover died. She was there when I broke down with my psychologist and exclaimed that I had nothing to live for. At that moment, very quietly, very bravely, she said, "What about me? You have me."

And I realized that I did have her, a beautiful child, my child, who had come back to me, the bright spot of brilliant light, the ray of hope that had penetrated my deepest despair. I did have something to live for. My life was something of value, and I wanted to share it with this young woman who was reaching out to me, a lifeline for me to cling to, a family for me to cherish.

It would be wrong of me to suggest that the terrible loss of those years apart was instantly forgotten, that all the wounds on both sides miraculously healed. That didn't happen. This is a real story. The important thing is that we began to work on the problems, began to build new foundations, gave ourselves the time that healing takes.

It would be equally false to suggest that finding my child, having her return to my life, solved all my other problems. I had lost the man I loved, the man I had planned to spend the rest of my life with. The manner of his passing was an enormous strain. The circumstances surrounding our years together and his death will always be marred by memories of how others intruded upon the most private and personal of relationships and prevented our being able to comfort and support each other as we would have, had we been left alone.

Other relationships had also left scars, other memories, ones that long preceded the events that sent me tumbling into despair in 1985, came to the surface and had to be dealt with, and, all the while, the pressures of my career, of earning a living and maintaining my self-imposed high standard of performance, continued.

But after that phone call on Easter Sunday and my reunion with Patty, I always had a purpose, a reason to keep going, to keep working toward a deeper understanding of myself and my experiences. I wanted her to know me, just as I wanted to know her. I wanted to see the dress she wore to her first prom. I wanted her to see me on the stage at Carnegie Hall. And so I began to tell her stories, the story of my life.

Part of that story is the story of a star, and I hope Patty will be as proud of that part of my life as I am. I remember walking with her in a mall once years ago. Herb and I had taken her along on a shopping trip, and we were walking just ahead of her, letting her dawdle and take in whatever caught her eye as we passed the stores.

In her excitement and wonder, she kept stepping on my heels. I turned to her and said quietly, "Honey, don't step on Mommy's heels, please. That hurts."

She looked me up and down, sizing up the reasons I might be mentioning this behavior to her. Then she said, with all the wisdom of her seven or eight years, "I see, the great Tempest Storm doesn't want to be upstaged."

I want her to know about my years on that stage she was so aware of, my successes, what I feel are my contributions to my profession. Any mother wants her child to understand her work.

But another part of my story is the story of a woman who happens to be in show business, who happens to have lived a public life. Yet, like all women, she has a private life. She has loved and lost, loved wisely and not so well. She has a childhood back there, filled with memories that are not the best, memories that her own child might now better understand. And she has hopes for the future, a future that she plans to make come true, just as she has made so many other dreams come true.

I want Patty to know both women, the public and the private Tempest Storm. I want her to understand how I lived so much of my life unclothed before a world that refused to see the real me, the woman beyond the performance, because of the stigma of my profession. As I have looked to find that real self, I have been amazed at much that has happened. I want to share that amazement.

I have too much to live for, not to tell about it.

# One

Finding out that Leonard Miller, Sr., was not my natural father shocked and upset me. I wasn't old enough to understand the difference in our surnames. I had been born Annie Blanche Banks, and Mother never changed my name to Miller even though she could have done so to avoid the inevitable explanation about my stepfather. That revelation is my earliest recollection from childhood.

I remember running, at age five or so, down the road to meet the man I thought of as my father when he came home from the fields where he sharecropped. I'd shout "Daddy! Daddy! Daddy!" as I ran. And there was something good and reassuring about having him pick me up, sit me on his shoulders and carry me to the house.

My Aunt Edna was the one who told me the truth. One day when I was announcing his arrival with my usual "Daddy! Daddy! Daddy!" she said, "That isn't your real father. He ran away a long time ago."

1

For a moment, I was speechless. Then I protested angrily, "He is my daddy!"

"No, he isn't," she said, and she looked at my mother. "Doesn't this child know he isn't her real father?"

My mother was shocked and uncomfortable, and she scolded Aunt Edna for ever bringing the subject up. Mother said she would've told me when I was grown up, when she thought I was old enough to understand.

I was devastated by this news. I couldn't sleep for several nights. When I did finally accept the fact that he wasn't my father, I began asking questions about the man who was and saying I wanted to see him. However, my mother refused to talk about him. She'd say, "Hush, child, don't worry about him. He's gone, and he will never come back." She'd gesture to my stepfather and say, "Just act like he's your real father, and everything will be all right."

But nothing was ever really right again at home. My step-father never seemed as warm and friendly and understand-ing after that. Maybe he changed or maybe I did. But, in many ways, his fatherly image was gone forever, and my life was irrevocably changed. I became a woman who would always search for the security and warmth that were snatched away from her before she reached the age of six.

After I started school, my stepfather expected me to do more and more chores around home. I became a real whiz at washing dishes, scrubbing clothes, even cooking. It wasn't difficult to become good at these things. I had plenty of practice. If I didn't work diligently, my stepfather would say, "I won't have a lazy person in my house. If you don't earn your keep, we'll have to find someplace else for you to stay." With that threat came dreams that I was without a home, wandering alone and cold in some strange place. Sometimes, I'd wake up, frightened that I would not be allowed to stay with my mother.

The older I became, the more I was expected to do. One of my most distasteful duties was killing the chickens we ate. I

2

hated that task more than any other, but I wouldn't stoop to begging my stepfather to escape doing it. I often cooked 'possum and sweet potatoes, but I never liked what I cooked. 'Possum and rabbit were gourmet foods at the time, far better than bean soup or pot likker, my stepfather said. But I longed for the day I'd never see another 'possum in a pan.

We made our own soap in a big iron pot in the backyard. We didn't have electricity or indoor plumbing. We washed clothes and ourselves in tin washtubs. I also learned to hoe cotton in the summer and pick it in the fall. I made fifty cents a day. It was hard work, backbreaking work. My half-brother, Jimmy, was born when I was seven, and I became a babysitter as well as a maid. Gradually, the thought of being someplace else wasn't frightening anymore. The harder I was forced to work, the more attractive leaving seemed.

For all I did, I drew little praise. In fact, it irked my stepfather that I couldn't pick or hoe more cotton than I did, and he didn't hesitate to let me know he was unhappy with me.

"You eat too much, Blanche," he'd say. "You eat a lot more than you earn. If you don't work harder tomorrow, you'll just have to eat less. That might not be a bad idea anyhow. I wouldn't want you to get all fat and sassy." Again, my stepfather's attitudes, his harsh demands and his refusal to praise and reward, probably had profound impact on my adult years, when praise, adulation, and handsome rewards seemed not so much luxuries as necessities to me.

When my stepfather talked to me in harsh tones with an odd look in his cold eyes, I knew he'd been back up in the pine grove where he had a small whiskey still. His drinking problem was a fact of life for our family. Of course, as I grew older, I learned to stay away from him after he'd been back at the still.

The worst of his drinking bouts came at the worst of times. When I was eight years old, my little brother, Calvin, died. He was just sixteen months old, and my mother was naturally very distressed at losing one of her children. I tried to comfort her, but my stepfather didn't. He drank until he couldn't stand up. Calvin was "laid out" in our home, as was the custom in Georgia at the time. But my stepfather showed no respect for Calvin or for my mother and her feelings. He never drew a sober breath between Calvin's death and the funeral.

Such terrible insensitivity should have made me understand what kind of man Leonard Miller was, but I was only a child and couldn't see what others, older and wiser, might have. Not until the summer after I finished seventh grade did I truly comprehend just how bad things could get in my home.

The early morning coolness was the only relief from the summer heat on a Georgia sharecropper's farm in the 1940s. It was in this pleasant beginning of a Saturday morning that I decided to wear the new white dress that had been a seventh-grade homemaking project.

I was proud of it. And I wanted that Saturday to be as perfect as the fit of the white dress. I wanted people to see it on me, Annie Blanche Banks, and I wanted them to admire it. Like most young girls, I was a little frightened about the changes taking place in my body, but, as most girls are, I was also secretly pleased with the transformation from girl to woman. I felt good about myself in that dress, and I wanted others to feel good about me, too.

But as I stood smoothing the skirt down in front of the only mirror in our cramped four-room house, the harsh tone of my stepfather's voice shattered the morning stillness. He was angry about the amount of time I had taken getting ready and hollering about what he called "lollygagging," which took in everything that wasn't exactly to his liking. On that particular morning, he was especially abusive in the way he talked to me. Even though he saw that I was wearing the nicest dress I owned, he insisted that I help hitch up the mule. So the day began with my hopes of being appreciated for my budding beauty dashed by my stepfather's inconsiderate treatment. He made me feel worthless and insecure.

"Look at you," he'd often say. "You can't wait to get to town and parade around for the young bucks, can you? Blanche, I'm worried about you, girl. You're gonna fall in with the wrong company and . . . aw, hell, c'mon out here and help me get the mule hitched up."

As usual, any concern, real or not, dissolved into a demand for work. He went out the door, and I followed. I didn't like the idea of helping to hitch up an ornery mule with my new dress on. The animal was dirty and stubborn and mean, and I didn't want to get near it. I wanted to argue, but it was better to take a chance on getting the dress soiled than to upset my stepfather. If he got mad at me, my mother would take sides with him, and I'd catch the devil for sure. I was careful, the mule was soon hitched to the farm wagon without my spoiling my dress, and we were ready for the five-mile ride to Eastman.

As my stepfather climbed up to the seat of the wagon, he laughed because I'd placed a folded blanket on the back of the wagon to sit on so I wouldn't get the dress smudged. Mother glanced back at me but didn't say anything. Like always, she climbed up next to Daddy on the front seat and put three-year-old Janice between them. Jimmy, who was seven years old, stood behind them, held on to the seat and listened to their conversation. As we moved off, I had some time to myself.

My mind shut out the jolting of the wagon, the conversation from the front seat, everything. My thoughts drifted easily to my friend, Betty Mae. I wished she could see the white dress on me. After all, she had helped me with the final alterations in homemaking class.

I liked Betty Mae very much even though she had a bad reputation. Kids at school said all sorts of things about her. Some whispered that she stayed out all night in a car with her boyfriend. Some said she could cuss like a sailor, but I'd never heard her say anything really bad. However, anytime I mentioned Betty Mae's name when Mother could hear, she'd fly off the handle and sternly warn me to stay away from her. Even though Betty Mae lived less than a mile away—closer to us than any other girl near my age—I seldom saw her except for the bus ride to school and in homemaking class.

Betty Mae was two years older than I but just a year ahead of me in school because she'd failed one grade. In a way, she was like the older sister I didn't have at home. We could talk. That's more than I could say for most of the kids at school. They liked to tease me about my large bust and crooked teeth. Because of that, I wore very tight brassieres and smiled very little. I talked even less. But Betty Mae was comfortable to be around. She had a large bust, too, so I didn't feel different. I wasn't so conscious of my crooked teeth, either, because I sensed that Betty Mae wasn't about to judge me on my teeth. I smiled more around her than I did around anyone else. With her, I felt happy and accepted.

As the wagon bumped along the shoulder of the highway to Eastman, I swung my legs off the back and thought about my last meeting with Betty Mae. Two weeks before that Saturday morning trip to Eastman, Mother had sent me up the road to borrow a cup of sugar from Betty Mae's mother. Even though it was hot and humid, I didn't mind the long walk because I looked forward to seeing Betty Mae. I hadn't seen her since school was out a month earlier.

She was just as happy to see me, shouting from the front porch when she saw me coming up the dirt road. She couldn't believe that I'd come to see her. I think she knew how my mother—and most mothers, for that matter—felt about her. I told her that my mother needed to borrow a cup of sugar, and naturally, she begged me to stay a few minutes to talk about what had happened since school let out. She told me how much she'd missed seeing me. I smiled and squeezed her hand.

She poured the cup of sugar and set it on the kitchen table. Then she picked up a magazine about movie stars and showed me the cover. Betty Mae and I shared a fantasy about going to Hollywood and becoming movie stars. We often talked about how we'd live once we'd made it in show business, about the fancy clothes, the big cars, and handsome men who would fill our days and end our poverty and boredom. Once we were stars, we were sure, we'd never feel out of place or lonely again.

She gave me the magazine, saying she'd already read it from cover to cover three or four times. Then she suggested that we go outside and sit under a giant oak shade tree where it was cooler and we could talk without her mother's overhearing everything we said. We were smart enough to know that people around Eastman, especially our mothers, would just laugh at our dreams, call us silly, and tell us to get back to our chores. Only when we were alone could we let our imaginations take over and transport us across the country to the place we really belonged—Hollywood.

She picked up a comb and ran it through her long hair as we walked outside. We sat on a couple of old chairs and gazed out at the fields. After a moment of just sitting there, she glanced at the house, lowered her voice and told me that things were not going well at home. She said she'd been fighting with her folks—again.

"I tell you, Blanche, I gotta get outta here."

"What do you mean, get out of here? You mean you're going to run away?"

"Maybe. I've got to do something. I'm just so durn tired of the way things are here. I want to go somewhere, do something, be somebody. I can't stay on this farm much longer. I just can't."

I asked her about her new boyfriend, the one she'd been telling me about just before the end of school. She smiled dreamily and told me how much she liked the guy. And she said he was willing to run away with her. But they had no money, no place to stay, no job and very little chance of getting one.

I remember the brazen statement she made about how she'd like to be in a fancy hotel room, making love endlessly. I laughed to keep from showing my embarrassment, but she went on talking shamelessly about such an adventure. She said making love was the most exciting thing she'd ever done.

I certainly didn't have any experience to allow me to agree or disagree with her on this point, but I've often wondered if it was this conversation with Betty Mae that linked men and sex so closely to the rest of my dream. I was young and impressionable, and I really trusted Betty Mae and looked up to her. I may have listened too closely. On this day, I steered the conversation back to running away. I'd thought about that, too, and I wanted to find out if she had a plan.

"I'm nothing but a maid," I told her. "All I've done since school let out is do laundry, scrub floors, wash dishes and look after the little ones. I'm just plain sick of it. But I don't know what else I could do. I don't know if anyone would hire me if I left home. In fact, I don't even know what kind of job I could possibly do."

"Scrub floors, change diapers . . ."

We laughed together. "Yes, I can certainly do those things."

We talked some more about running away. Then the conversation turned to Hollywood and being a movie star. If we were going to run away, we agreed that Hollywood would be the obvious destination for both of us. We talked about how nice it would be to have fine clothes, big cars and people to wait on us. "I could even have someone to scrub those clothes," I said.

"People in Hollywood don't scrub clothes, Blanche. They have washing machines like that one I saw over at Mrs. Varnadoe's house. That sure was a nice machine."

8

I threw in my wish for a personal hairdresser so I could get my hair done three times a day if I wanted. That jogged Betty Mae's memory about something. She'd seen a new style in one of the magazines and wanted to try it out on me. Betty Mae worked for perhaps half an hour on my hair, combing, curling and pinning it. Besides our dreams and frustrations, we shared a love for stylish hairdos, and we both spent a lot of time getting our hair exactly right. Because we did, we always looked nicer than even the rich girls in our school.

We became so deeply engrossed in our dreaming and our grooming that time slipped away from us. When we finally walked back into her house, I looked at the clock and saw that more than two hours had passed since I'd left home. I was frantic.

"Oh, God, Betty Mae! The time! Mother will kill me!"

We said a hasty farewell. Then I grabbed the cup of sugar and ran as fast as I could without spilling it. Mother was waiting for me at the front door, impatiently tapping her foot and demanding an explanation.

Breathless from running, I tried to explain that Betty Mae and I had just been visiting. At the mention of Betty Mae's name, anger blazed in Mother's eyes.

"Talking to Betty Mae?" she asked, her voice rising. "Talking to Betty Mae, the whore? I sent you to borrow a cup of sugar from her mother. I didn't send you to talk to that no-account girl."

I didn't know what a whore was at the time, but I knew it couldn't be anything nice. And I knew I had to try to get Mother to cool down a little.

"Now, Mother," I said, "you don't know Betty Mae . . ."

"That's what sort of girl I've raised, huh? She likes sitting around and talking to a whore? And look at your hair. What do you think you are, a movie star or something? You think you've got all day to play with your hair? There's chores to be done, Blanche."

"Mother . . ."

"You need a good thrashing, Blanche."

I tried to calm her down, but I'd never seen my mother so mad. Still berating Betty Mae as the lowest class of life on this earth, she picked up a slender piece of firewood from beside the kitchen stove and swung it at my backside. I tried to ward off the lick with my left arm. The log struck me sharply. Pain shot upward toward my shoulder.

I begged her to stop hitting me.

"You will not go over there again. Not ever!" she screamed as she swung the piece of firewood a second time. Again, I blocked it, and again pain shot through my arm.

I begged her to stop hitting me as tears streamed down my face. But she swung the stick again and again. She finally quit beating me when she saw blood on my arm. But she didn't apologize.

Through gritted teeth, she said, "Don't ever let me hear of you talking to that girl—that whore—again. Now promise me."

I felt like a traitor to my inner feelings, but, through tears and sobs, I agreed never to talk to Betty Mae again. But I knew I would. I would even if Mother beat me again.

Then I went to the corner of the room where I liked to sit and dream. This time, however, I slumped down into a chair and cried. This time, I didn't dream about Hollywood and lasting fame. I thought about the one person I could talk to, be comfortable with. But Mother absolutely hated Betty Mae, and she wouldn't let me explain my feelings.

To this day, I cannot understand my mother's hostility toward Betty Mae. I suppose she really was afraid that the older girl with the bad reputation would lead me into trouble. But my trouble came without any help from Betty Mae. If my mother had not worked so hard to isolate me from my friend, I might have had someone to turn to later when I really needed a confidante and an advisor.

As it turned out, Mother's attitude toward Betty Mae shut me off from the one person who could have filled that role. In addition, her fierce judgment of Betty Mae, tied, as it was, so directly to her sexual behavior, made me terrified of being judged with equal harshness if I had confided in my mother. Thus, I soon found myself in need of a loving and trusting listener, but my mother's attitudes left me needful and alone.

Sitting there on the tailgate of the wagon on this particular summer Saturday, I rubbed my left arm. The marks from the beating were still sore. I decided that I'd see Betty Mae again—if I didn't run away from home and never come back. Little did I know that the rest of that day would forever change my life in ways even Betty Mae could not have imagined.

Eastman bored me. It was small, sleepy and unexciting. Nothing ever happened there. Daddy tied the mule to a small tree near the back of the grocery store. Then he looked hard at me and warned me against wandering off where they couldn't find me because they might need some help with the kids.

The kids. All I ever heard from him was "Blanche, look after the kids." Or "Blanche, you eat too much." Or "Blanche, don't put on all of that damned makeup."

Good old Blanche. She always had to look after the kids. Well, right then, I wanted an ice cream cone. I had a dime, so I told Mother and Daddy I wouldn't be far away and started walking toward the ice cream stand.

The kid behind the counter hailed me in a way that was typical of the greetings I got from my schoolmates. He said something like, "Well, looky here. If it isn't old top-heavy herself, Blanche Banks."

Of course everyone in the place looked at me. Some snickered. I knew my face was as red as a beet because I never got over being hurt and embarrassed when my classmates called attention to my breasts. Still, I was too proud and stubborn to reveal how I really felt. So I told him to shut up and give me an ice cream cone. When I got it, all I could think of was getting away from that crowd. It felt like every eye in the place was on my chest.

After making what I hoped was a graceful exit that belied my inner shame, I walked slowly along Main Street and ate the ice cream. Then I turned down a side street and saw handsome Johnny down the block. He was tall and muscular and blond, and he was one of the most popular boys in school. Girls swooned over him. All of them wanted to date him even though he stayed in trouble most of the time. I heard talk that his father spent a lot of time and money keeping him out of deep trouble.

But he was a senior, and he was handsome. To that day, he'd never acknowledged that I, a soon-to-be eighth-grader, even existed. But on this day, he acted interested in me. I felt a faint hope that he would be different from the guy at the ice cream stand and the crowd who laughed at his crude joke. I dreamed for a second that handsome Johnny was seeing the girl I had seen in that broken old mirror earlier that day, a girl young and innocent and pretty, dressed in her freshest, prettiest white dress, sweet enough to be on her way to her first communion.

He was standing with four other guys—a man of about thirty years old who drove a taxi in Eastman and three teenagers I didn't know. He asked me where I was going. I walked toward him, saying that I was just walking around town.

He said that, considering the heat, riding would be a whole lot more fun than walking. He gestured to the car he was leaning on and asked if I wanted to go for a ride. For a moment, I was flattered that he wanted to be around me. After all, cars played a big part in the aspirations of this young girl who still had to come to town with her legs dangling off the back of a mule-drawn wagon. Then I remembered the talk about him. Some of the girls said he would go out with any girl who put out. Did he think I would?

Well, he had another think coming. Blanche Banks did not put out.

He asked again if I wanted to go for a ride. I shook my head and told him that I had to get back to the wagon and look after the kids for Mother and Daddy. He suddenly grabbed my arm and said, "Well, by golly, we are going for a ride. Right now! Let's go, you guys!"

With one quick yank on my arm, he pulled me into the back seat of the car. Stupidly, I asked how we were going for a ride in the back seat of the car. He said we could because all four of the other guys were going, too. He shouted for the older man, whom he called Charlie, to get the car started.

A cold, sickening fear gripped me when I realized what he meant. I tried to get out the opposite door, but one of the boys was pushing me back and getting in. The other two piled into the front with Charlie.

The car started rolling, and Johnny said they were taking me out into the hills "for a little fun—with all of us."

As the car began to move down the street, my mind said they weren't really going to do anything. Why, people would get put in jail for what Johnny was suggesting that they were going to do. I told Johnny just that.

Johnny put an arm around me and clamped a hand over one of my breasts. He told me to relax and enjoy it. He said that a girl in McRae had accommodated all five of them and she was all right.

The most terrifying fear I'd ever felt gripped me, and I wanted to strike out. I used my elbow and cracked Johnny a blow to the nose. I didn't hit him very hard, but almost instantly blood came gushing down over his mouth.

He cursed loudly as I glanced out the window. We were already leaving the business district. I wanted to scream, but before I could open my mouth, something cracked sharply against the side of my face. He had slapped me, and he said that what was going to happen to me would be worse than a bloody nose.

Another stinging blow numbed the side of my face. My head spun, and I almost passed out. When my eyesight cleared, I saw him holding a handkerchief to his nose, and I could hear his cursing.

I decided to try another tack. I told him that I was sorry about his nose and that I would try to help get the bleeding stopped. He swore at me and told me to get away from him. As he talked through the handkerchief, his threats about what lay in store for me became more graphic, more depraved, more unbelievable.

Chills ran up my spine as he gave me a cold, hard stare over the handkerchief. I bit my lip to keep from uttering the words that almost spilled out at that moment. I wanted to tell them that I was a virgin, that I was just in junior high, that I was much too young for anything they intended to do. But, somehow, I knew that such an admission might only make it worse for me. Maybe they would find my inexperience funny. Maybe they would like the idea that I was a virgin and enjoy themselves more. Nothing I could say would help me.

I panicked. I didn't know what to do. I knew I couldn't fight them all, and I didn't see any way to gain sympathy or an ally. As the car rumbled along a country road and Johnny tried to stop his nose from bleeding, the others joked and laughed about what they wanted to do to me. They were clearly looking forward to a good time. An empty, helpless feeling settled in my stomach, and I thought I might be sick. Then I wondered if I might be able to run when the car stopped. I was pretty quick on my feet. Maybe I could . . .

There is no way for a young, inexperienced girl to take control of such a situation. I couldn't really comprehend what was happening. But my mind kept grasping at even the feeblest hope of escape.

The car rolled to a stop in a clearing in a pine grove just off the main road. Johnny's nose had stopped bleeding. He looked at me coldly and told me to get out. I tried to apologize again for busting his nose. Then I tried begging. The cab driver had walked around the car and opened the door. Johnny got out and pulled me by the arm.

I kept begging them, looking at each of them for some hint of alliance, somebody to side with me, to tell them to leave me alone and take me back to town. But none of them showed even a flicker of compassion for me.

Johnny pulled me forcibly from the car. As my feet hit the ground, I made one desperate effort to get away. I broke free and ran for the pine forest. I took only about five steps before a battering ram hit me at the small of my back. Someone had tackled me. In spite of a bed of pine needles, I hit the ground like a sack of feed. The wind rushed from my lungs. I gasped for air.

Brutal hands turned me onto my back and began tearing my clothes from me. I made a desperate grab for my last garment. Then it was gone.

There was no escape.

On the ride back to town, I tried to comprehend what had happened to me. Now, I realize that I was merely a child and that I was incapable of true understanding. I'd been raped— brutally—by five men, one right after the other. They'd hurt me, physically and emotionally. The scars from that hurt would last a lifetime, I knew, but I couldn't know the ways in which that pain would manifest itself for years to come.

I'd heard about doing the things they'd forced me to do. To hear Betty Mae talk about sex, it was fun. But my experience had been a painful nightmare from which I couldn't seem to wake up. In fact, I felt like sleepwalkers must feel. I was moving. My senses were working. But I was not in control. I was not even fully aware.

I wondered what the police would say when I told them.

As if he were reading my mind, Johnny told the driver, Charlie, to pull the car off the road, that he wanted to talk to me. At first, I thought they were going to start all over with me, and I started to beg hysterically. I would do anything if they just wouldn't touch me.

"Shut up and listen, Blanche," he said as the car stopped. "We're through with you. We're going to let you off in town in a minute. But I want you to think about something before we let you go. Are you listening?"

I nodded. I would have done anything, said anything, at that moment just to get away from them.

Johnny grabbed me roughly by the chin, turned my face toward him and said, "If you go blabbing about this to anyone—anyone, you understand—you're a dead girl, Blanche."

He looked at me, and I could see real fear in his eyes, maybe worse than the fear I felt right then. I couldn't understand how anyone could be more frightened than I was, but Johnny was certainly scared.

"If you breathe a word about this to anyone, Blanche, you're dead. Do you understand?"

I nodded again, agreeing to anything to get out of that car. Alive. I believed him. Anyone who would do the things he had done to me would probably kill me, too, if he wanted to.

"Listen to me, Blanche," Johnny said. "Do you know this guy?" he said, reaching across me and putting his hand on the arm of the guy they'd called Butch.

I shook my head.

"Of course not, Blanche. Do you know why? He ain't from around here. He's from . . ." He stopped and gave me a crooked, nervous smile. "He's just visiting in Eastman, and he's going to leave as soon as we get back. He's going back to his hometown, Blanche, and if he finds out that I'm in jail, he knows he might end up there, too. He'll come back, Blanche, and he'll kill you. Do you understand that? He'll come back and kill you. He'll have to do that to keep from going to jail himself."

He clutched my jaw between his thumb and fingers and said, "He's mean, Blanche. He's as mean as hell, and he'll cut you open and watch you bleed to death. Show her the knife, Butch."

Butch pulled up the leg of his jeans and drew a knife from his boot. In my terror, it looked a foot long. The sharpened edge of the blade gleamed. He reached toward me and held it close to my throat.

"If you breathe a word about today, Blanche, you're a dead girl. Do you hear me?"

I nodded again. I just wanted to get away from them. I wanted to wash myself, try to mend the white dress they had torn. And go home. For once, home looked better than the outside world. At least I was safe from ruthless men there; at least nobody would demand sex from me.

Home. Oh, God.

I started to cry.

"Don't start that crap with me, Blanche. Crying don't do you no good, girl. It don't mean a damn thing to me. Just tell me if you understand what I'm saying about Butch."

I nodded one more time.

"Don't just nod, damn it. Tell me!" And with that he let go of my jaw and slapped me.

"Yes," I said, still sobbing, "I understand. I won't tell."

"That, by God, is more like it. OK, Charlie, let's go."

Charlie started the car and drove into town.

When I reached the ice cream stand, the smart aleck was gone. Only a girl I knew from school spoke to me. She asked what had happened. I told her it was nothing, that I'd fallen down. And I went into the restroom, hoping that no one else had noticed how I looked. I will never forget the shame that began to emerge from my numbness. What had I done to make this awful thing happen?

Once inside the restroom, I locked the door and stripped my clothes off. I felt unclean, isolated. I stood looking at my face in the little mirror. My eyes were red from crying, and

17

there was the faint outline of a handprint where Johnny had slapped me. I almost started crying again, but I knew someone might hear. So I bit my lip and tried to put the last hour and a half out of my mind. I was sure I'd be better off if no one found out. It was the only way I'd stay alive, I thought, as the image of Butch's cruel face and his gleaming knife passed before me again and again.

I ran some water on my underpants and used them as a washcloth to clean up as best I could. I also washed as much dirt from my white dress as I could. Then I dropped the panties in the trash can and put on my other clothes. A button was torn off the dress, but it probably would go unnoticed. My family tended to notice work I left undone, but they were never very concerned with dirt or tears or missing buttons on my clothes. My looking nice attracted their attention only because it must mean I'd been shirking chores or was putting on airs. I went through the ice cream parlor without anyone's speaking to me.

Back at the wagon, Mother was sitting with the kids on the tailgate. She said they'd been looking all over for me. If she noticed my soiled dress, she didn't let on. I told her I'd been walking around, that I'd fallen down by the railroad tracks and washed up at the ice cream stand. That was good enough for her.

If she'd questioned me right then about the dress and my appearance or if she had noticed the handprint on my face, I might have told her the whole story. But she was more interested in me because I could watch Jimmy and Janice while she went to the drugstore.

After she'd gone, I sat on the back of the wagon and tried to sort out my troubled thoughts. I wanted to tell someone what had happened, but I truly believed I'd die if I did. Besides, I knew Johnny's daddy was a powerful man in the county, and if his son denied raping me, his chances of being believed were better than mine. After all, it was common knowledge that his father had often had to buy

Johnny's way out of trouble. How was I to know that there wasn't a set fee he could pay and have even so serious a charge as rape swept under the carpet?

I thought about telling Mother, but I knew I wouldn't. I could imagine what she'd say: "Well, I told you what would happen if you kept company with that Betty Mae. Now it's happened, and you think we can get the law to do something to that boy?"

I could tell Betty Mae . . . if I ever saw her again. I really didn't expect to see her when school started. I was sure that she'd be gone before then.

Run away. It might be a solution for me, too. But I was scared of that. Why did Annie Blanche Banks have to be scared of so many things? I sat there, wrapped up in hurt, indecision, loneliness.

Then I remembered my dream—to be a movie star. I put the bad thoughts out of my mind, using what I now know was an escape mechanism. Then it seemed like a logical plan. I saw myself up there on the screen as the star opposite Clark Gable. And in my make-believe world, I was rich and famous. I could do anything I wanted . . . and I didn't think about rapists or hurt or loneliness. With money and fame, I could do anything! Such thoughts allowed me to repress the horror of the rape and my own sense of shame and isolation, but while that repression may have helped me deal with the short-term consequences, any psychologist could have predicted that the long-term consequences would be only more a devastating for my not facing reality at the time.

My dreaming was rudely interrupted. Jimmy said he wanted a drink of water. In that moment, the reality of what had happened began to dawn on me for the first time. What if I were pregnant? Besides the physical pain from the rape, an empty, hopeless feeling settled in the pit of my stomach once again. I needed to talk to someone, but there was no one in whom I could confide, from whom to draw understanding and empathy. Tears were streaming down my face. Little Jimmy looked at me and wanted to know what was wrong.

"Nothing, Jimmy, nothing at all."

I wiped the tears away and sat alone in the middle of town with my thoughts.

A nagging fear of pregnancy lingered for weeks after the rape. Not an hour passed that I didn't think about it. Several times, I awakened in the middle of the night, terrified. If I were pregnant, the secret would be revealed. Butch might return. I might die. What would I do if I were pregnant and Johnny and his friends left me alone, didn't kill me? I recalled the rumors at school about one girl who'd "disappeared" for several months. When she came back, one of her friends said that she'd had a baby and that it had been adopted out to a relative.

Well, I certainly didn't intend to have a baby. It would make me fat, my breasts would get even bigger, and everyone would talk about me more than they already did. I knew that I'd have to find some way out. I wouldn't want a baby if I were married, and I certainly didn't intend to have a baby from a rape. One thing the attack convinced me of was my need to escape, to find a better life. I would not, I promised myself, let anything hold me back. I would not be a helpless victim again. When my period finally started, I'd never felt so relieved. I walked far across a field, sat down under a shade tree and cried with happiness.

I didn't go to town on Saturday for several weeks. I didn't want to take the chance of meeting Johnny or any of the others. Most of all, I never wanted to see Butch again. He was the most evil, the cruelest person I'd ever known. Besides, once those boys realized I had not reported them, they might consider me easy and try to do the same thing again. It was a situation in which I had no viable options. I was trapped in ignorance and shame, confined by my mother's strong sense of indignation at the thought of wrong behavior on my part.

However, I wanted very much to see Betty Mae. I wanted to talk to her alone, to tell her what happened to me and ask her what I should do. But since I wasn't allowed to go to her house and because school was out for the summer, I knew that only a chance meeting would give me the opportunity to talk to her.

As it turned out, I saw her once—and only briefly—in Eastman about five weeks after the rape. Like always, she seemed happy to see me. She smiled and introduced me to a handsome, sandy-haired young man with her. She looped her arm through his and pressed herself shamelessly close to him. She bragged about how he held down a good job in Dublin, owned his own car and lived in his own apartment. From what she said, I figured she'd already spent quite a bit of time inside that apartment.

I wondered if my friend was breaking away from her family. I didn't have a chance to ask since she never left her new beau's side. Although I didn't know it at the time, that would be the last time I ever saw her. She left with her boyfriend and I was alone, my dreadful secret still locked inside me, looking down the street at a woman who seemed to relish the intimate contact that had proved so revolting to me. How could she have understood, even if I had had the chance to confide in her?

Near summer's end, I came very close to telling my mother the truth. She was in bed with a summer cold and headache, and while she was ailing, she treated me better than I could ever remember.

I sat on the edge of the bed that day, thinking about how young she looked. We were often mistaken for sisters. Mother was a very young thirty-one, and when I had the time to fix up my hair and put on makeup, I was a very mature-looking fourteen.

She was sitting up in bed, eating soup and crackers. I sat silently on the edge of the bed while she ate. Something prompted her to ask me if I thought she was too strict on me. I shrugged. On many occasions, I had wished that Mother would talk more about womanly matters. But her conversations always turned to discipline. It seemed that she was constantly trying to convince me that she held the upper hand and that the things she did were "for my own good."

She lifted the bowl to drink the last of the soup. Then she paused and peered over the bowl at me. "You think I'm just plain mean to you, don't you, Blanche?"

Right then, I wanted to tell her the truth. I wanted to say that I felt like a maid and that I'd thought about running away from home. Instead, I simply said that she acted like she didn't trust me even though I'd never given her any reason not to.

She put her hand on mine in a rare show of affection and said, "Oh, Blanche, I don't mean to sound like you can't be trusted. It's the others I don't trust. Like that girl up the road. She's just not the kind of person you need to keep company with. She's trouble, real trouble."

Again, I kept my feelings about Betty Mae inside.

Several times that day, I almost blurted out my story about the rape. I wanted to. Once, I opened my mouth to say, "Mother, something awful has happened to me . . ."

But the words just wouldn't leave my mouth.

Mother must have sensed my desire to talk. But, once again, she said the wrong thing. She asked me if I was going to "try to defend that whore again." She said the word whore with more hatred than I'd ever heard.

As I started to leave the room, she called after me. "She's no good, Blanche, no good at all. You stay away from her, you hear?"

I didn't answer her. I was too afraid that the truth would confirm her fears, would make her see me as she saw Betty Mae.

The summer was almost over when Daddy decided my future for me. He became more abusive after the rape. I think he suspected something, but I doubt that he ever came close to guessing the truth. The evil within my stepfather surfaced in the wee hours of a summer morning.

We had just two beds in the four-room house, one in each of the two small bedrooms. Mother and Daddy slept in one. The other belonged to the three of us children. Sometimes in the winter, all three of us would sleep in the bed for warmth. But in the summer the heat made such togetherness very uncomfortable. When it was hot, we alternated between the bed and a pallet made of blankets on the floor in the living room.

I'd chosen to sleep on the living room floor most of that summer. The doors to our bedroom opened into the kitchen and into the other bedroom, which meant I had no privacy at all. By sleeping in the living room, I could be alone, and I could move my pallet close to the front door where there always seemed to be a breeze.

One hot and humid night, I thought I was having a bad dream. It seemed almost like a repeat of the rape from two months before. Hands were clutching at my nightgown. But this time it was Daddy with the groping hands and heavy breathing.

Daddy had sat on the front porch earlier that night with a man from McRae, and they drank heavily of the potent moonshine Daddy brewed back in the pines. Daddy's walk was unsteady when he went to bed just after nine o'clock. Now, I could smell his whiskey-fouled breath as he crawled on top of me.

"Daddy!" I said in a loud whisper. "Get off me!"

He didn't say anything. He clamped one hand over my mouth and kept trying to pull up my nightgown with the other. He had his full weight on top of me, and I was afraid to move for fear of awakening Mama. What would she think of me if she walked in on this scene?

We struggled silently for a few moments. Suddenly, a plan formed in my desperate mind, just as plans had popped into my brain during that awful car ride. But this time I was determined to make the plan work. I had little to lose by going limp, so I quit struggling for a few moments.

At first, he was surprised, I think. Then he finally said something. "Good girl. Now you just be real quiet while I get these things off you," he said as his hand caught the top of my underpants and tried to pull them downward. To get them off me, he had to push his weight upward. That's when I struck a blow he'd never forget. My left knee came upward in as vicious a jerk as I could muster. He made a pathetic sound, rolled to one side and put both hands on his crotch.

"Get away from me!" I hissed in a loud whisper. "Get away from me or I'll scream!"

I could hear the bed springs in the other room groan as Mother turned over. Daddy quickly struggled to his feet and walked hunched-over to the back door and went outside to the outhouse.

I rearranged my clothing, and, in spite of the heat, covered up with one of the quilts that formed my pallet. I waited.

Finally, he came quietly back into the house and crawled in bed with Mother. I heard him groan once; then all was quiet. Sometime just before daylight, I finally drifted off to sleep again, knowing that my own home was no safer than Johnny's car.

Daddy was feeling mean the next morning. Between a hangover and a sore crotch, he growled from the time he got up until it was time to go to the fields. He told me to start hoeing in the back cottonfield and that I'd better "work like hell" because school would start the next week.

I nodded. It would be good to get away from the house, away from the babies, away from Mother—just in case she'd heard something the night before. And I would get to see

Nanny. Right then, I just had to talk to someone, and this elderly Negro woman was the only person besides Betty Mae I felt that I could confide in.

Nanny's house wasn't so far away from ours, but the only time I ever saw her was in the fields. She had taught me how to use a long-handled hoe to chop cotton. She'd taught me the balance points and the rhythm she used to get the most work out of the least effort.

Sometimes Nanny would couple the rhythm of chopping cotton with the beat of a song. When she did that, she was a graceful sight despite her bulk, ungainly walk, and constant complaints about arthritis.

On this day, though, I had something more important on my mind than chopping cotton. I didn't say anything through the morning, but while just the two of us ate our lunch—peanut butter sandwiches and lukewarm tea—under a shade tree, I started the conversation on a light note. I kidded her about her age as she plopped down wearily and began opening her lunch.

"Well, Missy," she said, using the nickname she gave all young girls. "I ain't but fifty-eight. So don't you go actin' like I'm some old, old woman. I've gotta a lotta livin' to do yet, honey. Fact is, I might even find me 'nother man. You know that last one done run off, hung out at that juke joint in town until he got in trouble, and now he's gonna be breakin' rocks for a long time to come."

She shook her head sadly and said, "Sure am glad I never married that man. I'd hate to have to tell everyone my husband is on the chain gang and a-bustin' rocks."

She laughed at her misfortune—if the loss of such a man could be called misfortune. When Nanny laughed, she quivered jovially and made others want to laugh with her. Her laughter finally subsided, and we ate in silence. That's when I made the decision to share my problems with her. I had to trust someone.

"Nanny, I want to talk to you . . . about something serious."

"Sure, Missy, what is it?" Her face, as changing as a sand dune in a wind storm, grew solemn.

I started talking slowly at first and then the words came tumbling out faster and faster. It was as if a dam inside me had burst, and I couldn't stop what rushed forth. I told her I'd been raped by some boys in town and that I was scared, that they swore they'd kill me if I ever told anyone. Before she could interrupt, I told her about the previous night and how I'd fought off the attempt by my stepfather. I told her I was afraid to go home.

"Oh, Nanny, I'm scared of everything," I said.

By the time I finished, tears were streaming down my face, and I was sobbing uncontrollably. Nanny reached for me, pulled me to her and held me tightly.

"Hush, child, hush."

She was the first person to realize that I was a child.

With my head buried in her shoulder, I told her I couldn't stay quiet anymore, that I had to tell someone.

"Lordy, Lordy, Missy, but you shouldn't have to even talk about things like this. You're such a baby."

She held me closer. Finally, my tears slowed and my sobbing subsided. Some great inner strength seemed to flow out of her as her dark features grew grim. The sandwiches and tea were forgotten. I talked. She held my hand and listened intently. By the time I finished, tears were trickling down my face again. She reached and wiped a tear from my cheek.

"Missy, you gotta get away."

"I've been thinking about running away," I said.

"You've got to get away," she said again. She shook her head sadly and looked down at the ground for what seemed like a long time. Then she straightened up and looked me in the eye.

"I'm gonna tell you something, Missy, and I want you to listen real careful, you hear?"

I nodded.

"You can't live around a man who wants to go to bed with you. You 'specially can't live around no man that's supposed to be your daddy and he's wantin' to do anything like that. You hear me, Missy?"

I nodded again.

"So you've just gotta get away. He'll come back, Missy, and he'll keep a-comin' back until he gets you. And after he gets you, he'll keep after you until you do move away. So you might as well go now."

Again, she was thoughtful. She asked me if there was any place I could run to. I told her I had only two friends—her and Betty Mae. Betty Mae was planning to run away, too, so she couldn't help me. And if I ran to Nanny's house, there was no telling what my stepfather might do.

Then I remembered Aunt Edna. But I told Nanny that if I ran there, Aunt Edna would give in to my folks' wishes, and I'd have to go right back home.

"I don't have any place to go, Nanny."

The tears started flowing again, and Nanny pulled me to her. "I don't know but one thing to do, Missy. I'll just get me a gun and kill that man."

I pulled back and stared at her in shock.

"No, Nanny!"

"Sometimes, Missy, it's the only way."

"No, Nanny! They'd put you in jail, and you'd be there the rest of your life!"

Later, as I remembered this conversation, I discovered that I truly was more concerned about Nanny's well-being than about the possible demise of my stepfather. I have held on to that memory because it helps me to believe that it is possible to remain a compassionate and giving person, no matter what the world offers.

As we packed up our lunch sacks, Nanny put a gentle hand on my arm and said, "Missy, the only way you're ever going to have any peace of mind is to get away from here. I don't know how you will do it, but you must go . . . as far away as you can go."

She looked at me with great concern. "You can make it out there," she said, gesturing to the rest of the world. "You're a smart girl, Missy, and you're very pretty. You ought to have something a whole lot better than this ol' cotton patch and a long-handled hoe."

She squeezed my hand one last time. She started to say something more, but her voice broke. She turned and walked back into the cotton field.

We worked through the scorching August afternoon. When we finally quit for the day, Nanny looked across the field at my stepfather who was hollering for me to "get back to the house and get supper cooked."

"He's an evil man, Missy," Nanny said. Then she cast her eyes toward the heavens and said, "He'll have to answer one day to the good Lord. Everybody has to answer to the man upstairs. But you can't wait for the good Lord to take a hand, Missy. You gotta get away. Hear me? Run, child, run. And don't you do no lookin' back."

I nodded.

She went one way, and I went the other. At the edge of the field, I turned and looked back at her. She was standing near the shade tree, and I could see her smile at me. For the last time.

Nanny realized the truth. That childhood summer was a nightmare from which I didn't awaken for many years. But the events of those months convinced me that I must leave my home. I had to get out or be destroyed. I never knew when my stepfather might again try to molest or beat me. The terror of rape was suddenly ever present in my house.

Through all the hard work and the grim poverty, my one solace had been my dreams of fame and fortune. They might seem silly now; others would have called them foolish even then. But in the forties there were no hotlines, no shelters, no counselors for a girl like me to turn to. So I used those

28

childish fantasies. They became my light, my only hope. I convinced myself that I could be a star, that such a life was my destiny, that I did not have to accept a life of pain and degradation. I did what Nanny said I must. I dreamed my way out of Eastman, Georgia.

# Two

The two nights after my talk with Nanny and my decision to leave passed peacefully enough. I worried that Daddy might try to force himself on me again, but he didn't. He stayed sober and took his frustrations out in another way. He ordered me around the house like I was a slave, just to keep me aware that he had the upper hand, I guess. I bit my lip and did as I was told.

Aunt Edna stopped at our house on Friday evening and asked if I'd like to go to town with her the next morning. I stifled the urge to jump for joy at the thought of an entire day away from the farm and away from Daddy. I was afraid he might ruin things by exploding in anger and forbidding me to go, but for some reason he kept quiet and didn't interfere when Mother gave me permission. Maybe he was afraid I'd tell her or Aunt Edna what he'd done. I was just thankful that I was going to get my chance at freedom.

Aunt Edna was my favorite relative, and we helped each other out. She was my ticket into town on many occasions, and I was her alibi while she was away from her husband.

Once we arrived in Eastman, she usually dropped me off at the movie while she disappeared with a male friend for a couple of hours. I asked few questions since there was no place that made me happier than a movie theater, where my imagination could keep strengthening my dreams of stardom. Besides, I was smart enough to know what was going on, but I wasn't going to spoil my trips to town by revealing her secrets. Aunt Edna treated me better than anybody else did, so I didn't see a need to judge her behavior. I would have done almost anything to keep her affection.

That Saturday morning, I awakened just after daybreak filled with a sense of adventure and just as much fear. I styled my hair and put on my makeup in a way that made me look older. I had a good reason for getting everything just right. I was going to try to find a job. But I didn't tell Aunt Edna. Busy with her own feelings of adventure and fear, she hardly spoke on the way to town. As soon as we arrived in Eastman, she pulled up in front of the theater, handed me a dollar and said she'd pick me up about two o'clock. For once, I wasn't interested in entering that magic place that had fed most of my girlish dreams. I turned away from the theater and set out in search of my first job.

Employment opportunities in Eastman were few and far between for a young girl in those days. I ruled out the family-owned businesses since all their openings got snapped up by relatives. And I didn't bother with the clothing plant because I'd heard kids at school say it always had more applications than jobs. I tried a dry-goods store and struck out. The manager asked if I wanted to leave my name, but I told him I needed a job right away. I talked to half a dozen merchants without finding anything promising.

Finally, I saw a sign in the window of the White House Café, a large restaurant on the main street: "Waitress Wanted." Coming from a family that didn't have the luxury of dining out, I'd never been inside the place, but I knew I could handle a job as a waitress. After all, I'd done plenty of waiting on people at home.

I opened the door to a whirlwind of activity. Just about every seat was taken. A man and a woman were trying to wait on perhaps thirty customers that Saturday afternoon. After the man at the cash register finished taking a customer's money, I asked him about the job. He introduced himself as J. A. Ross, the owner, and said, yes, he needed someone right away.

I told him I was ready to go to work that very minute.

"Ever worked in a restaurant before?"

"No, sir, but I'll work like the dickens."

He regarded me for a moment.

"How old are you?"

"Eighteen."

The job was so important to me I found lying about my age as easy as could be.

He said the job paid ten dollars a week plus tips, which sounded fine to me. He handed me an apron and said, "Take this plate to that fella in the plaid shirt by the front window."

"Yes, sir!"

For an instant, I forgot about my crooked teeth. I'd landed my first job, and I smiled from one ear to the other. I might just make my way to Hollywood, after all, if everything went this well.

By three o'clock, I must have put food in front of half the people in town, and I'd cleaned off enough tables to seat the Russian army. The work wasn't easy, but I figured I could make it on ten dollars a week plus tips. In three hours, I'd earned nearly two dollars in tips. Of course, it was the Saturday rush, and the tips would not be so good every day, but it was the first real cash money I'd ever earned that I could keep for myself, and I was happy. This simple job waiting tables in a small-town café felt like a real turning point to me. It was a victory over the man who had taken every penny I'd ever earned in the cotton fields, hoeing and picking.

When the rush was over, Mr. Ross locked the door and poured himself a cup of coffee, sat down at one of the tables in the back, and motioned me to a seat. He told me I'd done well and that I had a permanent job. I was basking in the praise that I so seldom heard at home when I suddenly remembered Aunt Edna. She would surely think I got lost! I told Mr. Ross that I needed to talk to someone to let them know I had a job. He smiled and told me to hurry back. I wondered if he knew I wasn't really eighteen.

When I finally spotted Aunt Edna coming out of the corner drugstore, the expression on her face told me that she was angry. I was scared, but I was also determined. Nobody, not even my favorite aunt, was going to stop me now that I had finally taken a step forward.

"Blanche, where in the world have you been? I've looked all over town for you. Now, come on, I've got to get you on home."

"Don't worry about me, Aunt Edna. I've got me a full-time job, and I'm not going home."

She was momentarily speechless. I repeated my news to let it sink in and told her to tell Mother and Daddy. She flew into a rage right there on the street and told me I could do the telling myself because I was going to go home with her. "What you do after that is your business, but first, you're going home with me. Now get in the car."

"I'm not going back, Aunt Edna. I've got a job and that's that!"

I started to tell her about the events of a few nights before, but I just couldn't. She would run straight to my mother. At that moment, I certainly didn't want to deal with anything other than keeping this job. My behavior probably seemed strange to her, since she didn't know what a bad summer I'd had. And she was my mother's sister, so she would naturally try to do what my mother would want.

She kept insisting that I return with her, but I didn't ever want to live with my parents again. In a desperate effort to win her over, I added that both of them beat me and made me work like a dog. She tried to reach a compromise, saying, "Well, I'm sure we can straighten all of this out and they'll treat you better. I'll talk to them for you. Now, come on. Let's go home."

"You just don't understand, Aunt Edna. I'm really not going home. I'm not, and that's final."

I turned and started walking back toward the White House Café. She followed me a few steps.

"Blanche, what about school? It starts next week, you know."

"I'm quitting school." This was a decision that surprised me. I'd been so eager to get away, I hadn't thought past the immediate needs: a job and, once I had that, a place to stay.

"Your folks ain't going to let you do this, Blanche. You're underaged. They can get the law to bring you home."

Cold chills ran up my spine when she said that. It was another thing I hadn't thought of. But I tried very hard not to let it show. "Then they'll just have to do it," I said, showing more bravado than I felt.

She said something else, but I didn't hear it. I was walking back toward the café, feeling a little more confident because I'd stood up to Aunt Edna. And I felt hopeful about my new life. Yes, sir, Blanche Banks was turning over a new leaf in her life, and nothing was going to spoil it.

Looking back, it is hard to imagine that I took this step so suddenly. My high hopes now seem so fragile that I shudder to think of all that might have happened to a girl so young and so full of repressed anger and fear. Yes, I was foolish, but I was also brave, I think, and very lucky. My escape didn't mean that I could shed the emotional scars of the world into which I was born, but it did mean I had a chance to find a better, safer world for myself. The foolhardiness of youth allowed me to be reckless; the fates were kind enough not to let that early recklessness destroy me.

The people at the café were happy to see me come back. They'd seen me arguing with Aunt Edna through the windows, but they didn't get nosey about it. They let me mind my business, and they minded theirs.

For the first time in my life, work was a joy for me. I worked as hard as I knew how right through to quitting time. When we finished, Mr. Ross said that since I'd already worked almost a full day, I could have a day's wages to help get me through the weekend. He handed me two one-dollar bills and told me that I might be able to get a room at Corinne Johnson's Boarding House just a couple of blocks away. Then he told me where he lived and said if I needed anything over the weekend that I should give him a call. I thanked him and left, feeling like an independent woman, ready to make it on my own.

The room I rented cost a dollar a day without meals or $1.50 with two meals included. I paid the dollar and decided to get by on what I could eat at the restaurant. Before the stores closed that afternoon, I bought a dress from a bargain rack. It didn't fit very well, and I'm not sure I ever wore it out in public. But buying the dress reminded me that I was doing something for myself, and that was a very good feeling.

Aunt Edna showed up at the White House Café just after the breakfast rush on Monday morning. I knew why she was there. I asked Mr. Ross for a few minutes off. He smiled like he understood and nodded. I followed Aunt Edna outside. She was furious. She said my parents blamed her for my leaving home and that if I didn't go home right then, she could never go back over there. I replied calmly that it looked like the farm had seen the last of both of us. She swore so loudly that a man walking by turned for a second look at us. She lowered her voice but kept right on ranting.

I explained to her again that I had a job, that I was better off, that my stepfather didn't have to worry about feeding me anymore and that I'd get along just fine. She again threatened that my father would send the law after me. She even suggested that he could ruin my job at the café if he sent policemen to ask around about me.

"If that happens," I said, "it will be the last time my parents ever see me. They might be able to make me come home once. But if they do, I'll just run away again. Next time, I'll run so far that they won't ever find me."

She said she was sure Daddy would go to the law.

Thinking quickly and fabricating a story as I went, I told her I had a boyfriend who'd asked me to run away to Alabama with him. I'm sure it sounded pretty flimsy, but I promised that as long as they left me alone, I'd stay in Eastman.

She left, but I knew she'd be back. She made three more trips into town during the next couple of weeks, but I stood my ground each time and told her nothing could make me go home. I figured as long as Mother and Daddy were sending somebody else to get me, I wasn't in that much danger. During that time, I met two interesting men. Both were much older, but that didn't keep them from asking me for a date. My life was moving too fast for me to understand all that was happening. I hardly had time to think. All I knew was that I had to go forward, not backward. The things that lay behind me were too hard to face.

The first man was Hoke Wynne. He was one of Eastman's most famous citizens because he'd robbed a bank in Cochran and spent several years in prison. He might have served a much longer sentence, but law enforcement people didn't believe he was really dangerous. So he served only a couple of years. Hoke was a dashing fellow who always had money, drove a nice car, and wore classy clothes. He doesn't sound like a good choice for a naive young girl, but it was because I was so naive that I associated his small-town reputation and his snappy dressing and flashy car with the Hollywood life-style I'd seen in the movie magazines.

I met him at the soda fountain in the corner drugstore late one Saturday afternoon, and he immediately tried to pick me up. He was a silver-tongued devil who could shamelessly flatter a woman. I felt my face get warm, and I knew I was blushing at such compliments from a strikingly handsome man. After all, I hadn't heard many compliments in my life. He asked me to go for a ride, but I remembered the last "ride" someone had taken me on. For long stretches of time I could block the rape from my mind, but eventually a word or a look would trigger the memories and my hard-won joy would disappear. I turned him down. He persisted, so I finally told him that I already had a boyfriend. Then I walked away before he could come up with another argument that would force me to make up another excuse.

The other man I met was Rural Giddens. His mother, a plump, kindly woman, lived in an apartment above the restaurant. Rural was a soldier home on furlough. He was a nice person, not as handsome or as dashing as Hoke Wynne, but he paid a lot of attention to me, and I liked that. It felt good.

Rural was easygoing, not pushy or self-centered, as many men are, I would later learn. I felt safe around him. Hoke worried me. I was afraid I might give in to Hoke. I really didn't want to do that. At least, not yet. So Rural was the sort of man to be around. He didn't set off the alarm I felt around Hoke, didn't remind me of the rape or my stepfather. I wanted to learn about love and sex, the kind of relationship Betty Mae believed in. But I wasn't ready just yet.

His mother told me a few days before Rural arrived that he would be coming home on furlough. "You two ought to get acquainted. You might hit it off," she'd said.

When he arrived in Eastman, his mother brought him to the café and introduced him to everybody who didn't know him, including me. During a lull, I sat with him while he drank coffee. He asked me about my quitting time. I told him, and he was waiting on me to get off four days in a row. I figured it was hard to go wrong with a guy when his mother was the matchmaker.

Mrs. Giddens was a serious woman who worried a lot. She worried that her son might be shipped out to the war in Europe. One day while he walked to the ice cream stand to get ice cream for the three of us, she said that he needed a good wife who would be waiting for him when he came home from the war.

I had no intention of getting married. At least, not for a very long time. I was too young, and I was just starting out on the journey toward my dream. But I thought about Aunt Edna's visits and the increasing threats to have the law take me back home. She came to town again on Friday—two weeks after I'd left home—and I knew another argument was in store. She came into the café just after the morning rush and motioned for me to come outside.

I told her I was very busy with my job, but she started giving me the same old threats. This time, however, she was very definite about what was going to happen.

"Blanche, if you don't come home today, your Daddy is coming to town on Monday morning to get the law to bring you home. He's very busy bringing in the corn, but he said he'd come to town Monday if you don't come home today."

I panicked, and I used the only excuse I knew would work. I told her I was married. She almost choked on that announcement. At first, she really didn't believe me. But I told her I'd married a soldier who was home on furlough, and when she pressed me for a name, I told her I'd married Rural Giddens. After all, sudden weddings were common in wartime. It was possible that I would be married.

Before she could say anything else, I ran back inside the café. As I cleaned off the tables, I tried to think of a solution. In my confused and frightened state, there seemed to be just one way out. I'd have to do just what I'd said I'd already done. I'd get married. Yes, I would do that before I'd go back to the farm. Going home was the last thing I'd ever do.

My new husband would have to be Rural Giddens. Hoke Wynne wasn't the marrying type. Besides, I wanted to be married only long enough to get my parents to leave me alone. That long and not a day longer. Rural Giddens had already talked about needing a wife, someone to write to him and to wait for him to come home from the war. Perhaps what I planned to do was coldhearted and selfish, but I was going to marry Rural. And very soon. He would get over what might happen to him if we married. I might never survive a return to my parents' home.

I didn't finish my full shift that day. I confided to Mr. Ross that I wanted to get married. I didn't tell him the name of my husband-to-be, and I didn't tell him my reason for getting married. He winked like we shared some secret and said, "Go ahead, Blanche. He'll make you a good husband."

I didn't bother walking to the rooming house. I had to be married by Monday. I went directly upstairs to talk to Rural. He was snoozing in an easy chair when I walked into the living room. I awakened him and teased him about wasting his furlough waiting for one waitress to get off work while all sorts of nice young ladies had absolutely nothing to do. He reached and took my hand in his, and he told me that I was the most beautiful girl he had ever seen and that he liked me a lot.

When I asked him how much he liked me, he said he liked me enough to marry me—if I'd have him. I asked him if he was sure, and he said he was. I told him that I'd marry him and he let out a whoop. He called his mother into the room, and I thought we were going to have a celebration right then and there. We went to get our blood tests that afternoon. We could be married Monday morning . . . before my step-daddy could round up the sheriff.

Again, things moved too fast for me to know what it was I was really doing. I was running so hard from my past that I couldn't slow down to consider the consequences of my actions. I'm sure I knew nothing of what marriage means. I certainly felt no commitment to Rural, although I did like and respect him and appreciated his kindness and gentleness toward me. I was in no position to be committed to anything other than myself. I had to survive, to make myself succeed, and I was willing to use Rural to accomplish that. None of my reasons for our marriage excuses my misleading him, and I was later to learn for myself the pain of such deceptions. Even now, I can only explain, not excuse.

The ceremony was a simple one, peformed by the justice of the peace at the courthouse in Eastman at about four o'clock on Monday. I wore a white dress I'd bought on Saturday, and Rural wore his Army uniform. After the ceremony, we went back to Mrs. Giddens's apartment, and Rural talked for hours about how we would save money while he was away, how we'd have a car and a house someday, and how he'd like to have two or three children.

I had other things on my mind. I wondered if my parents would leave me alone since I really was married. I wondered how I would react to going to bed with a man who wasn't going to rape me. But, mostly, I wondered if marriage was the easiest way out. Maybe I should have just run far, far away.

As night came, nervousness gripped me. The idea that my actions did have consequences loomed before me. I really couldn't go to bed with Rural. I had to find a way out. I didn't want to hurt him by leaving right then, but I didn't want to go to bed with him, either. Unwittingly, I had built another kind of prison for myself. I was as trapped now as I had been on the farm, safer, yes, but not one step closer to what I wanted to be. I told him that I didn't feel good, and I fell asleep on the divan. When he awakened me, I went to the bathroom and came back with the announcement that I'd started my period. Rural Giddens was a rare gentleman. He said that untimely event didn't matter, that we had our whole lives ahead of us. Guilty because I knew those lives would be lived separately, I accepted his graciousness and breathed easier.

I left early the next morning—with all of my belongings. I'd already told Rural that I was going right back to work Tuesday morning, so he expected me to leave early. He didn't wake up enough to see me gather up my things. Later in the day, Mrs. Giddens came into the café, obviously upset. She asked me why I'd moved out like that, and I told her that I just didn't want to be married. I told her that I was going home to my parents and would not be back to her apartment or to Rural. She had been nice to me, and I felt bad for them both. I hoped that they would just get on with their lives, as I had to do with mine.

I figured my strategy would work. If I went home, Rural would soon return to his base and leave me alone. Meanwhile, there wasn't much my parents could do to a married girl.

At last, perhaps I would be free from it all.

My return home was anything but peaceful. Daddy groused all the time. He called me "a sorry damned no-good runaway girl" and told me to get my work clothes on and get out in the fields. Mother put up the argument that I'd been gone for three weeks and the washing, ironing and cleaning had piled up. It was just like old times, hearing my parents argue over who would have my services for the day. I didn't say much. I had to stay at home until Rural left town. But once that happened . . .

Three days was all of the home life I could stand. Aunt Edna came by the house Saturday morning. I ran out to the road and told her I needed a ride to Eastman. Of course, she started telling me that there was no way she'd ever give me a ride into town again. But I changed her mind in a hurry when I started naming names of men I'd seen her with in town. She said I wouldn't dare start telling that stuff about her, but she knew I was desperate and just might. Finally, she agreed to pick me up half a mile down the road and take me to town. That way, she could keep me happy—and quiet—and not get back into hot water with my folks.

I was learning how to survive, how to get what I had to have. These are not life's only lessons, nor are they its most important ones. But when you are starting from the very bottom, when you have been hurt and abused and misunderstood for years, and when you are very young and essentially alone, surviving, getting what you have to have, is the first lesson to be learned. It has to be.

Mr. Ross smiled happily when I walked into the White House Café, tossed me an apron and told me to go to work. At the end of the day, we sat at a table, and I knew I couldn't avoid explaining my failed marriage. I decided I wouldn't tell him the whole story. I just said that I was much too young to be thinking about marriage and that Rural Giddens would get over me. Eventually, of course, he did, quietly obtaining a divorce and remaining the gentle, respectful man I knew him to be. Eventually I realized that I had told the truth: I was just too young for marriage.

Hoke Wynne heard about the end of my marriage, too. He came calling the day after I returned to the café. He asked me to go for a ride, but I turned him down again. I told him that, legally, I was still Rural's wife and that I could not be seen out running around. We talked for a long time. He told me that he would pick me up after dark and bring me home before sunup. So I finally agreed. After all, I needed someone to talk to, someone who didn't want me to be a slave or a housewife or even a waitress. When you are too young to settle down, excitement seems like the best alternative, and I'd never had much chance at it till now. Hoke seemed to promise excitement.

He picked me up just after seven o'clock, and we drove far out of town to the top of a breezy hill somewhere in Telfair County. We sat on the hood of his car and looked at the stars and a rising moon. The scenery, the setting, the mood were all beautiful, as perfect as anything I'd ever seen on those Saturdays at the movie theater. We talked for a long time, and I told him the truth about my marriage, that I'd married Rural just to try to break my parents' hold on me. He was a good listener, and I finally talked some of my problems and frustrations out of my system.

Then he told me about life in prison and how he had longed for a woman. "There were some weird men in there," he said, "but I like women. I couldn't wait to get out and meet someone like you."

Hoke was a charmer. He knew how to make me sympathize with him, how to make me feel comfortable and understood. He tried to get me to go home with him that first night, but I put him off. We continued to see each other and to ride around in his car, looking at the stars and talking about our lives. Those evenings were my first taste of real freedom, and no matter what his motives were, Hoke did listen to me, did understand, and did talk to me like I was a person, not a maid or an object. Freedom is heady stuff, and I was enthralled by the feelings of power and confidence being treated nicely instilled in me. One night, I went home with him. We made love.

I loved the way being with Hoke made me feel, and I knew he wouldn't want to keep seeing me if I refused him forever. It wasn't sex I wanted, for sure, but I thought sex was necessary if I was to keep feeling free, confident, and admired. It wasn't as bad as I'd imagined it would be. But it also wasn't as good as Betty Mae had said it would be. Even so, I moved out of the boarding house to save rent and lived with Hoke for several months, hoping to find that feeling that my friend had sworn was real.

By winter—when a person probably ought to appreciate a bed partner who is warm and giving—I was looking for a way out. Every day, I knew more clearly that I was not ready to be tied down. I needed freedom, and I couldn't seek it through Hoke. I had to find it for myself.

In January, I took a part-time job at a drugstore that didn't interfere with my job at the White House Café, and I moved back into the boarding house. The breakup with Hoke was not a bitter one. He never said so, but I believe he understood my desire not to be dependent on anyone. He was smart enough and sensitive enough to know that I was young and just starting out. He also knew I'd had some horrible experiences. He was good enough to let me go without the cruelty and harassment many men might have felt to be their due. Besides, I think I had slowed down what had been a pretty freewheeling lifestyle for him. After I moved out, we remained friends and continued to do things together. Once, I even went back and spent the night with him. He was the man who allowed me to see that sex needn't be painful and terrifying. But we both knew that we weren't meant to be together forever. For me, our relationship was a good lesson in the simple pleasures of romance, mutual attraction, and friendship. For Hoke, I suppose I was what he'd wanted in those months in prison, a caring, gentle woman to share some peaceful times with.

Eventually, I found a chance to move on. Myrtle Cook, a woman of perhaps thirty, came home one weekend after taking a job in an ammunition plant in Macon. I'd seen her around the café, and we'd become casual acquaintances. When I saw her on this particular weekend, I told her that my parents were hassling me and I needed to move away from Eastman. She suggested that I move to Macon and offered to help me find a job there.

I didn't have to think very long. Macon was a bigger city and was sure to have more interesting people . . . and it was in the direction I wanted to move—toward Hollywood. I still dreamed of being a movie star as I packed my belongings and caught a Greyhound bus with Myrtle and two of her friends. Macon was my next step.

Broadway in Macon was a bustling street in those days. The war was still on, and soldiers from Camp Wheeler jammed the sidewalks at night and on the weekends, looking for drinks, dancing and companionship. I considered trying to get a job in one of the bars, but I didn't—for a couple of reasons. First, the bar owners were very strict about checking birth records, Myrtle said. I wasn't yet fifteen, and I felt sure any lies about my age would soon be exposed. Second, I didn't drink and didn't want to start. And I had no desire to hang around with those who did. My experiences with my stepfather, unpleasant enough under normal circumstances, only got worse when he had been drinking his bootleg whiskey. I'd had enough of drinking men to last a lifetime.

While Myrtle tried to get me work at the ammunition plant, I started walking from business to business, looking for a job. My money was about gone when I finally resorted to the only place I was sure I could get a job—a restaurant. I found a job by sheer luck.

I walked into a small café just off Cherry Street and asked where I could find the manager. A tired waitress motioned toward the back. There was a door marked "Office," but just as I raised my hand to knock, loud voices came from the other side. A female voice was apologizing for being late, and a male voice was telling her to take her pay and get out.

The door suddenly opened and a tall, blonde-haired woman almost ran over me. She pushed me aside and stomped away. The door was still open. A burly, bald-headed man sat behind a worn desk littered with papers. He looked up and asked what I wanted. I said I wanted a job, that I was a good waitress and he could check my work record at White House Café in Eastman. He thought a minute and then said hiring me was a lot easier than going to the employment office and waiting for them to find somebody. I thanked him and hurried to work before he changed his mind or questioned me about my age. The job was a snap. I'd worked much harder at the White House Café.

When we got a break, I fixed myself a plate and sat down. It was good food, and I had a good feeling about landing this job. It was a good day, and it should have been. The date was March 1—my fifteenth birthday.

On that day, I made myself a promise never to be broke again. I didn't know if I could keep it, but I knew I'd sure try. As young as I was and as mixed up about many things as I now realize I must have been, I always knew it was important to work hard, to earn a living that would allow me to support myself, and I was always willing to do that. For years, I had worked my fingers to the bone without benefit or praise. That was work I resented. But, now, I was working to get somewhere, to be somebody, and I was finding out that it felt good to spend the money I earned. It felt good to be able to rely on myself.

About a month after I arrived in Macon, I found out that I was not far enough from Eastman. My parents came to town on a Saturday. I'd seen several people from Eastman in the restaurant, and someone must have told Mother and Daddy where I was working. They came in during a lull and said they wanted to speak to me outside. We stood in the spring sunshine, and they told me I had to come home because my mother was pregnant again.

I refused, telling them that I was perfectly happy fending for myself. I could see that Daddy was irritated by my determination to be independent, but he said nothing. They'd obviously agreed that Mother should try to convince me to go home with them, figuring I'd be more inclined to feel sorry for her and return out of guilt or loyalty. She said she might lose this baby if she had to scrub clothes and do all of the chores around the house.

Again, I said I wouldn't go. I did feel sorry for Mother, but I knew if I did as she asked, I'd never have a chance for a life any better than the one her request proved to be too hard to bear.

Daddy couldn't contain himself any longer.

"Well, by God, I know how to get you home," he said angrily. "I'll bet the law will bring you home. Either that or you're going to wind up in a reform school. Did you hear that, Blanche?"

"Yes, I heard you," I said, feeling suddenly tired of the whole struggle. "I heard it back in Eastman, and now I'm hearing it in Macon. You're just not going to leave me alone, are you?"

"No, by God, I'm going straight to the law."

I went back into the restaurant and went immediately to Mr. Brown's office. I told him I had to move on. A nice man, he offered to use his connections to do whatever needed to be done to keep my parents from interfering. I thanked him for the offer, but I knew that I had to leave. I had to make it impossible for my stepfather to find me and force me back into his cruel world. I'd come too far to stop now.

He grumbled that every time he found a good waitress somebody was just waiting to foul things up. Little did he know how drastically my stepfather could foul up my life. He paid me, and when I counted the money, I discovered he'd paid me two dollars too much. I tried to give the extra money back to him, but he gruffly told me to keep it for an emergency. I think such kindness from people I worked with was one reason I was able to keep going when I faced such overwhelming obstacles. For every bad experience I had, fate seemed to offer an alternative, a decent human being who treated me with kindness and respect. I was, in many ways, blessed, and I remember those people with gratitude and pleasure, all these years later.

Myrtle Cook, my roommate at the rooming house, didn't seem surprised that I'd decided to move on. But she argued against my leaving. She said that as long as my parents didn't know where I lived, how could they find me? Besides, she'd heard that Walgreen's drugstore on Cherry Street had an opening, and the pay and hours were better than the restaurant.

Walgreen's did have a position. I was hired and stayed in Macon five more uneventful months. But I'd made up my mind to leave, and I was only waiting for the first good opportunity. I didn't like the rooming house where we lived. The rules were just too strict. Besides, I always worried that my parents would come back to look for me.

I dated several men—mostly soldiers from Camp Wheeler—but they were not allowed inside the rooming house, not even to sit in the living room. If we weren't inside by eleven at night, we couldn't get in until the next morning. Sometimes, girls who were deemed too wayward were turned out of the place. At the time, I wasn't interested in spending the night with anyone, but something in me rebelled at such restraint. I worked hard and paid my rent, and I felt entitled to a little more freedom than the boarding house allowed, even if I wasn't planning to utilize it.

In the back of my mind, there was still that dream of making it in Hollywood. I was not yet of age, my teeth were crooked, and I didn't have the money to get there, but the dream was very much alive. Everything else I did was, consciously or unconsciously, preparation for the big move; each day was another day to position myself for the big break I knew would come.

Two events decided my next move for me. First, one of the waitresses at the café where I'd worked said my folks had indeed returned to look for me. That ominous news coincided with a marriage proposal from a young soldier named Bart. The war was on, everything was unsettled, and I shouldn't have been surprised that he asked me to marry him. It wasn't that different from the situation with Rural. But I was surprised; I was also different.

He said he was shipping out to Fort Benning, and he wanted me to go with him—as his wife. He was a handsome young man of about twenty-one. Many women would have jumped at the chance, but I really didn't want to make the mistake of marrying again without real love and commitment. However, a trip to Columbus, Georgia, certainly sounded interesting after six months in Macon. Columbus was, after all, one step closer to Hollywood.

So I told Bart I'd go with him, and we could talk more about marriage when we got there. At least I was more sensible than I'd been back in Eastman with Rural. I knew I was still running—away from my parents and toward Hollywood. Bart could only get in my way. But, again, I was willing to use him to get farther away from home and closer to fame and fortune. I was still hungry for the stuff that dreams are made of, and Bart's feelings were secondary at best. I knew he was young and immature and afraid of going to war without having someone to wait for him, but all of those conditions were temporary, which meant he had no permanent need for me.

I kissed him and went to the manager of Walgreen's to tell him I was quitting. I picked up my pay and went to pack my belongings. We caught a Greyhound bus just before dark. Good-bye, Macon; hello, Columbus. Even before the bus got out of Macon, I was planning my escape from Bart. Annie Blanche Banks was gaining confidence in herself, and the thought of a new town populated by complete strangers seemed more appealing than Macon and the prospect of a return visit by my parents. If I could figure out how to let Bart down gently, without any real damage to either of us, I would be safer than I'd ever been. Almost daily, I was feeling stronger, more sure of myself, and as we prepared to move west toward Columbus, in my mind, I was alone, beginning the next leg of my personal odyssey. To the west lay California, the land of my dreams.

As the bus rounded the station and pulled onto Broadway, I took one last look at Macon. Soldiers were filling up the street for another evening of revelry. Flashing neon lights beckoned to them and their money. Seeing Broadway in that light, I figured it must be a little bit like Hollywood, except that Hollywood surely would be much bigger, much better, much more interesting. I could hardly wait to see the real thing. Even though my ticket was good for just a hundred miles westward, I made a vow to spend as little time as possible in Columbus before moving on to Hollywood, where I would surely be rich and famous and happy.

# Three

My first glimpse of Columbus should have taught me something about the dangers of great expectations. Certainly, it looked no more like Hollywood than Macon did. Our bus arrived late at night, and the station was crowded with soldiers returning to Fort Benning. The dense cloud of cigarette smoke and fumes from the diesel buses nauseated me. All I could think of was getting my suitcase and getting out of there. Then it hit me—I wasn't alone.

Bart had arrived with his own set of expectations. He thought we were getting married. He guided me outside and said, "We've got to find you a place to stay while I check in at the base. It may be a day or two before I can come back to town. Then we can get our blood tests and find a justice of the peace."

In order to buy a little time to sort out my feelings and decide exactly what it was I was doing here, I said, "Listen, why don't you go ahead and check in, and I'll meet you back here two days from now."

"But what if I can't get back to town day after tomorrow?"

I smiled in what I hoped was a reassuring way. "Then I'll be here the next day and the next. I'll keep coming back until you do show up." I didn't know what else to do, so I thought I'd better postpone his inevitable disappointment.

He was uneasy. "I don't want to lose you, Blanche. You're the only girl I've met since I've been in the Army that I'd even think about marrying. I love you."

Even as he said this, I wondered how true it really was. He didn't know any more than I did about the kind of love people can make a marriage from. I just happened to be a woman who could give him what he wanted, what he thought he needed at the time—a wife to wait for him. In that sense, we were using each other to reach goals we'd set long before we met.

He was a kind and handsome young man, and, under the right circumstances, we might have fallen in love and found a way to share our lives. But the time and place were wrong, and there was no way our lives would have worked if we had stayed together. The new start I was seeking, the escape from my difficult past, was the most important thing to me, and I had to be alone to make that start.

"Look, Bart," I said, "don't worry. I'll get a room somewhere, and I'll be back. Promise." The lie made me wince inside.

An announcer on the public address system said the green Army bus in front of the station was the last one leaving for the base until morning. Bart kissed me one more time and said, "See you in two days."

He scampered onto the bus full of hope and trust I had instilled in him. I felt bad for him, but I also breathed a sigh of relief. It was good to be alone. Or was I alone?

A military policeman had been watching us, and as soon as the bus was out of sight, he walked over to me.

"Do you need a hand, miss?" he asked, gesturing to the suitcase.

"No, I can handle it. I just need to find the YWCA."

"If you want, I'll get you a taxi."

"Is it too far to walk?"

After he gave me directions, I said that I could walk that far. He followed me to the corner of the bus station, which made me a little suspicious.

"Was that your husband?"

I had learned enough about the way men operated to know where the conversation was leading, and I began to wonder if he would show up at the Y.

"Yes. I mean, he soon will be. We're getting married day after tomorrow. Surely you heard us making plans?"

He shrugged and walked back into the crowd at the front of the station. I breathed my second sigh of relief of the evening. Obviously, Blanche Banks was going to get plenty of attention. After years of being ignored and mistreated, I was finding that attention and affection felt pretty good in comparison, but I made up my mind not to rush into another quick marriage. Matrimony could wait. There was too much besides attention and affection that came along with marriage, and I wasn't ready for those pleasures and responsibilities. I wasn't ready to be tied down.

I picked up my suitcase and followed the military policeman's directions to the YWCA. I felt good about being in a new town . . . until I arrived at the Y and found it locked up tight. A sign said the doors would open again at six A.M. Down the street, I could see a clock with its big hands pointing at 4:30. I sat down on a bench and waited, contemplating how freedom felt as I sat alone in a dark and unfamiliar city in the middle of the night.

I made up my mind to find a good job, get a nice apartment, and find true love, if I could. Maybe the true love would take me to California, to Hollywood, to stardom. Now I realize how odd it is that I could be so clear-headed in deciding not to marry Bart and so unrealistic and starry-eyed about a true love making my dreams come true in

Hollywood in the next breath. But I had nothing to do while I waited for the sun to come up, so I resorted to the dreams about the future and what it held that had gotten me through much tougher situations than the one I faced on that Columbus bench.

The thing I was struggling to find back in Columbus was the hardest thing of all to find. I needed to know myself, needed to have an identity of my own—not one drawn from a man, not one spun out of a poor farm girl's fantasies inspired by fan magazines and Saturday matinees. Yes, I wanted comfort and security, and those things often got confused with men and the imagined world of fame and fortune. But the ensuing years would make crystal clear that the essential ingredient was to be self-knowledge. For that, I was to search very hard.

The last of the money I had brought from Macon went for a room at the Y once it opened. I had a roof over my head for an entire week. It was inconceivable that I would not find a job within seven days. But the inconceivable happened. By the end of that week, I was flat broke, my rent was running out, and I had not eaten in three days. Desperate and unable to ignore my hunger any longer, I wondered about Bart, and I walked back to the bus station. He wasn't there, of course, and there was little I could have said to him had I chanced upon him. He must have known by that time that Blanche Banks was not coming back, that she had no intention of becoming his wife.

I sat down and looked around. The air was the same blue mist of cigarette smoke, and diesel fumes permeated the entire area, but this time I was more nauseated from an empty stomach than from the smells and smoky atmosphere.

"Hi."

I looked over my shoulder. It was the same MP who'd been so interested the previous week.

"So you didn't get married."

I quickly lied. "Yes. Yes, we got married. I'm waiting on him right now."

"Where's the ring?"

"We, uh, didn't have the money for a ring."

"C'mon, honey, you can tell me the truth. You really aren't married, are you?"

"Yes. Yes, I am."

"I don't believe . . ."

"I don't care what you believe," I said. And I got up and walked away.

There is an important lesson a young woman on her own quickly learns. A bothersome male is usually easier to get rid of with a lie. For some reason, that type of man doesn't accept the truth. I was rid of him, but still that policeman bothered me more than my hunger . . . my hunger.

God, I couldn't stand it much longer. A block down the street, I saw a restaurant I'd passed a dozen times in the past week without ever going inside. This time, there was a sign in the window: "Waitress Wanted."

I went inside, picked up the sign from the window and took it to the only person in the place—a woman about forty-five.

"You've got a waitress," I said.

"When can you start?"

"I started about thirty seconds ago," I said, "if I can get something to eat."

She studied me closely. "Say, you do look sort of . . ."

I didn't hear whatever else she said. I passed out.

When I came to, I saw three faces looking down at me. A hand placed a cool dishcloth on my face and wiped my forehead.

"You OK?" asked the female voice.

"Yes, I'm OK . . . just hungry, very hungry."

"Here, let me get you into this booth," said a male voice.

Suddenly, I was sitting up. Hot food was placed on the table in front of me.

I ate. Like a pig! Never had food tasted so good!

"Better take it easy," said the female voice. "Don't want to overdo it. Too much food might make you sick."

I looked to see a round, friendly face.

"I'm Irma. I own this place. Well, me and the banker own it," she said with a smile.

"Thanks," I said. "Thanks a lot. I was so hungry. I haven't eaten in . . . say, what is today?"

"Friday."

I shook my head. I'd eaten Tuesday morning. I'd spent my last nickels and dimes for a couple of doughnuts at a bakery.

As I ate, I thought about Columbus, Georgia. I didn't know a soul there unless you counted Bart at the base and the MP who'd tried to pick me up. They certainly weren't people I wanted to be involved with or obliged to. I'd wanted a new start, but I wasn't sure I was prepared to be a loner. The past week had been too hard. I looked up at Irma, and I had the feeling that she could read my mind.

"Listen," I said, "I don't want this for free. I want to work for it. I'm a good waitress, and you can take it out of my pay."

"Honey, if you're a good waitress, you won't go hungry. At least not around here."

"Thanks."

"Say, what's your name?"

"Blanche Banks."

"When can you go to work?"

I tried to get up. "Right now."

She put a hand on my shoulder and pushed me gently back into the seat. "Don't panic. We're going to close in about thirty minutes. Can you be here tomorrow morning at 6:30?"

"Yes."

"Then you've got a job."

A job. Well, it might not be as good as the one I'd left at Walgreen's, and it certainly wasn't glamorous. There was no

58

fame or fortune involved. But I would survive, something I'd been beginning to have my doubts about earlier in the day. I went back to my room and slept like a baby. As long as I had a job, I would never go hungry again. By Saturday night, I had made enough money in tips to pay for my room through Monday. Things were looking up. I had a roof over my head, my stomach was full, and I was on my own, earning what comfort and security I had.

I worked in Irma's little café for about a month until I found a job in a jewelry store where the pay was better and I could make use of the two or three nice dresses I'd bought while I was working in Macon.

Irma didn't seem to mind when I told her I was leaving.

"You're welcome back anytime, Blanche," she said. "You're a good waitress, and you bring in a lot of business, especially those young Army boys who just want to talk to you."

There was something good and decent and secure about having Irma for a friend. I often wondered what it would have meant to grow up with a woman like Irma to guide me, to help me. I made it a point to stop by regularly, even after I moved out of the Y and into an apartment on Waverly Avenue, in the opposite direction from the jewelry store as the café. I didn't want to lose Irma's warmth and support once I'd found it, so an extra walk was a small price to pay.

Eventually, the job in the jewelry store became very boring. Even a small café like Irma's had more customers than the busiest jewelry store. I didn't meet many people. I spent my days wiping glass counters hardly anyone ever looked through and polishing gold rings that might never be worn. Partly in reaction to the boredom, I started dating Hank, who worked someplace across the river in Phenix City, Alabama. He told me several different stories about where he worked, so I was never sure. Of course, I should have known to listen, to hear the danger signals when a man can't even be straight about his work.

We went out to a movie one night, stopping at a drive-in restaurant. He parked at the farthest end of the service area, and like most young people, we used the darkness and our remote location as an occasion for what we called romance. We kissed, we hugged, we necked.

One of the carhops showed up at the window of the car and said, "Hey, y'all better break that up around here. The manager doesn't go for that sort of thing. He'll raise hell if he sees what y'all are doing."

Hank turned back square to the steering wheel, offered a few choice words about what the manager could do with the restaurant and drove away. He obviously felt good about putting the carhop in his place, even though the young waiter was only trying to warn us. Hank was a happy-go-lucky sort of man, and at that moment he was filled with bravado. His self-confidence was brimming over. What he said next shouldn't have surprised me.

"My place or yours?" he asked.

I hesitated. "We can't go to my place," I said. "My landlady watches me like a hawk. She doesn't have anything else to do, and she'd throw me out if I showed up with a man."

"Then it will have to be my place."

I didn't answer. I liked Hank, and I didn't want him to lose interest because I acted like a prude. But deep inside I was wishing we could have stayed at the drive-in, kissing in the soft darkness, maybe a little petting. Why did romance always lead to sex? He drove to a hotel. "This is my place," he said. He went inside to register us as man and wife. There was nothing I could do to stop what was happening. I was caught up in a chain of events I had no control over. Or that's the way I felt, at least.

We went upstairs and made love. I still didn't understand how Betty Mae could have wanted to do these things, but I did feel less lonely after I'd been with Hank. Sex seemed a small price to pay for feeling desired and appreciated, and I was daily coming to understand more clearly that the feelings of affection and warmth that came as part of sex were necessities to me. I could be independent—I wanted to be. But I did not want to be lonely. No one does.

A few days after my sixteenth birthday, I discovered I was pregnant. How many teen-aged girls have found themselves in this position? I'm sure they have all shared my fear, my guilt, my anger. Why did this have to happen to me? What did my future hold? I was just learning to take care of myself. I couldn't care for a child. It seemed that the longing for love would always extract a price, a high price.

When Hank came by that night, I told him.

"You're what? Pregnant? Good God, girl. Don't you know anything?"

"Please don't blame me. I'm sorry it happened. I guess I don't know enough. What are we going to do?"

"Wait a minute, Blanche. How the hell do I know that baby's mine? What am I supposed to do?"

"How can you say that? You know you're the only one I've been with. I work every day, and I'm out with you every night. When do you think I would see anyone else?"

He didn't argue. He knew I was right. But that didn't stop the pain, the sense of betrayal, I felt.

"Well," he said, "I don't want to get married."

"I don't either." And this was true. Still, it surprised me a little to realize I must have hoped he would want to.

"So what are we going to do?"

At least he was talking about us, not just me.

"I don't know."

We sat silent.

"Blanche?"

"Yes."

"What about an abortion?"

I'd never considered getting an abortion because I'd never been pregnant. I barely knew what an abortion was. But at that moment I was pregnant, sixteen, unmarried, and living payday to payday. I had to think about it.

"I'm scared. I don't know where to go. I don't have the money to get it done. And I don't . . ."

"Damn it, Blanche, quit saying 'don't.' We've got to do something. I don't know much about it, either. Look, let me talk to some of the guys at work tomorrow and I'll find out what we can do."

Not knowing what else to do, I let him take my fate into his hands.

Girls from Columbus went for abortions to a chiropractor's office in Phenix City, Hank said the next day. I detested going to Phenix City for any reason, and I was now more frightened than I'd ever been. The rape was not something I had to be responsible for. I was a helpless victim. An abortion I had to plan, I had to be responsible for. I needed someone to talk to, a sympathetic ear.

Hank was too angry to be the listener I needed. So I went to see Irma. When I told her I was pregnant, I immediately got the two things I needed most—sympathy and advice.

"Oh, honey, you're too young to be into anything like this," she said. "You're going to ruin your life if you're not careful."

"I'm past the point that I should have been careful, Irma. Now I need your help. Please go to Phenix City with me." I couldn't say the words, but she understood.

"For an abortion?"

"Yes."

She shook her head sadly. "You know, Blanche, there was a time when I would have given my eyeteeth to get pregnant. But I never did. Then here you are just sixteen and facing something like this. I tell you, there just ain't no justice in life."

"Irma, will you go with me?"

"Sure, honey, I'll go. What kind of friend would I be if I said no?"

The abortion took no more than fifteen minutes. It was over before I had time to understand it. Hank had given me

$125 to pay for it, and what had seemed an insurmountable obstacle ceased to exist faster than I could believe. As Irma drove me back to my apartment, I felt sore and nauseated. But I didn't feel in control. My life felt as far away from me as the pregnancy that no longer existed.

"You look awful, Blanche. Maybe you'd better stay at my place tonight."

"It's OK, Irma. I'm going to be all right. I just hope my boss at the jewelry store doesn't find out the real reason I took a couple of days off. I can't afford to lose my job now. That's for sure."

I'm sure I wanted to stay at my place only because I hoped Hank would come by. Otherwise, the security and companionship of Irma's place would have been irresistible. I'm also sure that the worry over my job was greatly exaggerated. As would be the case many times in my life, I took solace in having work to do.

So I went to my apartment and slept most of the next two days. Irma brought me a couple of meals a day, and I healed quickly. But Hank never came by to see me. He had seemed remote and cold the day he brought the money, and he refused to make the trip to Phenix City with me.

"That's women's business," he said.

It took a while for me to realize that Hank was not coming back. I didn't know how to call him or where to find him, so that was it. Scratch off one romance that could have been something special, or so it seemed to my starry, sixteen-year-old eyes. Those danger signals I should have heeded early on now echoed in my mind, and I knew true love was still nothing more than a picture I painted on the canvas of my imagination.

Unfortunately, that wasn't my only experience with the abortion clinic. I made two more trips across the river for abortions. The second was little different from the first: expectations of love and romance diminished into sex alone as I struggled not to lose a relationship; sex became pregnancy; pregnancy motivated the male's exit and my trip to Phenix City. The third abortion almost ended my life.

After nearly two years, I left the jewelry store and went to work in Archer Hosiery Mill. That, too, was a boring job. I sat all day long inspecting hosiery. It was a booming business. Nylon hose could be found only on the black market during the war, and when shortages of material finally ended, it seemed that every woman on earth wanted a dozen pairs of nylon stockings. Sometimes it felt like I was inspecting all of them, every stocking worn by every woman in America. At least the job paid well. A decent paycheck was something I'd learned to appreciate.

While working at the mill, I fell in love twice, first with Jack Locke, a soldier who was home on leave from the Army. His sister worked at the mill with me, and she introduced us. Jack said he'd met me at the jewelry store before he went away to basic training, a meeting I had no recollection of. Jack was young and sweet, and he really liked me. He said he'd known I was special from that first encounter, the one I couldn't recall. We dated a few times, and he asked me to marry him. I suppose both of us should have known better. We were very young and very insecure. In fact, it was our insecurity that made that feeling of being special so addictive to us both. I said yes for reasons I'll never understand. We drove to Phenix City with friends and were married. There is, of course, a touch of irony in my marrying in Phenix City, scene of so much grief in my recent past.

I should have been happy. There was the chance of joy to redeem the pain. Jack moved into my apartment, paying the rent for a month in advance. We'd already decided that I would stay in Columbus and work while he went to Fort McClellan, Alabama, his next duty station. But Jack seemed disappointed in me. I'd led him to believe that I was a virgin, again out of that familiar fear of losing the relationship if I wasn't exactly the woman I thought the man wanted me to be, and he wasn't happy when he learned the obvious. We didn't fight. We never became enemies. We just agreed that when he left town, he was single, as I would be. Jack got a divorce about a year later, and I found myself twice a failure at the institution I grew up believing was my ultimate destiny. The frightening thing was that I found myself in that position without ever having known real love, without having been able to sustain the romance and affection I craved.

My next romance came as I was on the rebound from the marriage to Jack Locke. His name was Buddy, and, although I'd known him for more than a year, I'd never felt drawn to him until after the break-up with Jack. His real name was pure Deep South, three last names hooked together, but everyone called him Buddy. He was a handsome fellow. Years later, when I first saw Robert Redford, I realized that he reminded me of Buddy.

Buddy, who was my boss at the mill, was married, which meant I was treading on doubly dangerous waters. At the time, however, I couldn't have cared less about that. My bad experience with Jack had probably made me a little desperate, a tad reckless. Buddy was the most gorgeous man I'd ever seen. He made a good living, and he was a skillful lover who taught me some of the pleasures of sex that I had so hoped to learn. I didn't mind competing with his wife for his time and affection, or so I told myself, over and over, each time doubts raised their ugly heads. If I'd thought, I might have been able to question how loving a person an unfaithful husband really is. But I wasn't thinking. I was feeling and acting.

He said he couldn't take me out in Columbus because too many people knew him. I didn't mind as long as I was with him. On our dates, we usually crossed the river to Phenix City where we dined in elegance and danced late into the night. Yet again, I decided to revise my opinion of the city. It became quite romantic, and I fooled myself into thinking my past experiences there were nightmares Buddy would rescue me from. After a dreamy, romantic evening, we'd return to my apartment and make love almost until daylight. He usually got home just in time to say good morning to his wife, shave, and get back to the plant. I teased him quietly during the day about how his eyes looked all bloodshot and droopy.

Having convinced myself that I was, at last, truly in love, I made a decision to do anything I could to win Buddy for myself. Sharing him with his wife wasn't enough. If I could get pregnant, I thought that he might leave his wife and marry me. After all, they had no children because his wife was unable to conceive, and he told me that he wanted children very much. I wasn't sure I did, but if a child would make him my husband, then I would bear his child. Instead of tracking my menstrual cycle for birth control, I did it to ensure that we made love during the most fertile time. Clearly, this was a bad decision, made out of desperation and immaturity by a young woman who confused infatuation and love.

Not long after I set myself on this destructive course, he picked me up as usual a couple of blocks from the plant. Normally, he smiled and said, "Hi, baby cakes." But on that evening, his face looked tense and worried, and he wasted no time in letting me know why he wasn't smiling.

"Listen," he said, "we've got to break up for a while."

"Why?"

"Well, my wife is raising hell. The boss is raising hell. Everything is hell, hell, hell."

"I thought you didn't care what your wife thought."

"It's more than that, Blanche."

"More than that?" I asked. "What else could possibly make you . . ."

"My job, damn it. The big boss called me into his office this morning and dressed me down. He said he knew you and I were sneaking off across the river and having a good time. He said one of the other supervisors had seen us over there. And he said he saw my car parked in front of your apartment at four o'clock in the morning. He's on to us,

Blanche, and he's a damned prude. I can't afford to lose this job. I've been working here for seven years, since I was eighteen, and I can't afford to lose it. With the war over, jobs are hard to find. I just can't lose it."

I sat there dumbfounded. It had never occurred to me that our relationship might end. I'd learned to lean on him, to count on him and, yes, to love him. Without warning, tears began to run down my face.

"Hey, look," he said, "it's just temporary, baby cakes. It isn't forever. Just give me a chance to get things straightened out."

"OK," I said, "but how long is that going to take?"

"I don't know . . . a few weeks, a couple of months."

"Oh, baby, I can't go that long without seeing you."

"Well, there is another way out of this."

"What's that?"

"I can fire you tomorrow morning. That'll solve all of the problems."

"What?"

"I'll fire you tomorrow morning right there in front of everyone. You find another job, and we'll stay together. It's the only other way I can think of."

At first I wanted to scream at him and tell him I had a good job, too, and I'd like to hold onto it. But I really wanted to marry him. Or so I thought. Perhaps I could go back to the jewelry store. I could certainly get a job at a restaurant. It would mean a cut in pay, but as long as I had him . . .

"OK," I said. "Fire me." I thought he would smile and hug me and tell me that he loved me. But he said tersely, "I think this will solve it." And he drove to my apartment.

When the car stopped, I turned toward him, desperately needing some show of affection. But he reached across me, unlatched the car door, pushed it open and said, "See you tomorrow."

I didn't even get a good-night kiss.

The next morning my lover walked up to my inspection station and said, "Miss Banks, you're fired. Go pick up your pay." And he walked quickly away.

The girl who worked across the table from me was shocked. "He can't do that. You're a good worker, Blanche. You ought to talk to the big boss."

"It's all right. I'll go."

"It isn't your work, is it? It's because you're seeing him. Everybody's been talking about it for months. That's what it is, isn't it?"

I smiled at her, thanked her for taking my side and left. I wonder now if she knew then what a big mistake I was making.

Buddy didn't bother to stop at the apartment for the next five days. I figured he was just playing it safe until the big boss quit watching him. I found a job at Choppy's Drive-In, but it was the late shift, and I didn't have a chance to look for Buddy again before the weekend. I waited all day Sunday and into the night. He didn't show.

It was time for my period, so I called in sick and stayed home Monday to see if he would come by. He didn't. To make matters worse, I didn't start my period. I worked and worried through that week and then another. After a couple of nights of torturing myself about how foolish I had been, I decided Buddy was gone for good. Lonely and afraid, I started dating a young soldier who frequented Choppy's Drive-In. My new fellow was all right, but he wasn't Buddy. I longed for him.

When I knew for certain that I was pregnant, I decided to make a bold move. I had no other choice, and I was angry. Buddy had misled me, caused me to lose the best job I'd ever had, and now I was pregnant. I began to forget that I had wanted to get pregnant, had planned on its happening.

I went to Archer Hosiery Mill to see Buddy face to face. When I walked in, he was surprised, unpleasantly so. I thought he might try to run, but he stood there with his eyes downcast while I approached.

"I'm . . . I'm sorry, Blanche. I wanted out, and I didn't have the nerve to come and tell you." He blurted this out before I could open my mouth.

"That's OK, Buddy. We've both got our own lives. Right now, though, we have a problem. You and I, understand?" I felt like everyone on that floor of the plant could hear what we were saying, but I didn't care anymore. "I'm pregnant, Buddy."

I purposely let my voice rise to make sure some of the women close to us could hear. In that plant, everyone would know by the end of the next break. I didn't want Buddy to have any hope of weaseling out of this situation.

"Shhhhhhh," he said. He took my arm and steered me toward an office he shared with another supervisor. There was no one there. He closed the door behind us.

"What are you trying to do, Blanche? Make sure I get fired, too?"

"That would be justice, wouldn't it? Maybe I ought to go into the big boss's office and shout that you got me pregnant."

"Blanche, goddamn it, I don't even know if you're pregnant or if I'm the one responsible."

"Well, I know, Buddy, and that's what counts."

"All right, what do you want?"

"We both know that we'll never get back together, so I certainly don't want any last reminder of you. I want to get an abortion, but I don't have the money."

"So that's what this is, huh, a shakedown?"

"Call it anything you want, Buddy, but I'm pregnant, and I don't have any money."

He was sweating profusely by then and becoming increasingly nervous.

"OK, OK, I'll get the money. Uh, how much does an abortion cost?" He pulled out a small wad of bills.

"About $150."

"Jesus Christ, Blanche, give me a break. I can't come up with that kind of money." And he stuck the bills back in his pocket.

"Get an advance in pay, Buddy. I know company policy. You've been here long enough to do that."

"Damn you, Blanche, you're shaking me down and . . . damn it, damn it, damn it."

With that, he went stomping out of the office. I sat down and waited, wondering if he really would try to get the money. The minutes ticked slowly away. I was afraid to face myself, to deal with the steps that had brought me to this position, so I focused on my anger at Buddy. I had to maintain that. If he saw how hurt and desperate and frightened I was, I would lose my control over him. Then I'd really be in trouble.

Nearly half an hour passed before he returned. He came inside alone, closed the door and held out his hand.

"Here. I got up $125, Blanche. It'll pay for the abortion, and that's all. No more. If you take this money, you'd better get out of my sight and never come back."

I took the money.

"Goodbye, Buddy."

"Don't ever come back, Blanche. If you do, I'll . . . I'll kill you, Blanche. I won't have my job, my marriage and my life all screwed up by a little whore like you."

I was stunned that he would call me something like that. What about my life, my job, my feelings? Why was he more important than I was? Who was he to judge me? My hand swung instinctively, and my palm ricocheted off his cheek.

"That was lowdown, Buddy, to say what you just said. You know I'm not a . . ." I couldn't bring myself to say the word. But I looked him straight in the eye and said, "Don't worry about me. You'll never see me again."

I left without looking back, hurrying by my former co-workers without answering their questions. I was concerned only with holding on to whatever shred of dignity I could muster.

My new boyfriend was sure to find out that I was having an abortion. I didn't see any way to keep him from knowing. With a toughness that sprang from feeling rejected, from having gotten a raw deal from Buddy, I decided to play hardball myself. I told my boyfriend I was pregnant.

"But we've only been going together for a couple of weeks," he said. "I don't understand . . ."

"I was supposed to start my period day before yesterday," I said, "and I didn't."

"Well, why don't we just wait a few days and maybe . . ."

"I'm going to see a doctor in Alabama and get a shot. It will make me start my period. But I've got to do it in a hurry. In a few days, it will be too late."

I didn't know whether there was an iota of truth in what I'd just said, but he didn't know the difference. He just wanted out from under the obligation, and I just wanted to survive, to come out of an ugly situation the best way I could manage.

"How much does this shot cost?"

I thought quickly. "Well, I've got to stay a couple of days to make sure I don't have convulsions," I said. "This is a new medicine, and it's very strong and very dangerous."

"So how much is it?"

"Fifty dollars."

He seemed relieved. "Listen, I'll take care of this. Just give me time to drive out to see my pa. He'll let me have the money."

Sure enough, he brought the money to Choppy's the next day. He was a nice country boy, and I felt a little guilty about using him this way. But I felt more anger at having been used myself, and he was a stand-in who unfortunately had to bear the brunt of that resentment. I told the boss my mother was sick and I needed to go home for a couple of days, and I went across the bridge to Phenix City to see the chiropractor again. Irma didn't go with me. She'd made the trip twice, and I felt funny about asking her again.

Something went wrong with that abortion. I knew it immediately. The bleeding didn't stop the way it had before. I stayed in my apartment for twenty-four hours, rolled up in a ball on the bed and groaning with pain. Thirty hours after the abortion, I was deathly ill. Every inch of my body was racked with pain. I tried to get out of bed to go next door to call Irma. But when I stood up, the room swirled around me, and I grabbed the edge of the dresser to keep from falling. I looked in the mirror. My hair was a mess, and my eyes looked black. Then I noticed my lips. They were turning blue.

"Oh, my God," I cried, "I'm dying."

My hand reached for the doorknob, but I doubt that I ever touched it. I was falling, falling helplessly into a cloud of numbness.

The next thing I saw was one of those little casters under the leg of the dresser. It was very clear, and the realization that I was not dead made me want to jump up and run out into the street and tell everyone that I was alive. I pulled myself back up to the dresser. I looked toward the window. Daylight streamed through the curtains. I didn't understand. It had been dark outside when I'd fallen. I must have been unconscious for a long time.

I still hurt. But now there was a strong determination to live. I opened the door and walked slowly but doggedly to my neighbor's apartment.

When the elderly woman who lived there opened the door, I said, "Call Irma," and passed out again.

My next bit of consciousness told me that I was in bed between cool sheets. People in white uniforms looked down at me. I went to sleep and slept for a long time. When I awakened, Irma was sitting at the side of my bed.

"Hi, it's Irma," she said.

"I know who you are."

"You didn't the last time I was here."

"Oh, God, Irma . . ."

"Hush, now. You're going to be all right. You had a close call, but you'll be all right. The nurse said to tell her if you came to, so let me get her."

In a few minutes, a doctor and nurse were at my bedside. They asked me a lot of questions, and I told them about the abortion. The doctor, a white-haired man with rudy skin, was obviously upset.

"We need to clean out that rat's nest over there. I wonder what it will take to get the authorities to do something?" he asked of no one in particular.

Then he sat down at my bedside and told me about what had gone wrong with the abortion. He finished up by saying, "The worst part of it all is that you'll probably never have a child because of this."

In a few days, I went back to work at Choppy's and settled into the grind of working until midnight every night except Sunday. There was nothing else to do. I couldn't change what had happened. I couldn't erase the abortion or the pain it had caused. I couldn't go back and relive the affair with Buddy, see him for what he was, see myself as young and wrongheaded and not ready for the consequences of my actions. I felt trapped again, like I was never going to get myself really started in the direction I wanted to go. Then, just when I thought I couldn't stand the boredom and repetition anymore, Jim Crowley came into my life.

He was a tall man, a Dennis O'Keefe type, who talked to me as if I were his daughter. He said he came from California. He never made clear what business he was in, but he drove a nice car and seemed to have plenty of money.

California? Money? Jim Crowley fit nicely into my plans. All those dreams of show business, fame, and fortune burst into vivid life again, and I was filled with hope for the first time in many months. But I'd become suspicious of just about everyone, and I didn't believe Jim when he said, "I'm going to be leaving for California in a few days. Want to go?"

I answered, "Sure, I'd love to go, but you're just pulling my leg. You aren't really going all the way out there."

"My parents live right there in Hollywood, Blanche, and I'm heading that way real soon. You just make up your mind what you're going to do."

I still didn't think he was serious. But he quickly proved me wrong. He came back the next day and said, "I'm leaving for California tomorrow morning. You've got to make up your mind. If you're going along, I'll pick you up wherever you say. But I won't be in town when this place opens tomorrow morning."

I'd been lied to so many times that I didn't trust him. So I didn't tell the boss I was quitting. At the end of the day, I said that I had a personal problem and needed my pay through that evening if he could give it to me. He didn't like it, but I'd done a good job for him. So he paid me. I was all set. If Jim Crowley came by my apartment the next morning, I was on my way to California. If not, I'd be back at Choppy's. At least I had learned one important lesson: always leave yourself another option; never count on any one thing alone.

Jim drove up in front of my apartment right on time the next morning. He smiled broadly when he saw me with my suitcase packed.

"I really didn't think you would go," he said.

"I've wanted to go to Hollywood for so long I can't remember the first time I wanted it. I'm so happy I can't see straight. Let me out of Georgia! California, here I come!"

His car was big and comfortable. As the car crossed the bridge, I took one look back at Columbus. I wouldn't miss it.

Jim was whistling happily. "We're going to have a good time," he said. "In fact, we're going to buy some new clothes for the best-looking gal in Alabama."

"Alabama?"

"Of course, Alabama. That's where we are right now. In a few hours, you will be the best-looking gal in Mississippi. And then you'll be the best-looking gal in Louisiana, then Texas, then New Mexico, then Arizona. In a few days, you'll be the best-looking gal in California."

Crooked teeth forgotten for the moment, I smiled.

We drove to Vicksburg, Mississippi, that first day. When he registered that night, he signed us in as man and wife. I knew I'd rather sleep with him than go back to Georgia. But I put him off that first night. I was testing him, making sure he meant the things he promised. I wanted to know now if he was just leading me on with false promises of California and new clothes. He took it pretty well, and the next morning he whistled as he shaved in the bathroom.

"We'll get to Dallas today if we hustle. It's Saturday, so the stores will stay open late. Dress stores is what I'm talking about. C'mon, let's dress you up like a queen."

The Dallas store was the biggest I'd ever seen. I looked and looked, and when I showed Jim two dresses I'd picked out, he laughed and said, "Two dresses? What are you going to wear the rest of this trip?"

By the time we checked out, I owned six new dresses, a couple of lacy slips, new bras that fit and fancy underwear.

"Now," he said, "let's find you a pair of patent leather high heels and a hat."

I squeezed his arm and said, "I'll take the shoes, but I won't wear the hat."

"Go on, honey, act like it's your birthday."

Stunned, I realized that the day before had been my birthday. I was nineteen.

After the shopping spree in Dallas, I didn't even think of putting Jim off another night. We made love, slept late the next morning, and took three more days to get to Hollywood. He made me feel special, safe, and secure. He was the first person to help me toward my dream, and dressed in the nicest clothes I'd ever had and basking in his obvious pleasure at seeing me transformed, I could only marvel at my good fortune as I came ever closer to my promised land.

When we arrived, I told him that I had to see the magic of Hollywood—even before we went to his home. He drove up one street and down the other. I'd never seen such sights. It was even more dazzling than I'd dreamed it would be.

When we finally went to his house, I met his parents. They were storybook grandparents—white-haired, quiet, courteous. He carried my bags inside and said, "This will be our room." I looked at his parents to see if they were going to ask about our marital status. They didn't, which surprised me. I soon learned why. Jim owned the house and paid the bills; that made him the boss, even where his parents were concerned. But I should have become concerned about what it meant for a man to need to be the boss to his parents.

Life wasn't all that bad at first. Jim took good care of me and the memories of tough times slipped away in the comfort of his home, cars and money. A couple of weeks after our arrival, Jim said he had to go to San Francisco on business. I still didn't know what his business was, and he didn't bother to tell me. He was gone a week. Then he flew back to Los Angeles for a few days. I was too busy enjoying my first small tastes of luxury to be concerned with Jim's doings.

One morning, he said, "I've got to fly back to Georgia to straighten out some business matters. You stay here with my folks and stay out of trouble. Understand?"

I nodded. But I was getting restless lying around all day, doing nothing and eating too much. His absence stretched into a week. I'd had enough. I caught a bus to downtown Los Angeles. I walked around for a while and wound up at Simon's Drive-In at Washington and Broadway. A familiar sign beckoned: "Waitress Wanted." In less than half an hour, I had a job. The manager said I could start that day at six P.M. I didn't bother to go back to Hollywood. I called Jim's folks and told them I had a job and would be in sometime after midnight.

For a week, I worked every night at Simon's until midnight. The crew was a great bunch of people about my own age, and it was good to talk to them after spending more than a month with only those old people and Jim, who was about forty-three. After Simon's closed, we went to an all-night doughnut shop, drank coffee and talked into the wee hours of the morning. Jim's parents didn't seem particularly disturbed by my hours. I suppose they were used to accepting their son's behavior without asking questions, and they treated me the same way. As for me, the work was good for me. I felt better than I had lying around the house all day. And I loved having friends again and spending those hours after work talking and laughing in the doughnut shop. It felt like it had been forever since I'd had any fun, and I liked having it.

Then Jim flew in during the middle of the night and found me gone. I hadn't told his parents where I was working, so all he could do was wait for me to come home. And that's when all hell broke loose. He was standing tall with his hands on his hips when I walked in the door a little after five A.M.

"Where the hell have you been, young lady?"

"Working."

"Working? Like hell! You've been out screwing around."

"No, I haven't. You don't know what you're talking about."

"Look at the time. Tell me where you work until five A.M. You're too damned young to get a job in a bar, so tell me what else stays open until this time of morning."

"I worked until midnight, Jim. Then I went to a doughnut shop and drank coffee with my friends until just a few minutes ago. I haven't been 'screwing around,' as you put it."

I walked toward the bedroom. He grabbed my arm and threw me onto the bed.

"I said you've been screwing around, and you're not going to make me believe otherwise. After all I've done for you, there's only one way to straighten you out."

His fist landed on the side of my head, and I saw stars. He fell on top of me and tried to jam his fist right down my throat. In the background, I could hear his parents screaming for him to stop, that I hadn't done anything wrong. Sitting astride me, he turned to his parents and said, "You two get out of here. I know how to settle things. I don't need your damned advice."

In that instant, while his attention was diverted, I struck back. I landed a blow to the side of his head, and, while he was leaning to his right, I shoved as powerfully as I could. He tumbled to the floor.

Quickly, I jumped to my feet. I saw him reaching for the nightstand, and I knew he kept an automatic pistol in the drawer. He'd shown it to me and said to use it if I ever had to. Right then, I wished I had it.

I ran out of the bedroom, almost knocking down the elderly couple that had been so nice to me. I was frantically pulling on the knob of the back door when I looked back over my shoulder.

"Blanche, goddamn you, you're dead."

He pointed the barrel of the pistol straight at my head and pulled the trigger. I braced myself for what I thought was coming. But I didn't see a puff of smoke or hear an explosion. All I heard was a flat click.

The gun had misfired.

Before he could clear the gun and get another bullet ready, I fled through the door, over a fence and barged head-long into a neighbor's house. They called the police and tried to get me settled down. Two policemen came to the door a few minutes later, and I told them what happened. They asked if I wanted to make a case against Jim Crowley. I told them that I simply wanted my personal belongings, that I wanted to move out and stay out.

They accompanied me back to the house. Jim tried to apologize, but when he saw that I wasn't going to forgive and forget, he told me that the only things I could take were those things I'd had when we left Georgia. Even so, I felt good about getting on with my life. I would make it without the false sense of security being with him had given me. After all, I was in California.

I rode downtown with the police and called a couple of the young people from work. They picked me up and let me sleep at their place for a few nights until I got enough money together to get a place of my own. Once again, Blanche Banks was broke and alone. But she was also wiser, and she was closer to her dream than she'd ever been.

In the next two years, I became old enough to work in cocktail lounges. I used the additional money I then earned to do several things. First, I bought some really nice clothes and tried to break into show business. But I had several problems: my teeth were crooked, and I didn't have the money to have them capped. Since I had no previous acting experience, no one seemed interested. At the modeling agencies, I was a joke, a freak with a forty-inch bosom that would never fit into their high-fashion dresses.

I saved up enough tip money by early 1950 to catch a train back to Georgia. Many times, I'd been homesick, and the trip back started off as a thrill. It didn't last long after my arrival in Eastman, though. My relatives still lived in poverty. They still wanted for all the things I'd learned to enjoy. They still suffered in more ways than I cared to count. If things had been better, I might have stayed home that time and never launched a show business career. But after visiting home, I went back to California with renewed resolve to get into show business. Eastman was as unbearable as I remembered it to be. I had to find a better life.

If I needed additional motivation, I wound up returning to California without enough money for the last meal before the train reached Los Angeles. Shortly after my return, I landed a job at The Paddock, a lounge with drinks and dancing in the front and bookmaking in the back. The pay was good, and I fell into a relationship with the owner, Lee Coopersmith. But my life did not fall into the old patterns. While I was working there, my first real chance at show business came.

Right: Family portrait
— Blanche, Mother, and
the kids

Below: A school picture
from Eastman

Bottom: A publicity
photo, early '50s

Publicity photo for my debut at Oakland's El Ray Theater

My early '50s look; Above: Promo postcard for Hoke Wynne's business

With Elvis in Las Vegas, a marathon of love

Right: In New York airport
with Stormy

Below: With a few of
the 1,500 male students
who mobbed me at the
University of Colorado

Samples from my portfolio, 1958-1969

Mickey Rooney, my first celebrity romance

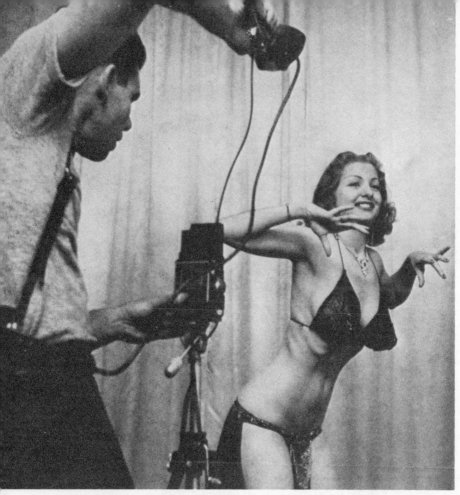

Photo session with Russ Meyer

My wedding to Herb Jeffries, May 1959

A working mother, Patty and I in my dressing room

Right: Patty and Herb

Below: Herb and I
performing together

# *Four*

The series of events that led me into show business and specifically into burlesque began in a way that made me suspicious. A regular at the Paddock offered to help me land a place in the chorus line at the Follies Theater. I knew him only as Denver. He looked like Robert Taylor, and he kept company with swaggering men who dressed in flashy clothes and drove fancy cars. I often heard rumors that he was somehow connected to the Mafia, and his appearance and that of his companions did little to dispel them.

Denver was supposedly the credit manager for a clothing store, but he never seemed to work regular hours. He was just as likely to show up at the Paddock at noon as at midnight. His salt-and-pepper hair gave him a mature, professional appearance that set him apart from his companions. Because Denver treated me like a true friend, I wasn't as shy around him as I might have been with other people who had his reputation.

One evening in the fall of 1950, Denver came to the lounge alone. He sat at a table near the back and ordered his usual cocktail, a martini. He drank regularly, but I'd never seen him drunk. That was another reason I liked him. I'd seen enough drunks—my stepfather and others—that I'd learned to dislike and distrust men who drank to excess. I put the martini on Denver's table and left with frosty mugs of beer for two customers at another table. As I started back to the bar, Denver motioned to me. The glass in front of him had not been touched, but, out of habit, I asked, "Another one?"

"No, I just want to talk to you."

"I've got customers."

"You've got exactly three customers, and I'm one of them. So sit down and talk, baby."

"Sorry, that's strictly against the rules."

"Be serious. Your boyfriend owns this place."

"I said it's against the rules."

"All right, then stand there and listen a minute."

I set my tray on his table and waited.

"Did anyone ever tell you that you ought to be in show business?"

"Oh, c'mon, Denver. Someone is always telling me that, but I've never had a break."

"Have you ever really tried?"

"I auditioned at a couple of places. But I wasn't willing to do . . . well, you know, some guy is always trying to get a girl into bed for some bit part in a movie. I wouldn't do that. I tried to break into modeling, but I have a problem there, too." Self-consciously, I looked down at my bust and added, "No one wants a model with a forty-inch bust."

Denver smiled and said, "So why don't you go where you're appreciated? Have you thought about burlesque?"

The very thought of it made me cringe inside. "Burlesque? You mean take off my clothes in front of a bunch of people? Are you crazy?"

The smile never left his face. "OK, then forget about stripping. How about dancing in the chorus line?"

"Chorus line?"

"Sure, I've seen you dance here on your night off, and you're a natural. It wouldn't take a whole lot of training for you to break into a chorus line. You've got a great body and a rare beauty about you. And I think you could smile if you really wanted to."

"My teeth are crooked, so I don't like to smile."

"Well, that wouldn't matter much in a chorus line."

"I don't know . . ."

"Listen, baby, they're hiring an entire new chorus line at the Follies Theater at Third and Main. A friend of mine, Lillian Hunt, does the hiring and firing and training. Right now, she's looking for young, good-looking dancers."

"Thanks, Denver, but I think I'll pass."

I walked away. He sat there for maybe fifteen minutes, sipping on the martini. I stood at the drink pickup station at the end of the bar and talked to Freddie, the bartender. He was telling me about a new sports car he was thinking about buying when he suddenly stopped talking and motioned over my shoulder.

"Denver wants you again."

"Freddie, why don't you . . ."

"He isn't going to bite you. See what he wants."

Denver's glass was still only about half empty.

"Another one?" I asked.

"Listen, Blanche. You really ought to talk to Lillian. She's a great lady, and she'll put you on your way to stardom. Lots of important people come to that theater, and they often come backstage to meet the dancers."

"Like who?"

"Well, Vic Damone was there the other night."

"Who else?"

"Mickey Rooney comes backstage sometimes."

I thought about it for a moment. Mickey Rooney? Maybe he could get me a break in the movies. I'd seen him in *National Velvet* and half a dozen other movies. No, I thought, what would he ever do for a girl from Georgia who never smiled? On the other hand . . .

"OK, Denver, if I decided to do this, what's in it for you?"

"Nothing, baby, there's absolutely nothing in it for me. Lillian's a friend, and you're a friend. I told her that I'd scout around for some dancers, and I've heard you say that you wanted to get out of here and into show business. Maybe it would be good for you and good for her."

"And how much does it pay?"

"You'll have to talk to Lillian about that, but one of the girls who just went to work there told me she's making forty dollars a week."

"Denver, counting tips, I make that much here."

"Sure, baby, but where is it getting you? You'll be here ten years from now, carrying drinks on a tray, looking at the same tired faces and making the same money. This might be a chance for you to make it big, Blanche. So what have you got to lose besides a little time?"

I started to walk away and tell Freddie to take Denver his next martini. But, somehow, I believed Denver was on the level, that he really wanted to see me break into show business. Besides, I could try it, and if I didn't like it, I could always return to waiting tables in a restaurant or bar.

"OK, Denver, I'll talk to her. No promises, you understand. If I don't like the deal, I'll just walk out and no hard feelings, right?"

"Sure, baby, sure."

He left without finishing his drink, and I figured he was gone for the evening. But he was back in less than an hour.

"You're all set, Blanche. Lillian is expecting you at the theater at three o'clock tomorrow afternoon."

"Just like that, huh?"

"Just like that, baby. Old Denver doesn't waste time when it comes to making money or doing a favor for a good friend."

The idea of dancing in a burlesque theater gave me cold feet. I thought about my mother back in Georgia. She'd kill me if she ever found out I was dancing in the skimpy attire burlesque dancers wear. Even though I wasn't in close contact with my family, what my mother thought remained important to me. In addition, I was always skeptical when a man offered something for nothing. I couldn't be sure, and even though burlesque was show business and I wanted more than anything to work my way to stardom, I just couldn't do it. I didn't go to the theater at the appointed hour, and it didn't take Denver long to find out.

He came to the bar and, as soon as he saw me, he pushed me firmly toward a quiet corner and said softly but angrily, "Goddamn it, Blanche, what are you trying to do, make an ass out of me?"

I didn't say anything.

"I go out of my way to try to get you a start in show business and you don't show up for a tryout. Well, hell will freeze over solid before I do anything else for you."

He paused a moment and then said, "I dropped in at the theater to see how you were doing, but all I got was laughed at. I really felt like a dumb-ass. Lillian said, 'What's the matter, lover boy, are you losing your touch with the ladies?' Well, I'm losing touch with you, Blanche. I'm getting the hell out of here, and you can thank your lucky stars that you're not a man. I'd beat the hell out of any man who went back on his word with me."

I'd never felt worse about letting someone down. After all, not too many people ever tried to help me unless there was something in it for them. I shouldn't have taken Denver's help so lightly.

I put a hand on his arm. "OK, Denver, I'll go. Tomorrow. I promise. Tell your friend that I missed the other appointment because I was sick, but that I'll be there this time. I'll do it for sure."

His face softened, and he smiled. Even though I felt a little queasy inside about going, I felt better about myself for trying to keep my word to Denver, and I was glad he was still my friend. I could use all the real friends I could get.

Just before three o'clock the next day, Lee, my boyfriend, who owned the Paddock, dropped me off at the Follies Theater. He smiled crookedly and said, "Have fun, sweetheart. Give it everything you've got. Maybe you can become a big star, make lots of money, and take me to Paris."

Lee had begun to wear on my nerves recently, getting more selfish and less lovable every day. I felt like I was involved in a replay of my previous relationships. As had happened with Buddy back in Columbus, Lee had led me to believe that his marriage was dead, a thing of the past, but I had finally realized that he would never leave his wife to be with me all the time. If the job at the Follies did work out, I might just go to Paris someday. But Lee Coopersmith would be the last person I'd want along. He'd better not count on me for his European holiday. Or anything else.

I stood across from the intersection of Third and Main and looked at the theater. It appeared dreary and a little shabby in the sunlight. Of course, that would change when darkness came and the neon lights began flashing.

I walked across the street for my first meeting with Lillian Hunt, who was a well-known trainer of chorus girls and strippers, I would learn. The young man at the stage door didn't bother to ask me what I wanted. He pointed down a hallway leading away from the stage. "Miss Hunt's office is the third door on the left."

"Must be a lot of girls looking for work these days," I said.

"Yeah, honey, there are," he said, his eyes glued to my bosom. "But there ain't many coming in here that look like you. I'd bet the shirt off my back that you get a job."

I was walking down the hallway when he said, "Damn sure ain't many like you. Honey, you've got it all."

I almost turned and smiled at him, because his comments gave me the boost in confidence I needed right then, even though they embarrassed me, too. But I didn't. I still had those crooked teeth. I wondered what Lillian Hunt would say about big bosoms and crooked teeth.

The third door on the left led into an office furnished with one desk and two chairs. The desk was littered with posters, papers and pictures. Behind the desk, a plumpish, red-haired woman about fifty sat in one of the chairs.

Without looking up, she said, "You looking for work?"

"Yes, ma'am."

"Don't say ma'am to me. I'm not as old as I look." She paused and then said, "How old are you?"

"Twenty-two."

She looked at me for the first time.

"Well, you're certainly pretty enough. But you sure don't look twenty-two, sweetheart."

"It's the truth."

"What's your name?"

"Blanche Banks."

"Full name."

"Annie Blanche Banks."

"Where were you born?"

"Eastman, Georgia."

"The date?"

I told her.

"You'd better be telling me the truth because I'll check."

"I'm legit," I said, using a term Humphrey Bogart had made popular at the time.

"Are you employed right now?"

"Yes. At the Paddock."

"Oh, yes, the cocktail waitress. You're the one Denver was telling me about, the one who didn't show up yesterday."

"Yes. And I'm sorry. I wasn't feeling well."

"Really? I thought maybe Denver scared you off with some of his wild stories."

"No, ma'am, I just . . ."

"Well, we'll see if you've got the stuff to make it in this business. Take 'em off."

"Take them off?"

"Yes, your clothes. Take them off."

"Take them off?" I asked again.

"Look, Blanche or Annie or whatever I call you . . ."

"Blanche."

"OK, Blanche, take them off. Every stitch, understand?"

"But why?"

"Because, by God, I said so," she said in a commanding voice. But then her expression softened and she added, "I want to see if you have any scars, birthmarks, stretch marks, fatty wrinkles, anything like that."

"I don't."

"Well, if you don't mind, I'll see for myself. Now take them off if you're looking for a job here. Or keep them on and start walking out the same way you came in. But do one or the other right now. I have a very busy afternoon."

With that, she went back to shuffling through the papers on her desk.

I began stripping.

God, I felt silly! She was old enough to be my mother, but I'd never felt so self-conscious. When I got down to my underpants, I hesitated. But only for a moment. All the old dreams, the years of turmoil and confusion, everything in my past had brought me to this moment. I had a chance to be in show business, and if all it took was undressing in front of a woman who might have been my mother, then I wasn't going to talk myself into refusing. It had become a challenge, and I wasn't about to turn back. I wanted the job very much. It was my way out of the Paddock and the dead-end affair with Lee, it was a way to earn the same money I was earning, and most importantly, it was a way to break into the career I'd dreamed about for years. So I placed my panties on the wooden chair and stood there as naked as the day I was born. Before she could look up, the door to her office opened, and a young man walked in.

"Lillian, that new backdrop is all screwed up," he said without any hint that he'd seen me. "We're gonna have to use just plain curtains for tonight's shows."

Modestly, I covered up as best I could with my arms and hands. He still didn't let on that I was even in the same room with him.

Lillian said, "Well, doll up the place the best you can. And get Zinger down here. He's supposed to be a good props man. I want that new backdrop in place by tomorrow night. It's the weekend and Lilly St. Cyr is opening, you know. She'll bitch to high heaven if we have just plain drapes behind her. You know how she is."

"OK, Lillian, I'll call Zinger."

He left, and Lillian Hunt, seeing me with arms folded over my nakedness, regarded me with open amusement.

"Don't tell me you've never stood naked in front of a man and he didn't get all excited about it?"

My face got hot, and I knew that the embarrassing moment had made it a bright red.

"Well, it's different around here," Lillian was saying. "These guys have more work to do than time to play around. Not that they won't try to take you out. But they don't have to ogle you. They see more than that every night of the week . . . except Sunday, of course, when we're closed."

She looked at me carefully as my arms dropped to my sides. She made a circular motion with her hand to let me know she wanted me to turn around. When I'd turned full circle and faced her once again, she said, "Get dressed and sit down."

Before I began putting on my clothes, I remembered the person I'd talked to at the modeling agency. I asked, "Do you think my breasts are too large?"

For the first time, Lillian Hunt laughed. It was such a hearty laugh that I knew everyone in the stage area must have heard her.

"Too big, my dear? Did you say too big?" Her stocky body rocked with more laughter.

"Listen, Annie Blanche Banks. Some women—indeed, most of them in this business—would kill to have what you've got. God didn't make boobs too big for my business. Have you ever really looked at strippers and chorus girls?"

I shook my head.

"Well, let me tell you about a girl who couldn't dance the first step. But she could walk and that created all of the excitement that was needed in a burlesque theater. She had a fifty-inch bust and, when anyone asked what sort of dance she did, her manager would say, 'Dance? She doesn't dance. She just crawls out on the stage and tries to sit up!' Of course, he was joking, but he kept her booked. Last I heard, she was . . . oh, hell, enough of this. Do you want a job?"

"How much does it pay?"

"Starting pay for a chorus girl is forty dollars a week. If you decide you want to try stripping, we'll talk about a pretty hefty raise."

"I'd like to try the chorus line."

She fixed me with a steady gaze and asked, "Do you have any doubts about yourself? I don't want to spend a lot of time training you if you're going to get cold feet—or tired feet—and walk out on me."

"Well, I'm worried about the dancing. The only place I've ever danced was at the lounge on my night off. You know, dancing with a guy."

"I'm not talking about your having doubts about learning, Blanche. I'm talking about inside yourself. I don't want you to chicken out when it's time to perform."

"No, I won't do that. I'm just worried about having enough talent."

Lillian didn't give my doubts much time to jell. She reached behind her and turned on a phonograph. A jumpy, bumpy tune filled the small office. Lillian Hunt came around the desk to stand beside me.

"Watch this step and see if you can do it."

She did a little skip step, then rocked her pelvis forward. It certainly was different—and more provocative—than anything I'd ever done on the dance floor. But I gave it my best effort.

"That's pretty awful," she said.

She repeated the basic motion, and I tried again.

"You're just a little too uptight. Relax. Relax and let yourself go."

She showed me the step one more time. I tried it.

She looked at me with an exasperated expression.

"You've been to bed with a man, haven't you?"

I hesitated for just a moment. It was a question I wasn't used to answering.

"Well, what the hell. Have you or haven't you?"

"Uh, yes . . . yes, I have."

"Well, thank God for little favors. For a minute there, I thought I might have recruited my first virgin for the chorus line." She smiled at the thought of such a development and then said, "Well, all we have to do is to get you to use the same motions right now. Now, let's see that pelvis move!"

She performed the simple move one last time. But it took me two more attempts before she finally nodded an OK.

"You might make it," she finally said. "But be thankful that you've got that great build and a rare beauty about you because your dancing has a long way to go."

I couldn't hide my disappointment at such an evaluation. She saw it and quickly said, "But, with the right training, you could become a headliner."

I shook my head at that suggestion. "It's all right. I'll be happy just dancing in the chorus line."

She slapped her hands together. "OK, let's see how good you might be at that. Let's see if you can kick your leg any better than you can rock your pelvis."

I kicked.

"Not like that," she said. "Take a little bounce step and do it this way." When she showed me, I was amazed at the agility of the heavy-set Lillian Hunt.

I tried it.

"Higher," she said.

I kicked higher.

"One more time," she said. "Higher."

I kicked again, going as high as I possibly could.

"Yes," she said, a smile crossing her face, "I think you'll do for the chorus line. It will take a couple of weeks to work you into the lineup, but your pay starts immediately. Part of your job is to watch every show until you start performing onstage. Understand?"

"Yes, ma'am."

"Listen, if you don't stop calling me ma'am . . ."

"I'm sorry, Miss . . ."

"Don't call me Miss. I haven't missed enough in life to be called Miss."

I stood there silently.

"What the hell's wrong with just calling me Lillian?" she asked, obviously irritated with me.

"Nothing, I guess."

"Well, fine. Call me Lillian."

I nodded.

She gestured to the chair where my clothes had hung, and she went behind the desk and turned off the phonograph. She sat down and pointed a stubby finger at me.

"Now listen to me very carefully, Annie Blanche Banks. Lots of girls come in here wanting a job. Most of them can dance. A few have real talent. But very few of them listen to—and heed—what I'm going to tell you now."

She paused a moment, and her expression became more serious.

"First, you weigh about 135 pounds, right?"

"That's pretty close."

"And you're about, hmmmmm, maybe five feet, six inches?"

"Yes."

"Don't put on one more pound, do you understand?"

I nodded.

"If you put on one more pound, you'll be fat. So watch what you eat. If your fellow brings you a box of candy, make sure he eats it before he leaves."

I nodded again.

"But don't lose too much, either. You're very close to being right. Men want a little flesh on their dancers. Slender women should try modeling."

Her eyes were riveted to mine. "I'm going to tell you one more thing you'd better never forget. Don't you start to drink heavily or just before you come to work."

"I don't even drink," I said.

"Good. Keep it that way. Don't let this job get you started. The people who work here may encourage you, but don't pay them any attention. Don't let the money you'll be making get you started either. Just remember, drinking and dancing don't mix. Say that over and over to yourself until you believe it. The last thing I need is a hungover dancer who falls on her rear end out there on the stage."

"Yes, ma'am . . . uh, Lillian."

"As long as you work at it, you'll be a good dancer. But if I ever find out you're hitting the bottle, I'm going to let you slide right on out of here and into the gutter. Understand?"

I nodded again.

"You might as well leave the cigarettes alone, too. All they'll do is make you short-winded, and you'll wear out before you make it through the whole show. A dancer has to be in just as good a shape as an athlete. Your body is your instrument. Take care of it."

She paused and regarded me for a few moments.

"I'm really going to try with you, Annie Blanche Banks. Are you going to try really hard for me?"

"Yes, I will. I promise."

She fixed me with that steady stare again. I looked her dead in the eye and never blinked.

Finally, she said, "Good. Here's a door pass. Come down here tonight and watch the show. Watch the chorus line. Watch every move they make. You'll be practicing with them tomorrow. And you'll be up there in a few days."

She stood up. "Practice starts tomorrow at 1:30 sharp. Be dressed and ready."

As I got up to leave, she put a hand on my arm. "You're different from most of those who come in here. You've got a fresh country look about you that will drive men crazy . . . if it already hasn't. And you've got a beauty that will make men drool, honey. You can make it in this business. And I mean you can make it big."

She smiled and added, "Now, come on, smile."

"I don't like to. My teeth are crooked."

"I'll bet we can fix that, too."

"Really?"

"Sure, I know a dentist in town who is the best. We'll see about it."

I left her office feeling better than I ever remembered having felt. I still didn't like the idea of dancing almost nude, but at least it was show business. Besides, Lillian Hunt truly seemed to care about my having a career in dancing. It wasn't just a two-bit job to her, and I intended to listen, to work hard, and to learn everything I could from her and all the other dancers. This was another real turning point in my life, and I was determined that it would be a turn in the right direction, toward the career and the way of life I'd been seeking when I first set out from Eastman. I couldn't wait to tell Lee Coopersmith that I'd be quitting the Paddock. I would never again wait tables, if I had anything to say about my future. And I was finally beginning to feel that I did have that say.

After watching both shows that first night, I went home and practiced the steps and kicks. I was perspiring freely and still dancing in the living room when Lee came by after closing the lounge.

"Hey, some of the guys asked about you tonight."

"Good," I said as I continued dancing.

"I want you to give up this thing about dancing and come back. You're a drawing card. The people like you."

"I'm not going back to the Paddock, Lee. I don't intend to wait another table. I'm going to make it in the theater."

"Make it in the theater?" he asked, his voice rising in anger. "You're going to be just another goddamn stripper, showing your ass to everyone in town, that's what you're going to do."

"So what's wrong with that, if that's what I want to do? Why shouldn't I try to make my own career?"

"To hell with your career. Get back to the Paddock. And do it tomorrow night, do you hear?"

"I'm not going back, Lee."

He stood there for a minute, trying to stare me down, waiting to see if I'd weaken. Undoubtedly, what he saw was not what he'd expected. He walked toward me.

"Say that again."

"I said I'm not going back."

Without warning, his hand swung around in a lightning-quick arc and struck me on the left cheek. I spun around and landed on the sofa on my right side.

He reached for me. My voice dropped an octave and I said, "Get your goddamn hands off me, Lee. Don't you touch me again!"

I seldom swore, and I'd never used that word in his presence. His body froze.

"If you so much as touch me, I'll have Denver drop you in a ditch out in the hills."

It was his turn to be stunned. "What?"

"Denver," I said as harshly as I could. "He doesn't like you, Lee. He thinks you're a drunken sissy, and he's just looking for a reason to beat the hell out of you. If I tell him you hit me, he's liable to shoot holes in you. You understand that, don't you?"

Lee had often talked about what a tough guy Denver was reputed to be. He backed away from me.

"That's right, get the hell away from me. Get out and don't come back. A man doesn't get but one chance to slap me around."

"Aw, honey . . ."

"Don't try to sweet talk me. Just get out."

He stood there for a moment. He could see I was serious.

"OK, sweetheart. Go ahead. But you won't make it. You'll come crawling back, looking for a job, looking for me. You can't make it, not even in that goddamn business."

I stood my ground and didn't bother to answer.

He turned and walked to the door. He hesitated and looked back. When I didn't say anything, he left.

I locked the door, took a hot shower, crawled in bed and slept like a baby. I didn't need Lee Coopersmith. From that point on, it would be Blanche Banks and her career. From now on, I would not retreat from my own goals for fear of losing a man. Any man who was afraid of me when I was in control of my career wasn't a man I'd want anyhow.

Lillian Hunt was obviously pleased with my first day at rehearsal. She stopped calling me Annie Blanche or even Blanche. She called me Ann, and at one point during practice, she said to one of the other dancers, "Ruth, you'd better get with it. This is the first day Ann ever stepped on a stage, and she's making you look like a rank beginner."

I appreciated the praise, but I wondered how Ruth was going to take that kind of criticism when it was delivered in front of the other dancers. As it turned out, it didn't matter. While I was dressing, one of the stagehands told me Lillian wanted to see me before I left.

"Ruth won't be coming back tomorrow. She quit. But that's just as well. She wouldn't have made it on the stage. God gave her two left feet and a brain about the size of a pea. Good riddance!"

I didn't say anything, but I noted that Lillian saw brains as necessary to success as a dancer. I wouldn't hide my brains from her.

"I need you tonight, Ann."

"But I've rehearsed just one day."

"I don't care. You've done well, and I need you tonight. We can't do the routines with less than eight dancers. Without you, I'll have just seven."

"Just one day of practice . . ."

"But you can do it."

"I'll try."

In one evening, I won Lillian Hunt's respect as a performer. I mustered all of my concentration and tried like I'd never tried before. When my feet ached between shows, I remembered Lee Coopersmith, my stepfather, all the men who'd seen me as an object and not as a human being, my old schoolmates and other people who'd ridiculed my large breasts and crooked teeth. And I danced every step like it was the most important thing I'd ever done. I wanted perfection. Even the other chorus girls complimented me on how I'd managed to master the routines in such a short time.

My reward came quickly. Lillian moved me to the center of the line—the most coveted spot—on my third night. After the fourth night, she said she wanted to see me in her office after the last show. She was seated behind the desk when I entered. She looked up from some paperwork.

"Ann, you're really a talented young lady. You're by far the best student I've ever had . . . and don't forget I've had some good ones."

"Yes, I know you have."

"I want you to think real hard about something. I want you to have your own act and start stripping."

"Lillian, I can't. I just can't. My mother would . . ."

"Your mother can't see you. We need a new act, a new face out there." She paused and looked at my bosom. "Hell, the truth is, we need someone to knock their damned eyes out. And you're it."

"I don't know. I just . . . "

"I'll train you and pay you sixty dollars a week right away."

"I don't know."

"Remember that dentist I told you about?"

My heart jumped. "Yes."

"I've already talked to him. I'll get you an appointment, and you can get your teeth fixed starting tomorrow afternoon. I'll even get things arranged so you can pay for it on time with the extra money you'll be making."

I had all I could do to keep tears from spilling out. I swallowed hard and didn't trust myself to say anything. Lillian took my silence for reluctance. She couldn't have known what an obstacle those teeth had been to me. If I did as she suggested, if I did become a stripper, I would be able to use my money for myself, to give myself a smile. No wonder I couldn't speak.

"I'll tell you what to do," she said. "You think about it and let me know. Meanwhile, you can dance as long as you want in the chorus line whether you ever become a stripper."

"I don't need to think about it," I said, finally trusting my voice. "I'll do what you want. But I want to start getting my teeth capped right away. I guarantee you that I won't smile a single time until I get them fixed."

She smiled broadly.

I couldn't keep from smiling, too.

The transition was remarkable. Suddenly I didn't have to rehearse with other dancers. I worked on my own routine with Lillian constantly coaching and encouraging me.

After my first lesson in provocative dancing, Lillian motioned me to a seat in the front row of the theater.

"You've got to loosen up a little, make your movements smoother. Just remember that the men in the audience come here to see you. They've paid good money to see you. Give them a show! Let yourself go!"

"I think I'm getting the hang of it."

"I know you are. I just want you to relax a little. Don't be so stiff. And don't think you have to do things the way other strippers do. You must adapt the basic steps to your own talents and your own feelings. Make the dance be you! Understand? I want you to be such an individual and become such a good dancer that you can look back someday and say, 'Nobody does it like me!' Hear me, Ann?"

"Yes, I hear you. I'd like to be that good."

I rehearsed twice a day—one hour before the chorus line showed up and another hour after they finished. I borrowed an old outfit from one of the other strippers, but I didn't like it. It didn't fit very well, and it was held together with straight pins.

So Annie Blanche Banks, the Georgia farm girl, decided to put her training from Dodge County High School to good use: I could make my own outfits.

"You can't just go out and buy things like that," Lillian had told me. "There's a woman in Huntington Beach who makes all sorts of costumes, but they're expensive, and it takes a while to get them. You'll have to borrow some things from the other strippers."

"It's OK. I'll make my own outfits."

"Make them yourself?" Lillian asked in a tone that indicated she doubted me.

"I'm pretty good with scissors, needles, and thread," I said. "I'll just have to find someplace to get the right material."

So I looked at the costumes worn by other dancers. Then I went shopping. I bought material, snaps, lacy trim, and needles and thread.

Lillian was amazed.

"You're the first dancer I've ever trained who made her own costumes. I shouldn't be surprised, I suppose. You're different in a lot of ways."

I'd been rehearsing only a few days, and things were moving incredibly fast. But I was hardly prepared for Lillian's next statement.

"I have one more challenge, Ann."

"What's that?"

"The back-up act is moving to the El Rey Theater in Oakland to open on Monday night. You're the replacement. Think you can handle it?"

A new confidence was building inside me. I'd worked hard on my routine, and my costume was finished. Besides, I felt like I could fly to the moon if Lillian told me to.

"I'll do it," I said, "but I won't smile."

We both laughed. And for good reason. My first appointment with the dentist was set for the next morning. We knew it wouldn't be that long before I could both dance and smile.

# Five

Burlesque shows begin with lesser known performers and lead up to the star attraction. Since I was the newest dancer at the Follies Theater, I was the first stripper to perform that night late in 1950. I stood in the wings and shivered while a couple of comedians, Eddie Ware and Billy "Zoot" Reed, warmed up the audience. I liked the idea of opening on a Monday night because it gave me a few nights to smooth out my act before the larger weekend crowds filled the theater. Of course, I also liked the idea of my name's appearing on the marquee for the first time. I'd stood on the street earlier that day looking at Ann Banks up there and admiring it, even though few who saw it would know who I was.

As Eddie and Zoot wrapped up their act, the lights on the stage dimmed. I was next. Eddie, a really nice guy who'd encouraged me as a chorus girl, knew that I was nervous. He walked past me, touched my hand and said, "Give 'em hell, honey. You can do it."

Then the spotlight shot its lavender beam at the part in the curtains where I was supposed to appear. Lillian Hunt, standing beside me, touched my shoulder and gave a last bit of advice: "Just relax and do your thing."

I almost smiled. But then I remembered that all of my teeth weren't capped yet, so I kept a straight face as I glided onto the stage to the notes of "Deep Purple," doing a full turn to show off the purple gown I'd made especially for the show. I heard the announcer say my name and call me "an up-and-coming star of burlesque." The show was on.

But the applause seemed polite. Almost too polite. This wasn't the response from the audience I'd learned to expect from watching other solo performers. Then a voice near the front said, "Holy cow! Look at the build on this one!" That brought another round of applause, this time louder and spiced with wolf whistles.

Many things came together in the next few moments.

I was as green as spring grass when it came to stripping. I'd practiced my routine no more than a dozen times. If my name had not been on the marquee, I might have gotten cold feet before I ever stepped out on the stage that night. But the reaction of the audience did something for me. It washed away any doubts I'd had. They liked me, and I intended to give them the best show they'd ever seen.

My hips gyrated with a seductiveness I didn't know Annie Blanche Banks of Eastman, Georgia, could ever muster. My hands moved like they were guided by their own choreographer. My feet glided with a confidence I'd never felt before. The purple gown came off. The roar was deafening. Goose-bumps of excitement rose on my skin. As "Deep Purple" ended, I stood there in a net bra, a rhinestone-covered G-string and a see-through skirt of purple chiffon.

Then "St. Louis Blues" came pouring from the speakers, and my body, my hands, my feet began the second part of my act. As I peeled away the skirt, the crowd roared again and voices encouraged me to take it all off. Of course, everything didn't come off in those days. The net bra and the G-string had to stay on. So it was up to me to give them a show they'd remember. My dancing had to be the thing to satisfy them.

I could feel a chemistry with the audience that night. And I was happy that they had given me such a hearty welcome to the stage. When the music died, the crowd stood and cheered. I gave one more bump and grind and ran offstage. I couldn't keep from smiling, no matter what my teeth looked like.

Lillian was waiting for me.

"My God, you were great!" she said, a happy smile lighting up her chubby features. "Listen to them. They want you back. Here, wrap your gown around you, take a bow, give them one more good look at you and then get off-stage before some of them try to attack you."

As I walked back onto the stage, the applause was truly music to my ears. They were still shouting "More! More!" as music for the next act began. In the dressing room, I soaked up the praise of the other performers. Even a couple of the stagehands stopped long enough to offer compliments. Finally alone, I looked at my nearly naked image in the mirror and winked at myself. Aloud I said, "Annie Blanche Banks, you're a vamp!"

Lillian Hunt seconded that statement the next day at practice. "You're a natural-born tease, Ann. You're in the right business." Then she said that still another dancer would be leaving for Oakland the next week. It was a normal rotation between theaters, and I would be given the chance to move up.

I wondered who would have to perform before me and how that dancer might feel about dancing ahead of an absolute beginner. I'd already noticed the little jealousies among performers, and I really didn't look forward to animosity because of my rise in the performance order. On the other hand, I wasn't willing to take any backward steps in my career to salve someone's hurt feelings. I was on my way at last.

Within a month, the dentist had finished working on my teeth, my career was taking off, and I had plenty to smile about. If there was a drawback at that point, it was my name.

Lillian called me to her office one afternoon and told me that we were going to have to come up with a stage name that would grab people's attention. We talked for perhaps an hour. We looked at a list of current burlesque performers—Torrid Terry Lane, Gay Dawn, Icel, Kasha, Countess de Risque, Lady Godiva. I told her I didn't like the single names or anything like Lady Godiva. We kicked names around for a while and almost settled on Sunny Day. But I held back on even that one. I didn't feel like a sunny day, even though I knew it had stage appeal.

Finally, she said, "You know, you really dance up a storm. Maybe we could name you Stormy something-or-other. Maybe Storm would make a better last name. Hmmmmm. Let's see, what kind of first name would go with that?"

That name clicked. Lillian could see that I liked it. We talked some more and finally, she said, "Oh, it's so damned obvious! Why didn't I think of it an hour ago?"

"Think of what?"

"Tempest! That's stormy, too. It's perfect! Tempest Storm!"

I rolled the name around in my mind. Tempest Storm, huh?

"Well, how do you like it?"

How did I like it? I loved it. And it has never lost its appeal to me. I legally changed my name to Tempest Storm in 1957, and I would see it on marquees from coast to coast—in Las Vegas and Atlantic City, in Los Angeles and New York, in Miami and Buffalo and Dayton and Chicago and San Francisco—and in London, England, where the European press flocked to my opening night. It is a name that has never left theater marquees, so it must have been the right choice.

Being a burlesque dancer meant being pursued, truly pursued, by men. Famous men. Rich men. Ordinary men. All of them had one thing in mind—sex. But thanks to Lillian Hunt and other veterans in the business, I learned early on what these men and their pursuit meant. I decided to play my hand carefully, not to go overboard like some and sleep with everyone who took me out on the town.

Even though it was fertile ground for superficial relationships, there was also a certain respectability about burlesque theaters in those days. Men sometimes brought their wives to the Follies back then. I remember Edward G. Robinson and his wife showing up a couple of times. And Burt Lancaster and his wife came to see me one time shortly after I got my own act. What I remember most about Robinson was that he was every bit as mean-talking and ill-tempered as his screen characters. He must have enjoyed being the bad guy, even in real life. Maybe that made him happy, but I didn't enjoy talking with him.

Lancaster, on the other hand, seemed to have a great sense of humor and did not talk to the dancers like they were some lower form of life. He told me that I had real talent, which, of course, meant a lot to a young woman just starting a career.

My first romance with a celebrity began the night I met Mickey Rooney. I'd seen him in a number of movies and had always liked *National Velvet*, in which he starred with a very, very young Elizabeth Taylor. I'd been dancing about two months when he came backstage after the last performance. One of the chorus girls said, "Mickey Rooney is out here and wants to see you right away."

I'd met enough stars by then that some of the awe had faded. I almost told her to tell him to wait if he wanted to see me. But Mickey Rooney was a big star, and if he wanted to take me out, I knew what that could do to my career. Being seen with him meant bits in gossip columns, photos in magazines, perhaps a break in other types of show business. I was learning how to handle my career, how to use the press to further my reputation and enhance my image. Very quickly, I had realized that there is much more to a career in burlesque than performing.

"Tell him to come on in," I said.

I was fully dressed and ready to leave, but I decided I'd rather talk to him in the privacy of my dressing room. He entered with his famous All-American smile splashed across his babyish face.

"Hi, Tempest," he said. "The show was great, and I thought you might like to celebrate with me. What do you say? Dinner?"

Mickey was just out of a highly publicized divorce from wife No. 3 (Martha Vickers), and his sexual exploits with the young ladies of show business were quickly becoming a Hollywood legend. But that didn't bother me. I'd become a good dancer. I'd taken a name with stage appeal. I'd done just about all I could do on my own to become a star. I'd reached the point in my career that I needed to be seen with name entertainers, to be talked about, to be publicized. And I knew it. So I agreed that a little celebration was in order.

He took my arm and escorted me through the people still congregated backstage. I could feel their eyes on me, and I knew they were thinking, "Well, there goes Rooney with another conquest." But that's exactly what I wanted—for them, for everyone, to talk about Tempest Storm.

We dined that night in a small, out-of-the-way restaurant in Santa Monica. There was nothing wrong with the food or the atmosphere, but I would have preferred one of the better-known spots where celebrities dined. As we drove back along the freeway toward Hollywood, he asked if I'd like to have a drink at his place. I knew where that could lead—to the bedroom. And I was determined that if it was going to lead there, then Mickey Rooney would have to do a whole lot better than a mediocre dinner in an out-of-the-way restaurant in Santa Monica. He wanted something from me, but I also wanted something from him. I wanted to be sure I didn't come out the loser in the relationship. This may sound harsh, but the world of show business can be a tough world. It's important to know how to protect yourself and your interests.

"I'm really beat tonight, Mickey, but I'm sure I'll feel a lot better tomorrow night," I said. "Tell you what I'll do. I'll meet you at the Interlude tomorrow night, and we'll see what happens after that."

The Interlude was one of the most prestigious clubs in town, and I knew that if I met him there, we'd also dine there. Yes, I was learning how to play the game of show business dating.

At the Interlude the next evening, Mickey was pacing nervously around the lobby when I arrived about ten minutes late. I had the feeling that his nervousness was about more than my being a bit late. While we dined, he kept looking around and commenting on who was there. Suddenly he said, "Oh, God, there is Dick Williams, that gossip columnist from the *Los Angeles Mirror*."

"So? What's wrong with that?" I asked. This was just what I'd been hoping would happen.

"Oh, we'll probably make the papers, that's all."

"Is that bad?"

"It's my agent. He'll raise hell if he sees anything in the paper about my being out with you. He said I was going to ruin my *National Velvet* image if I was seen out on the town with you."

This was my first brush with the stigma of being a stripper. I let it pass because I hadn't dealt with it enough to get angry. But the stigma was destined to become one of my most constant companions. No matter how successful I was to become, no matter how much class my act became known for, some people have never been able to deal with me, Tempest Storm. They can see nothing except their own image of "a stripper," and society has conditioned them to see that as a negative image.

At the Interlude that night, Mickey introduced me to several other stars who frequented the nightspot. And when we left, he drove straight to the Beverly Hills Hotel. "I started to ask, 'Your place or mine?' but I decided it might as well be mine. I maintain a suite here. I hope that's OK," he said.

It was OK. I liked Mickey Rooney. He'd treated me decently, and I needed him.

Once in his suite, he wasted little time. He mixed me a drink—which I really didn't want—put a record on the phonograph and waltzed me around the room. He was a couple of inches shorter than me, and his gaze became fixed on my bosom as we danced.

"Damn! All that meat and no potatoes," he said with a big grin. As the song ended, he let his face drop down until it was buried in my cleavage. To Mickey Rooney, that was foreplay.

Within a few minutes, we were in bed.

Mickey was right about the gossip columnist. In the *Mirror* the next day, it was reported that "one of Hollywood's biggest names showed up at the Interlude (wearing elevator shoes, of course) with one of the rising stars of burlesque (a performer known for her stormy dances)." That wonderful way gossip columnists have of being both obilque and crystal clear meant any idiot could have figured out who Dick Williams was talking about.

Mickey didn't come by the theater that evening. He called and said his agent was in a rage. But I didn't intend to leave him alone. Not only did I know the publicity would help my career, but I was also yearning to strike back at the stripper's stigma.

"Aren't we going out tonight, honey?" I asked in my most inviting voice.

"Well, I don't know . . . aw, hell, yes," he said. "How about . . ."

"How about Ciro's?" I interrupted. Ciro's was every bit as swanky as the Interlude and attracted just as many of the stars.

"Oh, well, uh, sure, baby. Sure. Why not?"

His stuttering told me that he would have preferred a more isolated restaurant. But he agreed, and I met him there after my last show. Of course, we were seen, and, of course, we were talked about again. And after a scrumptious dinner, we went to his place, and I made love to him with an abandon I'd never known. It was wild and wonderful, and when I left, he was draped across the bed as limp as a wet dishtowel.

That's the way I planned to keep him. I wanted him to stop paying so much attention to his agent and do what I wanted to do. Mickey became bolder about where he took me after that frenzied session. We were seen together almost every night. I thrilled at the attention, and he thrilled at our lovemaking afterward. We'd reached a wonderful working agreement.

About three weeks after our love affair started, Mickey showed up at the theater one night with a box almost as tall as he was.

"Got something for you, baby. Something very special for a very special lady in my life. Go ahead, open it."

When I did, my mouth dropped open in shocked disbelief. It was a full-length mink coat. My first mink coat. A wonderful mink coat. A mink coat that said I'd hit the bigtime.

I kissed Mickey long and passionately, then said, "You won't live through this night, lover."

He held his head with both hands and joked, "You know, I think I feel a headache coming on."

When I walked out of my dressing room with that coat on, the chorus girls screeched with admiration. And when I left his place that night, he wouldn't have felt it if an elephant had stepped on him.

119

At the theater the following evening, I decided to do something different with my act. What better way to show of my new coat than right out there on the stage? So I put the purple gown aside for one performance. The coat wasn't purple, but I turned in one of my best performances by stripping from that coat. The crowd ate it up. Gay Dawn was the headliner that evening, and after my mink coat performance, her dance drew much less applause. As I came offstage at the end of my dance, she was already complaining to Lillian Hunt, who was holding my coat. And as she heard the continuing applause, she really sounded off. Later, Lillian warned me never to upstage a star attraction. That's when I made up my mind to be the star of the show. To be at the top very soon.

Mickey Rooney and I saw each other for about three months. I sensed that we were drifting apart even before a gossip columnist reported that he'd given me a mink coat that wasn't entirely paid for and was already chasing another woman.

A later report in the *New York Post* said:

"Rooney started dating stripper Tempest Storm. He was thoroughly familiar with what it took to woo a stripper—for instance, a floor-length mink coat that set him back $10,000, according to one of his managers. Of course, he made only a small down payment, but it was a serious enough investment to convince friends that Rooney would soon be escorting the young lady to the altar.

"As fate would have it, Tempest Storm was not destined to become Mrs. Mickey Rooney No. 4. It's doubtful if Rooney even continued making payments on the coat after a tall, statuesque redhead named Elaine Mahnken caught his eye at a [golf] driving range one afternoon."

Well, Elaine Mahnken became Mrs. Mickey Rooney No. 4, but I kept the mink coat. I don't know how many payments Mickey made or didn't make. I don't even know if the newspaper report was accurate on the money details, but I kept the beautiful coat. Anytime I wore it, I remembered Mickey Rooney. We remained good friends, but the coat was a reminder of how he played me for what he wanted and how I played him for what I wanted, a reminder of my growing savvy about life in show business.

Even though our affair eventually cooled, my career didn't. In fact, another break came my way because of the "assets" that kept me out of modeling. Dick Williams and some of the other well-known Hollywood gossip writers got together and decided to have something called the "Mickey Awards." The name had nothing to do with Mickey Rooney. It was just a coincidence that I was dating him at the time an absolutely funny show was put together.

The Mickey Awards was a spoof of the Academy Awards. The writers thought up all sorts of crazy awards to give out to get the big stars to attend the ceremony. For instance, Phil Harris got an award for getting the most phone calls at the Brown Derby. Some of us thought he'd planted someone to call him every few minutes. But only at an event as zany as the Mickey Awards would he ever have been recognized for something like that.

The writers also had the idea to give out an award to a girl with a big bust. This award would go to whoever had "The Two Biggest Props in Hollywood." The first time I heard about the Mickey Awards was when Williams, the same reporter who first linked my name with Rooney's, came to the Follies one night to look for the right woman for that award. Of course, there were others in the show with busts every bit as big as mine. A few had even bigger "props." But he picked me. I didn't react like someone who'd won the Miss America contest. I took it in stride. I figured I might get my picture in the papers, and that kind of publicity could help my career. I had no idea of the impact that title would have.

I was still a brunette at the time, and, on the night of the awards, I wore an elegant champagne-colored, lacy strapless gown with a flair at the bottom. It was the sort of gown that showed my "props" off best. My hair was piled up on top of my head in a chic bouffant. And I could smile because my teeth had been capped.

Perhaps my biggest surprise was to learn that Dean Martin and Jerry Lewis would escort me into the awards dinner at Barney's Beanery, one of Hollywood's most famous clubs. I'll never forget that night. Jerry and Dean stood on either side of me as we awaited our turn to enter the small stage around which a crowd of people and several newsreel crews were gathered. Both Movietone and Paramount news cameras were among those filming the awards. And I remember Jerry looking across at me and Dean and saying, "She ought to win an award—for two very big reasons."

Once we reached the podium, they joked constantly. I had prepared and memorized an acceptance speech, but I never had a chance to open my mouth with those two swapping one-liners and keeping the crowd in stitches.

Several people told me that Movietone News could go a long way toward making me a star. Before the days of television news, it was the most widely viewed news source in the country. At first, it didn't mean that much. A couple of days later, however, one of the girls in the chorus told me that she and her boyfriend had been to the movie matinee that afternoon and my "props" award had been shown.

I ran down to the theater and sat through what seemed like the most boring movie in history to see myself on the big screen. Perhaps I was biased, but I thought I really looked good standing there between Lewis and Martin as they cracked jokes about big bosoms. I was like a star-struck teenager. I went back half a dozen times just to see Movietone News before the clips changed a week later. I could hardly believe that the girl on that screen was me, the same girl who not so long ago had sat in a shabby theater in Eastman, Georgia, fueling the dreams that kept her going by imagining herself up on the screen before her eyes.

Another big break soon came my way because of an unusual series of misunderstandings and backstage jealousies. Lilly St. Cyr was in town to headline the Follies' lineup and, because of all the publicity and my increasing name recognition, I'd moved up to be the number two act, dancing right before the star attraction. Before Lilly's very first show, a new stripper named Suzy danced with a costume held together with straight pins. As she danced, she pulled the pins out, dropped them on the floor and tossed her clothing offstage.

We didn't know it at the time, but Lilly St. Cyr stepped out of her shoes near the end of her act and danced barefoot. And just before she finished, she picked up a pin in her foot. It was painful, and she was thoroughly embarrassed to have to stop her dance and remove the pin from her foot. When she came off the stage, she was furious. In her anger, she made a very serious mistake. She accused me of dropping the pins on the stage. If she hadn't been such a snob, perhaps I wouldn't have reacted as I did. But she didn't deserve much consideration because she didn't give much.

"That's a damned lie," I said, my own anger rising. "I don't use pins. I never have. I have enough class to make my outfits, so you, Miss St. Cyr, had better get your facts straight before you start pointing a finger at anyone."

Lillian Hunt stepped between us and tried to settle things down. Later, I told her what had happened, and she told Suzy to stop using straight pins to hold her outfits together. But it didn't end there. I didn't like Lilly, and she knew it. Two nights later, she flew into a rage about how I was using my hands during my act.

"Tell her to stop running her fingers through her hair," she told Lillian. "That's part of my act. She's stealing it and using it before I go on."

Right then, a Georgia sharecropper's daughter had had just about all the bickering she could stand.

"Listen, you so-called star," I said. "I was running my fingers through my hair—and right here on this stage— before I ever heard your name. You're out to pick a fight with me, and, by God, you've found it."

Again, Lillian Hunt got between us, but not before one of the columnists overheard what was said. So I made the gossip sheet in another way—as a backstage battler. When that came out in the papers the next day, Lillian called me to her office. She motioned me to sit down and said, "We've got to find a way to keep the peace around here."

I told her that I was not the problem, that perhaps she ought to be talking to Lilly St. Cyr.

"That's the second time she's bad-mouthed me," I said, "and I've had about enough of it."

"Look," said Lillian, "I've got an idea that might work out all the way around. I'm going to send you to Oakland."

Before she could finish, my temper boiled over, and I told her again that if anyone ought to be shipped out, it was Lilly St. Cyr.

"Just wait a minute," she said in a patient voice. "I'm trying to tell you that you're going to be the headliner up there. Do you understand? The headliner. The main attraction. The star."

It took a moment to soak in. Me? The main attraction?

I couldn't believe it.

"Tempest, you're too good to be dancing second to anyone. You've made a name for yourself in just six months, and from here on, you ought to be a headliner everywhere you go. Nobody does it like you. You're one of a kind."

I was still in shock. Then she said the magic words: "Your pay will double immediately."

Money. I'd worked up to $175 a week, so it meant my pay would go to $350 a week! I could buy a car to go with the mink coat Mickey Rooney had given me.

Me! The star!

For the first time, I hugged Lillian Hunt.

"Thank you," I said.

She smiled and said, "Forget it. You've earned it. Now stay away from Lilly one more night, then you're gone. When you come back to L.A., you will be the headliner.

When I reached my apartment that night, I didn't take a shower and dine as I usually did. The excitement I felt was one of the greatest feelings I'd ever known. So I started packing for the trip to Oakland. Then I had a thought. I wanted to call somebody and tell them that I was a star. That seemed very important at the time. But I couldn't call my mother. I still hadn't told her that I was working in burlesque. I'd long since lost track of Betty Mae. And Hoke Wynne. And all of the others.

There was no one to call, no one to hear my shout of victory. All I had were the crowds, the applause, the glittering cities and movie stars. Somehow, it didn't seem right that I had no one with whom to share the biggest break of my life. The stigma of being a stripper had put me in life's lonely lane, and I wondered if I could handle it.

# *Six*

When I arrived in Oakland, my name was already in place on the marquee at the El Rey Theater. Tempest Storm was, in fact, the only name on the marquee. But I had little time to bask in the knowledge that I'd finally arrived as a headliner. Russ Meyer, who eventually became one of the best-known cheesecake photographers and erotic movie producers of all time, was putting together a slick magazine about the El Rey, and since I was the new headliner, it was important for me to be included.

During most of that first week, I spent the days posing for Meyer and the nights performing. The photo sessions could be tiresome, and posing didn't earn me any additional money. Still, two things that furthered my career came from those long hours under hot lights. First, it was nice to see some really professional glamor photos of myself. Second, many of the photos appeared in *French Peep Show* magazine, a widely circulated publication. This exposure definitely increased the numbers of those who instantly recognized my name.

My first engagement in Oakland lasted about six weeks. This first trip outside L.A. as a dancer also marked another first for me. I bought my first car, a gorgeous red 1951 Cadillac convertible. I had no credit references at that time since I hadn't been earning a decent salary long enough to establish credit. But the manager of the dealership where I bought the car had watched my performance at the El Rey, so he took care of financing the car.

I had also become a redhead for the first time when I began performing in Oakland. My natural brunette hair was long and glossy, but I wanted desperately to be a redhead. Lillian Hunt had encouraged me to stay a brunette. She said I looked like Hedy Lamarr with my dark hair. I preferred red hair, though, and I think mine was a wise choice. The change drew many compliments, and, except for a couple of brief periods in the 1970s, I've been a redhead ever since.

From Oakland, I moved east—not to New York or Boston, but to Denver. It wasn't exactly Broadway, but I found that performing in clubs was much different—much more tolerable—than performing in theaters, the only places I had performed up to that point.

My contract at the Tropics nightclub was supposed to last four weeks, but I stayed two additional weeks because of packed houses every night. It was my first venture into nightclubs, and I quickly noticed that audiences there were more appreciative and better mannered than those in theaters.

I also noticed that more women attended nightclub performances. So I made it a point right from the start to try to be a lady about my act. Sexy? Yes. Teasing? Yes. Vulgar? Never!

From the very beginning, I had been a class act, and I intended to stay just that. I worked hard to build an act that would not offend women, that I hoped would set me apart from the many other dancers in the business. The attitude—and the act—I developed in those early club engagements would keep my act popular and my name respected long after other strippers caved in to the sort of performances they felt were necessary to compete with the boom in porno movies.

During my third week in Denver—and after several articles about my dancing had appeared in Colorado newspapers—the editor of the University of Colorado's student newspaper, the *Flat Iron*, came to the club to catch one of my shows. Afterwards, he talked to me about posing for what he called "cheesecake photographs." The *Flat Iron* didn't use nude pictures, he said, just skirt and sweater pictures. I told him I would be happy to pose, and we made a date to meet a few days later on the campus.

I called my agent to make sure it was OK. He loved the idea so much that he began calling newspapers in the area to let them know that I would visit the campus for a picture session. When word got out that a stripper was coming to the University of Colorado, the dean came down hard on the editor. He said the deal was off. "I'd really like to do it," he said, "but the president has forbidden it. He says there's no way he will allow a stripper to come onto the campus."

The stigma of being a stripper had struck again. Well, I decided to strike back.

"Just a minute," I told him. "If you're willing to go through with it, so am I, and your dean just doesn't have any choice."

"Are you serious?" he asked.

"Sure I'm serious," I said. "Look, that's a public college. He can't keep me off the campus. I can walk around the campus all I want, and you can take pictures if you want. And your dean doesn't have to like it. What's he going to do? Have me arrested for walking around on property that belongs to us taxpayers? I'll bet the newspapers would love that!"

"Well, I don't know . . ."

"All right, it's up to you whether you show up. I plan to be there at noon tomorrow, just as we planned."

I really didn't know whether he would show, but I wouldn't have missed it for the world after being "forbidden" to go there. I wore a silky, white summer dress, put the top down on my red convertible, and took a leisurely drive to Boulder the next day. I had no trouble finding the campus or the little park where the editor had suggested we meet.

I parked the Cadillac on a street that bordered the park and waited. At exactly noon, a heavyset fellow walked toward my car. I didn't know whether he was friend or foe, but he had a camera in his hand, so I assumed he was with the paper. He smiled and introduced himself as the editor of the *Flat Iron*.

"Since you're here," he said, "we might as well get a picture or two."

We walked through the little park, looking for an ideal spot for a photograph. While we walked, he told me that my presence was welcomed by the students but frowned on by those who ran the university.

I told him that I liked to make big shots frown.

It was very quiet on campus, but just when we'd chosen a setting for the first picture, I heard a noise that sounded like a mixture of thunder and a crowd cheering a touchdown run. I looked toward the main part of the campus and saw what must have been three thousand students heading my way like a herd of stampeding cattle.

"It's the student body," the editor yelled frantically. "You'd better make a run for it!"

"What?"

"Run! Get in your car and go! These kids will mob you!"

I'd never been mobbed, and I didn't know what a terrifying experience it could be. Within a few seconds, I was surrounded by screaming, wild-eyed students.

"We heard you were coming," shouted one young man. "Can I have your autograph?"

I didn't have time to answer him. The editor was frantically pulling me through the crowd. But it was slow going. Suddenly a big, muscular guy appeared.

"He's a boxing champ," said the editor. "Let him help you."

The big guy picked me up and sat me on his shoulder. But just as soon as he started making a little progress, someone tripped the boxer, and we both hit the pavement in the midst of that sea of humanity.

I scrambled to my feet and ran for the car. Somehow I managed to reach it with little more than a few scratches and bruises. I climbed in and started the motor, but I couldn't believe what I was seeing. A dozen students piled into the open convertible with me. Some of them dove in headfirst, and I could see legs sticking straight up from the back seat.

I put the Cadillac in gear and began to drive. I didn't know exactly where I was going, but I knew I had to escape the mob. It's a miracle that I didn't run over anyone. As I cleared the largest group and began picking up speed, one boy who had been sprawled across the hood slid off and hit the ground with his feet running. He kept up with the car for a few paces and shouted breathlessly, "You're the sexiest woman I've ever seen." Under other conditions, I might have smiled and blown him a kiss. But right then, I was totally unnerved.

About three blocks from the mob, I stopped the car and said, "You guys have got to get out of here. I'm going back to Denver, and I'm taking no passengers."

A chorus of "Awwwwww" came from the students packed around me in the car. Reluctantly, they climbed out, telling me all the while how much they liked me and how they wished I'd come back for a visit sometime.

I tried to smile, but I was shaking like a leaf. I really didn't realize until the next day what a unruly mob it had actually been. Pictures in the *Rocky Mountain News* showed the dining room where many of the students had been before they mobbed me. The place looked like it had been bombed. Tables and chairs were upended and food trays were scattered everywhere.

Even though I seemed to be very popular on the University of Colorado campus, I never considered going back—not even in disguise.

After Denver, I had a successful four-week engagement in Portland, Oregon, before I returned to the Follies as the star attraction. It was good to be back in L.A., even though it meant performing in a theater, and I'd come to prefer nightclubs. My name had been splashed through magazines and gossip columns, and everyone knew who I was, even though my brunette hair had become flaming red.

Columnists rehashed my affair with Mickey Rooney and wondered who Tempest Storm might tempt this time. Such publicity packed the theater night after night, but not even the most far-out columnist would have guessed that I was on my way to becoming involved with Sammy Davis, Jr.

Not long after I first went to California and started working at Simon's Drive-In, I met the Triener Twins, Claude and Cliff. They were well-known black musicians in the Los Angeles area, and they frequented the drive-in while I worked there. They invited me to parties, and sometimes I went to their house for dinner. They treated me like family, and even before I went into show business, I became intimate with Claude. It was a good—although not public—relationship. He was kind to me, and, after my shattering experience with Jim Crowley, I needed a friend.

Such a relationship might seem shocking since I grew up in the Deep South where blacks and whites were separated in everything. But certain events in my life had a profound effect on how I regarded the races. First, white people always seemed to abuse and ridicule me. I was never close to my own family. White kids in school ridiculed me for my crooked teeth and big bosom. Five white guys raped me. Marriages to two white men had failed. And Jim Crowley, a white man, had tried to kill me. In my childhood, I found true friendship with only two people: Betty Mae, a white girl with a bad reputation, and Nanny, the old black lady with whom I chopped cotton and shared my troubles. Black people never ridiculed me or assaulted me. Perhaps those I met in California had had enough ridicule and bad treatment of their own so that they didn't feel like dishing it out, even to a white girl from Georgia.

By the time I first met Sammy Davis, Jr., at a small club where he was appearing with the Will Maston Trio, before I went into show business, I felt quite comfortable with him. His race was not an issue. After my return from my first tour out of Los Angeles, Sammy came by the theater one night and stayed afterward to talk.

He was still singing and dancing with the Will Maston Trio at a club in Los Angeles, and his rise to stardom was just beginning. In many ways, he was young and insecure just as I was. Perhaps that's why we became good friends and lovers. Sammy was comfortable to be around. His lifestyle was easy-going and full of laughs. His friendships were strong, and when he threw a party, some pretty big names showed up. Among others, I remember seeing Eddie Fisher, Debbie Reynolds, Janet Leigh and Richard Egan at various of his parties.

Our involvement had ended by the time he became involved in his well-publicized affair with Kim Novak, but I heard about it first-hand. Sammy called me one night, and he couldn't hide the fear in his voice. He said certain people were upset about his dating Kim Novak and someone was going to kill him if he didn't get married right away and end their affair.

I said, "So what are you calling me for?"

"Because you're my friend."

"Oh," I said, "I thought you were proposing."

"And if I was?"

"You know the world isn't ready for you and me as man and wife."

He laughed, and I felt like maybe I had helped take the edge off of a bad situation. But the conversation turned very serious again as he told me how a couple of thugs had backed him up against a wall and told him he'd lose his other eye if he kept messing with Kim Novak.

"Do they know about us?" I asked.

"No, but if you don't tell me how to get out of this, I might squeal when they come back."

At the time, we had to be concerned about our affair's ever becoming public knowledge—for him because of the threats and for me because of possible damage to my career. Of course, those concerns would not amount to much today since some of Hollywood's biggest stars have been quite open about biracial affairs, and it is not uncommon now for stars of different races to marry and have families.

In 1970, Sammy was playing at Carnegie Hall, and he invited all of those closest to him to be there. He bought me a plane ticket, put me up at the Waldorf Astoria, and sent a limousine to pick me up. I wore a gorgeous royal blue-and-white evening gown and a long white mink coat to his show that night—not a bad outfit for a sharecropper's daughter from South Georgia.

Sammy started celebrating a little too early and got thoroughly soused, so when we reached the Waldorf after the show, I turned to his girlfriend—a chorus girl who later became his wife—and said, "He's all yours, dear."

I knew he wouldn't be much of a lover that night. But we met at his suite the next day, and we made love. That reunion high up in the Waldorf was very sexy and romantic, and it was our last time. Even though we never made love again, our friendship remains strong to this day. I still love him, and I treasure the closeness we had as two insecure rising stars. I'm also proud that we didn't let society's inhibitions hamper us from caring for each other. It's people such as Sammy who have been like an extended family to me.

As my passion for Sammy Davis, Jr., cooled back in the early 1950s, I continued performing at the Follies, and I turned my affections toward John Becker, a former singer and burlesque straight man who had performed for several years under the stage name of Johnny Del Mar.

When I first met Johnny, he was a bartender at a little club next door to the Follies. Between shows, it was the most convenient place for me to get a ginger ale. Johnny was a dark and handsome man of about thirty. He had been married to Arabella Andrea, a stripper who performed along the West Coast. After their divorce, he had given up the theater to be a bartender. He said he was happy to make the change.

However, he knew the burlesque business like few other people I've ever known. Besides advising me about my act, he coached me endlessly on my diction. If any of my Southern accent remained, I credit him with ridding me of it.

Within a few weeks, we became very close, and I moved in with him. Both of us worked nights, and the days were pleasant and relaxed. Somewhere along the way, I started calling him my manager and let him make many of my decisions and coach me in everything from costumes to the music I used for my dance routines. He was very good as both a lover and a manager.

After six months of living and working together, we decided to get married. We drove up to Las Vegas in early 1953 and married in one of those little wedding chapels that used to be so popular.

Almost immediately, I became aware of two things.

First, his ex-wife had not given up on getting him back. When we were just going together, she'd make her presence known once in a while by showing up at the Follies or at the bar where he worked. I think she was more or less willing to tolerate our affair as a temporary arrangement. But the moment we were married, she became more visible, a constant pain to me.

And, second, Johnny became an insanely jealous person. I had seen a bit of that jealousy while we were living together, but nothing I had seen before could have have prepared me for his temper tantrums after our wedding. My work brought me into close contact with many celebrities, and Johnny just couldn't handle my visibility and the kind of teasing and titillation necessary to staying on top in my career. Perhaps I could have handled one of these problems, but together they nearly drove me up the wall.

In a move to escape his ex-wife's presence and to placate his jealousy, I agreed to buy a theater in Portland, Oregon, renovate it and even perform in it. I paid $15,000 for the theater and spent a few thousand more fixing it up.

I played there for several weeks when it first opened, and we raked in the money. We had our investment back in a very short time. But as the weeks turned into months and the crowd kept coming, I noticed that we seemed to be making less money. Nothing I could do would make Johnny account accurately for what we took in. If that wasn't enough of a headache, his ex-wife made frequent trips to Portland to work at a theater just down the street from ours. I despised the woman, but I didn't know what to do about her. Even with her presence, I tried to find happiness and contentment in our having our own theater and a beautiful home in Portland.

My agent in Los Angeles began showering me with offers in other cities. I told Johnny to book some good performers, that I was going on the road for a while. I knew I couldn't keep building on the terrific start I'd made if I never danced outside Portland. Life on the road is hard, but it is part of the business. Each time I came back from a trip, I'd hear stories about Johnny's taking other women to our home. Each time he denied it, and I would drop it, not wanting to face yet another serious problem.

The real irony is that I turned down many offers for dates with some of the most famous men in this country. I stayed so straight for Johnny Del Mar that I didn't even have dinner with any of those men. With his wild jealousy, I didn't want even the hint of a love affair.

After three confrontations about his affairs, I reached the point that I couldn't stand living in our house any longer. I couldn't avoid feeling that other women had been there every time I was performing out of town. So we moved into a penthouse in one of the hotels in an effort to "start all over."

But peace just wouldn't come to us.

One night, the doorbell rang, and Johnny opened the door. There stood his ex-wife with a glass in her hand. She had threatened many times to pour acid on my face, so I was hysterical when she threw the contents of the glass at me. It turned out that the glass held nothing except water.

Even so, I was terrified about what she might do next. Johnny agreed that her harassment had gone far enough. He had her arrested and asked that she be placed in a mental hospital. Of course, since I was involved in the precipitating incident and was married to Johnny, I signed the papers, too.

We went to court where she was judged to be somewhat mentally unbalanced. However, the court ruled that she was not enough of a threat to be put away. They let her go. In *Life* magazine a month later, a story came out labelling me as "John's other wife," who had tried to have his first wife committed to a mental institution. Meanwhile, his ex-wife sued us for $50,000 for false arrest. After spending a small fortune on attorney fees, we eventually settled out of court, paying her $1,500 and her attorney $1,500.

Having gone through this turmoil and the attendant publicity, I'd had enough of Portland. I told Johnny I had to move. We sold the theater and went to San Francisco in what I considered a last chance to save our marriage. We leased a club called the Streets of Paris on Mason Street. I worked at the El Rey across the bay in Oakland, even though Johnny kept demanding that I perform in our club. We argued a lot about that, and I finally told him that the club we owned simply wasn't the quality kind of place that was right for my act. It didn't have the clientele or the seating capacity to afford me as a headliner. That brought a bitter argument from Johnny. I figured the real problem was that the club simply wasn't bringing in enough money to keep him supplied with women.

The whole conflict came to a head one night right after a press conference. I'd told Johnny that I could not have dinner with him because I was having dinner with a couple of columnists from the big newspapers in the bay area. For some reason I was never able to understand, my plans made him very angry.

After the press conference and my dinner with the reporters, I went to the club to meet him when he locked up at midnight. He'd had a couple of drinks, and I knew this might be a very long night. Johnny was one of the nicest people in the world when he was sober, but give him a couple of drinks and he could be as mean and abusive as anyone I've ever known.

After locking up the club, we went to a place called Coffee Dan's to meet Phil Downing, head of the burlesque performers' union. When the waitress brought the menu, Johnny, still showing the effects of his drinking, asked sarcastically, "What are you going to have to eat, my darling wife?"

I said, "I'm not hungry, Johnny. I've already eaten. I told you . . ."

"Goddamn it, you're going to eat!" he said loud enough that others could hear. "Now tell the waitress what you'll have."

"But I'm not hungry."

"You're eating!" he shouted.

138

I knew everyone in the restaurant was looking at us, and I could not hold back the tears.

"Johnny, please . . ."

"Come on, Johnny, leave her alone," Phil said, trying to get him to quiet down. "I don't want to interfere in something between you two, but this is ridiculous. She says she isn't hungry. Why don't you just leave her alone?"

Johnny's eyes blazed with anger, and I thought he was going to hit Phil. His jaw muscles flexed as he said, "Why don't you just stay the hell out of this?"

Then he turned to me and began calling me every bad and profane name any woman has ever been called.

Phil walked out.

I cried.

Johnny ordered a plate of food and told me to eat it. I refused. He swore some more and then said, "Come on. I'll straighten you out at home."

I was glad to get out of there, but I was even gladder to know that it was finally over between Johnny and me. I would never suffer such humiliation again. I just had to figure a way out before I killed him. I was that hurt and angry. Perhaps I should have refused to go home with him that night, but I didn't. He ranted and cursed me all the way there. Finally, I got tired of crying. He was still calling me dirty, filthy names that one human being should never call another. Something in my own temperament snapped.

"Damn you, Johnny!" I shouted. "Damn you! You've embarrassed me, insulted me, shamed me. I've had enough. Enough!"

At that moment, I would have shot him if I'd had a gun. But there was none. I did see a pair of scissors. I grabbed them and tried to stab him. He jumped out of my reach, and I threw the scissors at him. They hit him handle first without hurting him. But given an additional one-half of a rotation of the scissors, they probably would have pierced his heart.

139

He sobered up in a couple of heartbeats. He looked stunned. He looked from me to the scissors to his chest. Suddenly, he put his hands over his face and said, "Oh, honey, I'm sorry. God knows, I'm sorry. I didn't mean to blow up like that. Please forgive me. I love you. That's why I get like this. Please forgive me. You're my beautiful baby. I love you, and I can't live without you."

I turned away from him. He came up behind me and put his arms around me. "Please? Forgive me?"

"Just leave me alone, Johnny. Just get away from me and leave me alone."

"I'm sorry. Please believe me."

He went to bed. I went into the living room and sat on the couch for a long time. I didn't think much. I didn't need to. I just sat there, my mind already made up.

We had breakfast together the next morning just as if nothing had happened. He made a lot of small talk, and I answered only when I thought it was necessary to keep him from blowing up again.

Before I went to the theater that night, I stopped at the club and asked him for the keys to the car. I didn't want to make him suspicious, so I said that I wanted to gas it up. I drove back to the apartment, packed my wardrobe into the trunk and gathered up my personal things. I stood looking at the apartment. It held a lot of memories—good and bad. Then I went out to the Cadillac. It was mine. The clothes in the trunk were mine. That's what I had left from two years of marriage. But it was enough for Tempest Storm. I could always make money. What I needed was love and understanding. And I wondered if I'd ever find it.

I checked into the Leamington Hotel near the theater in Oakland. But Johnny Del Mar just wouldn't leave me alone. It didn't take him long to figure out that I was gone and not coming back. I wouldn't answer his calls to the theater, and he didn't know where I was staying.

A few nights after I'd left him, I left the theater to find my car missing. My first thought was that it had been stolen, but then I figured that Johnny had come to Oakland with an extra set of keys and taken it. By then, I had an attorney, Nathan Cohn, and I called him. He called Johnny and gave him an hour to get the car back to Oakland or face arrest. The car was returned very quickly.

Because I was afraid he would come back, I checked into the St. Francis Hotel in San Francisco. Even with that precaution, I came back to my suite one night and found the door open. I went downstairs and told the maid that she'd left the door open, but she said, "Oh, no, ma'am, your husband was up there. He said he was your husband so I let him have a key."

I checked my suite and found no one inside. So I called Nathan Cohn again. While we were talking, there was a knock on the door. I asked who it was and a voice responded that it was Johnny. I told my attorney.

He said, "Just stall him and keep talking. I'm only a couple of blocks away. I'll be right there."

When he arrived, I opened the door to both of them. Nathan told him that I had nothing to say to him, but Johnny pleaded for me to come back to him.

I told him flatly I would never return.

Before he left, he tried to make me feel bad by saying that I was leaving him out in the cold after he had made a star out of me. I told him that he'd helped me, yes, but that I'd more than paid his way. Besides, I was well on my way to stardom long before I met him.

To get away from him, I moved into a house high up in Twin Peaks in San Francisco and tried to keep the address secret while I waited for our divorce hearing. But when I went out of town for a four-week engagement, I returned to find my house ransacked and the car missing again. That was the straw that broke the camel's back.

I called Nathan and told him to get my car back for the second time and speed the divorce along. A couple of weeks later, we went to court. The divorce was granted on St. Valentine's Day of 1955.

I was so relieved to be out of that violent, abusive relationship that I asked Nathan Cohn to have lunch with me to celebrate. Nathan had to attend a different celebration—a victory luncheon at the Palace Hotel for newly elected San Francisco mayor George Christopher. He invited me to go along. When we arrived, we discovered that Nathan's table was at the very front of the room. We walked toward the table, and heads began turning and conversations stopped. To this day, Nathan swears that it was the best celebration a newly divorced woman ever had. I stole the show from the most powerful politicians in the city.

The divorce wasn't the end of my association with Johnny. After I returned to Los Angeles, he tried to run me off the freeway one night. I got off at Wilcox Avenue where the police station was and filed a complaint. The *Herald Examiner* carried a front-page story the next day with the headline "Tempest Storm Fears for Her Life."

On another occasion, Johnny called my apartment one night more than a year after our divorce and threatened me. I was headlining Minsky's Revue at the ChiChi Club in Palm Springs, California. He said that I ought to make that night's performance my best because it was going to be my last.

Of course, I was scared. I called the club and had security people meet me when I arrived. They did, but when I went onstage for my show, Johnny was sitting in the front row with his arms crossed, staring at me. I was petrified. I was afraid he would take a shot at me from the audience or something else too awful to imagine. At that point, he seemed really crazy.

As soon as I finished my number, security came by my dressing room to escort me to meet some people in the lounge. As my friends and I stood talking, a fist suddenly came through the crowd at me. I don't know whether Johnny aimed poorly or whether I ducked the punch, but it landed on one of the security men. They picked Johnny up like a sack of Georgia cotton and tossed him out into the street with a stern warning never to come back.

Still, he wasn't through. He showed up at the Sands Hotel in Las Vegas while I was performing there. I was dating a man named Larry, one of the managers of the Desert Inn, and after I finished my show at the Dunes, we walked over to the Sands Hotel for a midnight snack. In the dining room was Johnny Del Mar. Larry and I ate and left. We were waiting for the valet to bring Larry's car around when I heard a familiar voice say, "Here, sweetie. I forgot to give you something." As I turned around, he threw the contents of a glass in my face.

You can imagine the panic that gripped me. After the incident with his ex-wife, when she pulled a similar stunt, I had an unholy fear of someone's trying to ruin my looks and therefore my career with acid. As it turned out, Johnny's glass held just a drink. But I was scared enough to run— around the car and back into the hotel. Someone called the police, and the next day they told him to get out of Las Vegas and stay out.

That was the last time I saw him for more than twenty years. In 1980, he showed up while I was headlining "Burlesque, U.S.A." at the Sahara Hotel in Reno and asked for a ringside seat. After the show, he came backstage and said hello. He said he still loved me, that he'd always loved me. During the conversation, he revealed that he had married an English girl and that they owned a string of beauty salons. He said that if I ever needed him, all I had to do was call.

I told him that I just might do that.

"You still owe me, Johnny Del Mar," I said. "You still owe me a hell of a lot."

It felt good to put the bad memories behind, to have a new, happier memory to modify the torture I recalled from the months that followed my leaving him. Johnny looked just the same, sort of like a young Gene Kelly. At that meeting in 1980, he seemed mellower and quite sweet. His offer to help me was, I think, his way of finally recognizing my hard work and all that I did for him all those hard years ago. I'd never interfere in his present life—it sounds too stable and too good for me to cause any problems—but I will always be glad that he made the offer.

In 1980, I didn't need any help. "Burlesque U.S.A." was a wildly successful show that toured legitimate theaters for seven months. My costars were Robert Alda, Red Buttons, and Eddie Bracken. After touring, we went to the Sahara in Reno for nineteen weeks and on to the Sahara in Tahoe for nine more weeks before closing.

When the political elite of San Franscisco were making me feel like a princess on the day of my divorce from Johnny, I felt real hope for the future. When I saw him again, years later, in 1980, I could truthfully say many of those hopes had been realized. "Burlesque U.S.A." was evidence of that. But I still hadn't found the whole, fulfilling relationship that would bring me the happiness of a lasting marriage.

# Seven

After my divorce from Johnny Del Mar, the possibilites of life suddenly seemed more numerous and more exciting, probably because I was finally able to notice what the world had to offer. Although I'd become accustomed to being in the spotlight off the stage as well as on, I wasn't prepared for the sudden rush of attention focused on me by some of show business's biggest stars as soon as the papers revealed that I was a single woman again.

The first celebrity I went out with after the divorce was Hugh O'Brien, whom I had met at the Fairmont Hotel in San Francisco in 1955, while I was appearing at the El Rey Theater across the bay in Oakland. By that time, my position as a top-billed star of burlesque made it necessary for all of my phone calls to be screened. When Hugh called the first few times, I simply declined to speak with him from habit because so many men called. If I wasn't immediately interested in meeting someone, I simply didn't talk to him. When you've just gotten out of a bad marriage, you are ready to demand a lot from any new relationship.

But Hugh O' Brien was a persistent man. He finally sent me a big bouquet of flowers with a note saying that he'd like to take me to dinner. Flowers always get my attention and soften my heart, and the next time he called, I spoke with him.

We made a date for dinner at the Papagaya Room in the Fairmont Hotel, one of the most popular late-night dinner spots in San Francisco. It turned out that Hugh, who made something of a career of his bachelorhood, was as in love with romance as I have always been. That first night and throughout our relationship, he made every effort to please me, catering to my taste in food and wine and taking the time to explore emotions, to get at feelings. His sensitivity was especially important to me in the difficult time after my divorce, and Hugh made me feel so special and secure that I could have spent my life with him. His special qualities of sharing and concern were a part of his lovemaking too, and even after our affair ended, we kept in touch, maintaining a strong mutual respect and fond memories of our time together.

The qualities that made Hugh O'Brien so special to me were not, I think, surprising. I had come out of a violent, destructive marriage. Many times the humiliation of that night in the restaurant when Johnny demanded that I eat or the terror of the evening he tried to run me off the freeway came back to me in vivid detail, making me afraid to risk any emotional involvement at all. To have a man treat me with concern, respect, and gentle passion was an important part of the healing process all women who leave an abusive relationship must go through.

One of the most frightening aspects of the struggle to leave such a relationship is the tendency to go back, to try again, to get trapped a cycle of fear and reconciliation. Because I wanted so badly to have a marriage that worked, I found myself in the middle of a reconciliation attempt with Johnny shortly after I stopped seeing Hugh. Ironically, it was this mistaken attempt to hold onto a bad relationship that led me to my first meeting with Nat King Cole, who was to become one of the most special people in my life—exactly because he treated me with all the love and compassion that had been missing in my marriage. In 1955—some months after our divorce—Johnny asked if we could go to Lake Tahoe together to take in a couple of shows. He called it a first step in reconciliation. Having seen a better kind of relationship in the time since the divorce, I really had no desire to get back together. But a die-hard romantic like me is as big a sucker for a former lover's heartfelt plea as she is for flowers. A weekend away from Los Angeles seemed like just what I needed, and I traveled with the faint hope hidden deep inside that maybe things could be different in new surroundings, without all the pressures and resentments.

Our first stop was the Cal-Neva Hotel where Nat was headlining a show. Included in the cast was Mitch DeWood, a comedian I'd met during one of my nightclub tours. Mitch came to our table to say hello and brought Nat King Cole with him. Nat was one of the most captivating men I've ever met. Although he wasn't as charming as Hugh O'Brien or as much of a comic as Mickey Rooney, he had an unbelievable sex appeal, a magnetic aura that drew me in immediately, in a way that no man had ever done before. The power of it was a little frightening, to tell the truth, and later in life I would learn the dangers of such sudden and irresistible attraction. But with Nat it was pure magic, and the magic was good, as if there were only good spirits waving their wands over us on that first night.

His speaking voice was as soft and smooth as velvet as he said hello and shook my hand. That should come as no surprise to anyone who has ever heard him sing. The beauty of his voice came through even on his records, but its impact in person only reinforced my initial response. Even though

I'd heard people describe him as ugly, I saw nothing to suggest why. Maybe that's because, from the very first, I looked beyond his outer features and sensed his inner goodness. He was courteous, charming and absolutely mesmerizing.

After only a few minutes of conversation, I never again saw him as anything but beautiful. I'm sure it showed in my smile and the way I gazed at him from the moment we were introduced. My feelings did not go unnoticed or unanswered. There was a real chemistry between us. He sensed my attraction toward him and told me my eyes were like emeralds.

I felt that he had truly connected with my soul and that the connection had irrevocably changed me. It was the most powerful feeling I had ever experienced, but, at the same time, a warning sounded in my brain. I said to myself, "Tempest, people have been tarred and feathered and run out of town for what you're thinking." (And that image was not merely a figure of speech in the 1950s.) Even though I'd already been intimate with two black men, this was different, stronger. I could not control my feelings, and I knew it. I also knew that the relationship I was already imagining could be dangerous, but nothing would have kept me from following my heart's desire and exploring this passion fate seemed to have sent me from the blue.

The hotel's showroom was packed for Nat's performance that evening, and when he sang many of my favorite songs, I melted. In addition to everything else that was going on, I was getting to be a member of the audience, something I didn't, as a performer, have much opportunity for. The very strong and very real connection between an appreciative observer and a good performer that had been crucial to my success on stage from the very first night I performed solo was now working in reverse. Nat King Cole was wooing me from the stage, and I loved it. I acknowledged his attentions with a smile and grew flushed at the prospect of where our feelings might lead.

The only thing that kept that performance from being perfect was a heckler in the audience. He was obviously a racist who didn't like Nat's music, and he became louder and more abusive as the show went on. Finally, Nat stopped and asked that the heckler be removed. It was a gutsy thing for a black entertainer to do in those days, but Nat did it—with class—and I admired him for it. Thus, in a very short time, the initial physical and emotional attraction deepened and took on a richer quality as I learned to respect this man for the struggle he had been through and continued to undergo. I began to feel a kinship with this performer who labored under a stigma of his own.

After the show, Johnny and I went backstage. While we waited for Nat to come out of his dressing room, Johnny walked away to talk to a couple of the musicians he knew, and I borrowed a pen to scribble a short note to Nat. Rarely in my life have I been so forward. Usually, I am a more traditional woman, waiting to be pursued and won over. But this was too powerful to wait, to play traditional courting games. I wanted Nat to know how I felt.

I told him he was a great singer, a fine entertainer, and one of the sexiest men I'd ever seen. And I asked if we might meet somewhere alone. I also wrote down my Los Angeles phone number.

When he emerged from his dressing room, he came straight to me. As I made small talk, I pressed the note into his hand. He smiled, pocketed the note, and made the rounds to talk to other admirers. His smile assured me that my message had been well received, and Nat's discretion prevented what might have been an ugly scene with my ex-husband.

Two days later when I was back in L.A., Nat called me, and we talked for an hour. By the time the conversation ended, we'd made a date for a late breakfast at his hotel after the last show the following night. I headed back to Lake Tahoe—alone. All these years later, I can still feel the sense of urgency with which I made that trip, and it was important, I think, that it was an urgency to get to something rather than away from something bad. I had moved with that other urgency, the desperate need to escape, too often in my life, and it felt good to have such an attractive force pulling me toward it for a change.

Nat traveled with an entourage of five men at that time, and I knew that some of them would find out sooner or later that we were meeting. But the power of this attraction was too great for me to worry about what others might think. Even though Nat was married—and supposedly off-limits to me because of the color of his skin—I wanted him as I had wanted no other man I'd ever met. He was kind and gentle, and he was good for me. Those qualities were enough for me to fly in the face of taboos dealing with adultery and race.

He told me that I was the most beautiful woman he'd ever known, and our lovemaking was vibrant, warm, and wonderful. When I was with him, I felt truly connected to another human being, safe at last from the terrible loneliness of my life. His body was as velvety smooth as his voice. He made me feel like a princess, and he surely was my king. Never had a woman found herself so suddenly awake and living all her romantic dreams come true.

After we first made love, he asked me, "Are you really sure this is what you wanted?"

"More than anything in the world," I said. I had never spoken truer words.

"Being with me could ruin your name, your career, everything."

"And I could ruin your marriage and get you run out of town."

"We make a hell of a team, don't we?" he asked, those dark features breaking into a devilish grin. "Well, since we've gone this far, why turn back?"

"Yes. Why turn back?"

Then we made love again. Just gazing into his eyes and feeling them meet mine honestly and openly, just touching and holding one another, gave me a feeling like I'd never before known with a man. At long last, I was beginning to understand what made Betty Mae so enthusiastic about being with a man, what made Nanny ready to find another one after so much pain and trouble.

We saw each other as frequently as we could arrange to, not an easy task with two busy careers to schedule around. And it was inevitable that people—at least those closest to us—would realize how we felt. Nat came to see me while I was starring in Minsky's Revue at the Dunes Hotel in Las Vegas. He came backstage after the 2:30 show, and we talked for a few minutes. Of course, there were several people with him, including one white man who always seemed to be wherever Nat was. I later learned that most black entertainers in that time kept at least one white man around who served as a public stand-in, making it easier for a black man to go certain places and to appear in the same group as a white woman.

Nat and I talked for a minute, and then he and his entourage waited while I dressed so that we could go out. Nat and I had agreed that if we were seen in public, we would be part of a crowd, as much for his protection as mine. After all, Nat never had a tarnished image. Only insiders of the entertainment world knew about our relationship.

Nat offered no unusual show of affection toward me when I came out of the dressing room that evening, but as we left to go across the street to the Sands Hotel, he could not resist squeezing my hand and saying, "I'm glad to see you. I've missed you so much." I didn't notice at the time, but the pit boss of the Dunes saw what Nat did, and I would certainly hear about it later.

Nothing spoiled that evening for us. We dined in elegance at the Sands, and I was pleased that he had enjoyed my show so much. His pleasure brought back all my own feelings from that first night when I saw him sing in Tahoe. Of course, I found the perfect opportunity to give him my room number. When he slipped in during the wee hours of the morning, we stood silently for several moments, holding each other and marveling at our happiness.

"God knows, I wish this could last forever," I said. I'd often wondered if he'd ever considered divorcing his wife. I was certainly serious enough to want a more open and more permanent relationship, and my strong romantic streak kept sending out its little messages about true love and lasting happiness.

But Nat didn't offer any indication that divorce was a possibility for him, and I never pressed him about making our relationship permanent. I was enraptured by what we were able to share, and I was overjoyed to be so pleased with lovemaking at long last.

The next day, the pit boss cornered me before my first show, and I could see that he was angry. "What the hell's with you, Tempest? Are you trying to ruin your career?"

"What are you talking about?" I asked.

"I've watched you flitting around like a butterfly—Vince Edwards, Johnny Ray, that prince from Saudia Arabia. But that thing last night was the last straw."

"One more time, Charlie, what are you talking about?"

"You and Nat King Cole, that's what I'm talking about. Don't you know that dating a Negro can put your career on the skids quick, damned quick?"

"That's ridiculous," I said. "There was a whole group of us who went over to the Sands, ate dinner, and watched a show."

"But I saw you holding hands with him."

"Nat's a friend, for God's sake. A friend! Can't you understand that?"

"Yeah, well, maybe. But one of the bellboys saw him going through the lobby at two A.M. I don't suppose he was just looking for a men's room, now was he?"

My patience exploded into a fit of temper.

"Listen, Charlie. When we get right down to the nitty-gritty, I don't think it's any of your damned business."

"Tempest, Tempest," he said condescendingly, "you just won't listen, will you? OK, sweetheart, it's your career, not mine. So screw it up if you want to."

He walked away, leaving me red-faced and so mad I didn't know what to do. Why did men always assume they knew what was best for me? Men had sure had some funny ideas about my welfare in the past. I could damned sure take care of myself and make better decisions about how to treat myself and run my life than they had made. Besides that, would he have been talking to me that way if I had been a man? Men could see several women, however casually or seriously, and everybody patted them on the back and admired their prowess. But let me be seen with several men or even one man somebody didn't think I should be seen with, and my career was headed down the drain. How could I win?

No one was going to keep me from seeing Nat King Cole. Nobody. He was the only man who'd offered me love, affection, and understanding without asking for my soul in return. He was the quiet, stable influence on my life that I'd desperately needed for a long time.

I felt tears trickle down my face, and I rushed into my dressing room and cried. I cried for myself. I cried for Nat King Cole. I cried for a world that wasn't ready to understand what he and I had together, for a world that was bound and determined to crush my ideals of romance.

Our rendezvous didn't end. I flew to Philadelphia when he was appearing at the Latin Casino. Nat arranged for a suite at the Warwick Hotel and welcomed me to his bed. After that, he'd send for me at every engagement, wanting me to be a part of his career, his world. I went as often as I could, for I wanted to be a part of all that was him. We met frequently at the Sands Hotel in Las Vegas. Although we

always took separate suites, Carl Cohen, one of the managers who always took care of my accommodations, knew
about Nat and me.

Years later, I heard that one of the supermarket scandal
sheets published a story about my connection to Sammy
Davis, Jr., and Nat King Cole, but I never saw a copy of the
story. I know it would only have made me angry and sad,
because those papers never want to tell the story of friendship and love. They want to turn those things into something twisted and ugly. They want to cheapen real human
emotions. The real tragedy is that their readers let that happen. I'm happier knowing inside myself what I shared with
these men and what those things we shared meant to us. Let
the scandal sheets tear these relationships down for
strangers if they must. I won't let them do it to me.

Their story may have grown out of one of my trips to see
Nat at the Sands Hotel in 1956. Although segregation was not
a major issue in the West at the time, managers at many of
the hotels—including the biggest—knew that they had to
keep up appearances for the sake of those who had very
strong feelings about it. That was just good business sense
to them. The Little Rock school integration case had stirred
up old prejudices, and black entertainers were often denied
seating for shows. Some hotels in Las Vegas still required
that they enter and leave by the back door.

I remember once when Pearl Bailey went swimming in a
pool at one of the biggest hotels. All of the whites left the
pool, and the management, in a move to appease some feelings, had the pool drained the next day. It was not a good
time for many people even in the glamorous world of show
business, where we sometimes forget that such problems
ever had an impact.

It seemed so unfair. Tempest Storm, the fair, red-haired
stripper, could get anything she wanted in Las Vegas. When
I arrived at a hotel, dressed in beaded gown and white
mink, people applauded and hotel employees scurried about

to do my bidding. This was one place the stigma of being a stripper seldom reared its ugly head. But when Nat King Cole tried that night in 1956 to get a table at one of the hotels, he was turned down.

Sammy Davis, Jr., once told me that if you cared about someone of another race, you couldn't stay uninvolved in the way they were treated by your own race. He was right. Something about Nat's being turned down for dinner reservations clicked with me, and I couldn't let it pass. I called the maitre d' who had refused Nat's request and asked for a table. I think she knew Nat and I were friends. She asked if the table was for me. I said it was for Nat King Cole. She asked if I would accompany him. I said I had a show to do at the Dunes and that I would be joining him later in the evening. She put the table in Nat's name and let him have it. I'm sure she didn't like it, but she did it.

The next day, a bouquet of flowers was delivered to my room with a card that said simply, "Stay alive. I love you. K.C." Those were the initials that had appeared on other of the flowers I so loved getting and that Nat was so thoughtful about sending. I never told him how good it felt to bring those goody-goody hypocrites to their knees, to see them squirm as they tried to protect prejudices that should have disappeared long before that night in 1956. I wish I had. Knowing Nat and loving him made me all the more determined that my career would be the one that finally toppled my own nemesis—the stripper's stigma.

Through it all, I never met Nat's wife. The closest I came was at the Ambassador Hotel in Los Angeles. Nat was opening there, and I went because he wanted me there. I sat at a table with friends on one side of the room, and she sat with some of her friends on the other side. If she ever knew about Nat and me, I never heard about it, not even from Nat. Our time together was too precious to let any of the outside world's complications intrude. Maybe that's the mark of true love—the two people's emotions are so strong that they can block out all the interference that seeks to work against them. They can cast a spell with their love and ward off evil, or at least that's the way it seemed when Nat and I were in each other's arms.

Our feelings for each other never diminished, but the realities of our careers made being together more and more difficult. Both of us were professionals, dedicated to excellence at what we did, and we were mature enough to know that we had to continue working at our art, at staying on top. Maybe that's the other sign of true love, knowing how to let the loved one live the life she needs or he needs, how to give that person the freedom to be the one you fell in love with in the first place. It is a rare combination, those two qualities, and Nat King Cole is the man who made me believe I might just find them and live happily ever after, after all.

Finding that feeling and not being able to make a life with the one who inspires it is a double-edged sword. You are torn between the desire to have that feeling permanently and the desire to be with that person, the one who can give it, however fleetingly. After knowing Nat King Cole, life was never quite as satisfying, but I did have a greater faith in the possibilities of romantic love. I never stopped yearning for him and wishing our affair could have gone on forever.

My name continued to crop up in gossip columns. Some of the stories were true; some were not. I'd like to separate fact from fiction, to make clear my sense of the difference between true love and casual relationships. It would be unfair to the memories of my feelings for someone like Nat not to make the difference clear.

My name was once linked romantically to singer Johnny Ray. We met in 1952 in Hollywood. I was performing at the New Follies Theater when my press agent said that publicity pictures of Johnny and me together might help both our careers. The setting was Florentine Gardens, a posh night club in Hollywood. After the photo session, Johnny and I dined together and enjoyed the evening. But that's as far as it went. He kissed me when we parted and, for the sake of anyone watching, I held onto his hand until I stepped out of reach.

It was the sort of thing that might make people talk, but I was surprised to find out later that we were listed as possible lovers. The photos taken that evening surely helped my career, and we remained friends. But any stories about us having a love affair were fabricated. If it were true, I certainly would own up to it. After all, I still think Johnny Ray is a handsome, desirable man.

John Fitzgerald Kennedy was a young senator from Massachusetts in 1955 when I was performing at the Casino Royale in Washington, D.C., a nightclub known for featuring big name singers. I didn't care about politicians at the time, so I wasn't particularly impressed when a tall man came backstage and asked if I would like to meet Senator Kennedy.

"Not particularly," I answered.

The man said he was an aide to Kennedy, that they had watched my show, and the senator wanted to meet me.

I asked a question I often asked about men who saw my show and wanted to meet me: "Is he married?"

"Well, yes, he is, but that doesn't matter," said the aide.

"It matters to me," I said. "Tell the senator I'm not going out with a married man, regardless of who he is."

The aide left, but I couldn't resist peeking out past the curtains to see this senator. Perhaps I expected to see a much older man, but, whatever the reason, I was captivated by his stunning good looks.

The aide shook his head and talked to his boss. Then they left, and I figured that would be the last I ever heard from him. But I was wrong. The following night, the young senator was back with his full entourage. They saw my show, and immediately afterward, the same aide came backstage. He repeated the invitation to join the senator.

"That was a pretty quick divorce," I said with noticeable sarcasm.

"The senator didn't get divorced," the aide said. "He's Catholic and doesn't believe in divorce."

Again, he offered the invitation. I came within a heartbeat of telling him to forget it, but then I remembered the handsome man I'd seen the night before. So I went to his table and found him to be as charming and witty as he was handsome. The aides moved to another table and left us to talk alone. We made a date for the next evening, my night off from the Royale, after he used his considerable powers of persuasion to calm my fears about his marital status.

It was an exciting evening, but at the time I didn't think it was important enough to make the effort to remember times and places or the people we saw. After all, John F. Kennedy was just one of many men I had dated, and at the time many of them were more famous than he. Besides, even though he told me he would someday be president of the United States, I filed that remark away in the same category with all the statements by actors who told me they would win Academy Awards.

Our relationship was never smooth. He would be warm at one meeting and stormy at the next. One problem was that my notorious habit of being late collided with his impatience and penchant for punctuality. On one occasion, he sent an aide into the club to get me. The manager of the club was talking to me, and it took a long time for me to get out to the limousine. Jack's face was red, and he barked angrily, "Goddamn it, you kept me waiting!"

When he was angry, he was even more handsome and appealing than when he was happy and flashing that famous smile. However he was, he melted me like butter over an open flame. In many ways, he was like a little boy who wouldn't grow up. In other ways, he was one of the most mature men I've ever known.

That youthful side of him came through one evening after we'd finished dinner and his driver was taking us for a leisurely drive through Washington. We were passing a little park down near the Potomac River, not far from the Washington and Jefferson Memorials. Suddenly, he told his driver to stop.

"Come on, let's get out and walk around," he said.

It was a balmy night, and he said, "I'll race you to the river."

I stayed in excellent physical shape, as dancers must, and figured I could outrun a senator who sat behind a desk all day. So I pulled off my high heels, tossed them back into the limousine, pulled my evening gown up to my thighs.

He said "Go!" and we ran.

Less than a hundred yards from the river bank, we were running side by side and holding hands when my foot hit a tree root and I fell. His hold on me was broken, but he came back, collapsed beside me, and said, "I hope you're all right."

"Yes," I said, "I'm fine."

Light from nearby streetlights let me see the intensity in his eyes. "Yes, by God, you are all right," he said, and he kissed me long and passionately. Then he picked me up and carried me to the car. He told his driver to take us to the Mayflower Hotel, where I had a suite.

Once in the privacy of that suite, we used the opportunity that being away from the world's eyes provided, and I realized that he was a fine figure of man, in better shape than most who sit behind a desk all day. Later that evening, he told me that he was not happily married, that Jackie was cold toward him. I held my finger to his lips to silence talk about his home life. I made him forget all of that in another rush of lovemaking. It was that same old inescapable problem of trying to block out the outside world, trying to create a private haven.

In my memory Jack Kennedy's sex drive lives up to the legend that has developed around it since his death. The man just never wore out. Years later, I read in Lance Morrow's book *The Chief* that former Prime Minister Harold Mac-

millan of Great Britain quoted Jack as saying that he got
headaches if he didn't have sex every day. My experience
with him makes me hesitant to dispute such a statement.

Then there was Elvis Presley.

Nineteen fifty-seven was an important year for me. My
career in burlesque had mushroomed, and I was making a
breakthrough appearance in Las Vegas. In honor of that occasion Major Riddle, manager of the Dunes Hotel, where I
would be headlining in Minsky's Follies, hosted a cocktail
party for celebrities and the press at the Beverly Hilton Hotel.
Even Walter Winchell showed up to report on my opening.
My breathtaking climb to the top of burlesque was a real
story, and Major Riddle wanted to make the most of it. I, of
course, was thrilled to be headlining at the Dunes because
there just wasn't a more exciting place to be.

In only six years, I had become a superstar. Fans and
professionals alike considered my dancing the best in burlesque. I finally felt that I had come into my own. The dark
curls of my youth had given way to flaming red, and I had
come to appreciate life in the fast lane—the clothes, the
travel, the attention, the men. In short, I was single, sexy,
and yearning for the good times that would make up for all
those hard years back in Eastman, Georgia. Nothing could
have pleased the lonely daughter of a Georgia sharecropper
more than to have her childhood dreams of show business
and romance come true, and for me they had. I was being
hotly pursued by millionaires arriving in private planes and
by some of the biggest names in the entertainment world. I
had arrived.

One of the consequences of being a superstar was the
constant threat to my privacy from all sorts of admirers:
slick-talking Romeos, stage-door Johnnys bearing flowers
and gifts, and just plain kooks. Anyone in my position had
to worry about the kooks. That's why any hotel where I
stayed assigned bodyguards to me each time I left my room.

The hotel management also made sure that the switchboard operators screened all of my calls.

Thus it was that my calls from Elvis Presley came through a hotel operator. Shortly after I opened at the Dunes, the switchboard rang my room.

"Hello? Miss Storm?"

"Yes."

"This is the switchboard. Mr. Elvis Presley would like to talk to you."

"Yes, I'll talk to him."

Elvis Presley. In the seconds it took for the operator to connect him, my mind flashed on the gorgeous young man named Elvis who seemed to have every American female under thirty wailing at his feet wherever and whenever he performed. Well, he might have others longing for him. But not me, not Tempest Storm. I knew that I could live out the fantasy of those women if I really wanted to. After all, I could have my pick of celebrities, and Elvis wasn't that big a star at the time. All I had to do was let him talk, let him make the proposal, let him find me at the right time and the right place. He wasn't so different from the other rich and famous men who had pursued me.

I'd tempted Elvis a couple of evenings earlier, just as I'd intended. I was more familiar with the show business scene than he was, and I wanted him to know who had the upper hand.

My early show at the Dunes had ended, and I dressed in a gold lame outfit. Elvis and I were scheduled to have some publicity pictures made, and I wanted to be at my sexiest best, both to tease Elvis a little and to get the most out of the publicity opportunity.

As I left my dressing room, an overly eager publicist cornered me and said Elvis was waiting. Acting just like a publicist, he began telling me how elegant he thought we'd look together. Then he leaned close and said in a voice lowered to a confidential tone, "He is the hottest singer on the scene right now, my dear. You know what photographs with him can mean to your career."

The publicist wasn't the brightest guy in town. I didn't mind being photographed. I certainly understood how being pictured with other stars and having juicy bits of gossip about me featured in the media fired the imagination of the public and made them want to see my show. When my fans stood in line just to get in, my salary—already past $3,500 a week—would keep growing.

But there was no need to tell that to the publicist. Like many men on the fringe of the entertainment business, he assumed he knew more than I did about my career. I knew that I couldn't have come so far so fast without learning as much about the business of burlesque as about dancing. And I certainly intended to use what I'd learned to stay around now that I'd made it to the top.

Standing next to the publicist, I could see the dark, handsome features of Elvis towering above a circle of chorus girls just down the hallway. I knew by the smile on his face that the young women were flattering him endlessly. My companion bubbled on about how Elvis and I would look "absolutely elegant together." I nodded my agreement. If nothing else, I wanted to spoil all of that attention Elvis was getting from the chorus girls.

The publicist giggled at his own cleverness and scurried away to pull Elvis from the clutches of the young dancers from the chorus line. Even with his dark skin, Elvis blushed deeply when he saw me. I could tell he was trying not to look at my plunging neckline as he said in a deep but boyish voice tinged with a southern accent, "Hello, Miss Storm. Your show was the greatest."

My best smile in place, I linked my arm through his and turned toward the photographer. "And I love your singing, Elvis. Right now, though, I'm famished. I want to get this over with."

As the photographer's flash winked, Elvis asked what I would be doing later. I coyly told him that I already had plans. It was true. I'd planned to dine with Major Riddle and an oilman from Texas who'd sent flowers to my dressing room the previous night. I suggested that we might get together another time. Then I guided his arm around my waist and told him to think naughty thoughts, "like we just got out of bed together."

His face reddened again. He turned toward the camera and didn't look away until the photographer had finished. His uneasiness made smiling a breeze for me. Not only were we going to get some great publicity photos, but I was also going to linger in Elvis's mind as a different sort of woman, someone not ready to swoon at the opportunity to be near him. After several flashes, I put one hand on the upper part of his bare chest above the opening in his silk shirt. Still, he didn't look at me. I finally called a halt to the picture session and turned to leave. "I'll see you soon," he said as we parted.

I returned to my dressing room and donned a slinky, skin-tight evening gown with a plunging neckline. When I entered the cocktail lounge, I saw Elvis again. Major Riddle, the oilman, and a newspaper columnist from Los Angeles were sitting with me when Elvis, surrounded by half a dozen chorus girls, entered the lounge. The group was just getting seated around a table across the room when Elvis spotted me. He immediately got up and came to my table. He knelt at my side, flashed that unforgettable grin, and asked if he could join us.

"What will all of those young ladies do without you?" I asked.

"Oh, they'll be around later."

I looked at my companions. The hotel manager and the oilman shrugged. The newspaper columnist said he certainly didn't mind. In fact, he said he looked forward to sitting with "two of the hottest names in Las Vegas." He obviously figured to get some material for a future column out of such a session. Of course, I didn't mind. I was intrigued by the handsome Elvis.

For perhaps half an hour we talked about attendance, the economy, and what was happening in burlesque. Elvis, as shy as he was, became more animated as the conversation continued. He even recounted his harrowing escape from a crowd of delirious young women at the Paladium in Los Angeles a few weeks earlier.

Toward me, he certainly became more aggressive. He sat close to me, touched my hand suggestively a couple of times. I don't think the oilman was happy with Elvis's presence. Perhaps he had some plans of his own. But it was obvious that Elvis was going to stay until the others left or until I departed. Finally, they excused themselves. Once we were alone at the table, Elvis didn't waste any time letting me know what was on his mind. He said he wanted to see me away from the hotel, away from the lounge, away from other people.

I asked in my most teasing tone just what we would do, enjoying my power over this man who held so much power over so many women. I shall never forget how his face reddened and he struggled to express himself. "Well, we could, uh . . ."

I didn't intend to let him off easy. "We could do what, Elvis? Go to some secluded place and make mad, passionate love?"

Elvis was a fresh and wonderful person at the time, and he stammered again as he tried to express himself. I made it a little easier for him by saying that's what most men had in mind after they watched my show. "That's something we have in common," I told him. "Members of the opposite sex lust after us. They don't seem to understand that what we do on the stage is an act, a performance."

I pointed to his booth where the troupe of female admirers waited. I knew they would wait all night if they thought they

**164**

had a chance to take Elvis to bed, and I told him so. As his face reddened again, I added, "And I'll bet at least one of them has visions of marrying you and living happily ever after."

I understood the dreams a starry-eyed young chorus girl might be dreaming. After all, I was young and not long out of the chorus line myself.

"Well, now, Colonel Parker says I shouldn't even be thinking about . . ."

I had heard tales about Colonel Parker, Elvis's manager, friend, and father figure. "I'll bet he wouldn't like your getting all romantically involved with the wrong woman, would he?" I teased.

Elvis said he usually did what he wanted to do, that he was free to dine with whomever he chose. And if he felt like seeing someone that Colonel Parker didn't approve of, then he'd just leave his security men at the hotel and do what he wanted.

I said, "Elvis, that's sneaky."

He said he'd do it anyhow.

Wanting to know just how successful I had been at arousing this legendary sex symbol, I couldn't resist asking, "Would you sneak out for me?"

He suggested we get together that night, but I demurred. I had another show to do, and I needed my beauty sleep. Then I smiled at him and said, "But tomorrow is another day."

Indeed, there were other days. Elvis and I became almost inseparable. We dined together, danced together and laughed together. As much as I enjoyed the feeling of power that came from having the idol of millions idolize me, I also felt real compassion for Elvis. I understood the pressures of being a star, of having fans who felt that your onstage persona was theirs for the asking offstage. I also knew what it was like to be constantly concerned about your image, to calculate the effect of every appearance, onstage and off. I knew the pressures of the business we shared, and I knew how difficult that business made having genuine personal relationships. So, gradually, I felt myself growing closer to Elvis, and I became less concerned with playing games and more interested in a real relationship.

The one thing Elvis and I had not done was make love. When I received a late-night phone call from him, remembering our past conversations, I didn't have to be a mind reader to know what he wanted to talk about at that time of night.

"Tempest, honey, I'm busting out of here tonight, and I want to see you. Real bad," he said.

I had been coy long enough, so I consented. But still concerned with my image, I added, "You can't come through the lobby. No man has ever been seen coming into my suite, and I'm not going to start with you."

"That's just as well," he said. "Colonel Parker is raising hell about us already, and I'd rather come in the back way."

Thus, from the very beginning, our intimate relationship was, in part, controlled by our public images and by those concerned with protecting and maintaining them. This was to be a lifelong pattern for us both.

I reminded Elvis that there was an eight-foot security fence behind the hotel. He said he would climb the fence if I would just tell him where my suite was located. I promised I would open the drapes and turn on some lights so he could see me. Then the phone went dead.

Elvis.

God, what magic that name bore! Even though I wouldn't have admitted it to anyone, I was thrilled at the prospect of what the next few hours might bring.

Peeling off my evening gown, I hurried toward the bathroom and took a quick shower. Afterward, putting on a flowing blue negligee with lacy white trim, I looked about me in wonder. I was living in the most luxurious surroundings—a suite with chandeliers, a marble bath, and all of the plush trimmings. And now Elvis Presley was on his way to my place. It was as if all my childhood dreams of stardom and romance were coming true.

I stood before the mirror and admired the negligee I'd bought in Los Angeles a few weeks before. I loved it. But I decided that it wasn't sexy enough for Elvis, who was only twenty-one at the time. So I changed one more time—to a blue shorty that would show off my legs better. Then I put every hair in place. After all, if Elvis Presley was going to leave his security men behind and climb a fence behind my hotel, I wanted him to remember—for all time—that first glimpse of me when he came around the swimming pool and looked through my patio door. I wanted it to be just like a scene in a movie, the kind of scene I had imagined back in Eastman as I thumbed through my dog-eared movie magazines for the hundredth time.

In a way, I had created this scene. I had taken control of Elvis's interest in me, and I had decided how far and how fast our relationship would move. I had considered the business side of it, how being seen with Elvis and having my name linked with his in the press would affect my career. I was smarter than those teen-agers who screamed when he appeared and those chorus girls who lingered about in hopes of the smallest attention from him. Even though I wasn't much older than those women and even though I might have been stuck in the chorus line myself if I hadn't been able to dance my way to headliner status, I did feel that I could control this situation. After all, I had learned very early that I had to take control, that I had to shape my own destiny.

It was nearly three in the morning, and there was no one at the pool. So I pulled the drapes open, dimmed the lights, and waited. Stormy, my tiny toy poodle, nestled into my lap. For all the fancy surroundings and the celebrity of the man I expected and despite my confidence in myself and my control over my emotions, I was just like any other woman in this situation, dressed in my best, groomed to perfection, waiting for my date, hoping to have my dreams come true.

Perhaps fifteen minutes after Elvis hung up the phone, I saw a leg slide over the top of the fence. Then he stopped, hanging comically with one leg at the top of the fence and the other pointing toward the ground. Obviously, he was hung on something. I couldn't keep from smiling at the sight of my glamorous date's daring arrival. He wiggled first one way and then the other. Finally, he dropped to the ground and walked around the swimming pool.

I considered leaving the lights down low and letting him worry a bit. But I really liked Elvis, so I turned up the lights and stood. At first, he just stared. Then he smiled broadly and reached for the handle on the sliding glass door. As he crossed the threshold, Stormy barked loudly.

"Tell that damned dog to shut up before everyone in the hotel is looking this way."

I shushed Stormy as Elvis closed the door and pulled the drapes. "Well, you're certainly a mess," I said, gesturing toward his torn trousers. But he couldn't have cared less. I'll never forget that naive country boy's saying, "Well, I'm as horny as a billy goat in a pepper patch. I'll race you to the bed."

So much for the way I would have written this scene. He grabbed my hand and started toward the nearest door. I told him that it led to the hallway. He swore and turned toward another. I said that was the bathroom door. He smiled, and Stormy started growling to let me know that she wasn't happy to have a visitor. She was a possessive little dog, but she would have to go. She ran away when I tried to pick her up, but on the second try, I nabbed her, dropped her into the living room and closed the door before she could scamper back into the bedroom. She immediately started whining and scratching at the door. Our romantic evening was about to turn into a silly comedy sketch.

Elvis complained about the distraction, but he wasn't distracted for long. I knew how to turn the tone back toward romance. He was the impatient lover that night. As the sounds of lovemaking grew more intense, so did Stormy's growling and scratching. Once Elvis asked if I would mind if he strangled Stormy, but I managed to take his mind off the dog.

Later, we lay side by side while our breathing slowed. It was a tender moment between two people who understood the lives they each were leading in the fast lane of a very busy highway, a life that could also be very lonely. As with any lovers, for Elvis and me these special moments after lovemaking were the time for talking, for sharing feelings, for holding on to that feeling of closeness the physical intimacy helped to create.

He kissed me and said he wanted to be with me as often as our schedules allowed, but that he'd have to be careful because Colonel Parker was in a huff about me. I knew what was coming—the stigma I often dealt with, that of being a stripper.

The gossip columns had labeled Elvis and me "breakfast pals" and had speculated that things might be getting serious between us. The colonel pitched a fit, Elvis told me.

"He said, 'If you keep hanging around that stripper woman, those screaming teen-agers are going to quit screaming. And when they stop screaming, they'll stop buying your records and then where the hell are you going to be? Back in Memphis driving a goddamn truck!' I'll tell you, Tempest, he was really in a rage," Elvis said.

I asked if he thought our being seen together could ruin the sales of his records.

He said that if Colonel Parker said it, he believed it. "He's been right on everything so far," Elvis said. "He's made me what I am."

That wasn't what I wanted to hear. I wanted Elvis to say that it didn't make any difference. I wanted him to say that my way of making a living was all right with him, that I could take off my clothes as a performer and still be respected as a person. What I wanted from Elvis at this moment is what I have longed for throughout my career—respect for me, as a person, rather than the assumption that I was only a stripper, a woman without feelings, emotions, needs of my own.

But that wasn't the way he felt, and because he was fresh out of the sticks and still believed in the tooth fairy and Santa Claus, he couldn't hide his conviction that Colonel Parker was right—that a relationship with a stripper, no matter how big a star she was and no matter how sincere her interest in him as a person, would ruin his career.

Looking back on my relationship with Elvis, I now realize that his dependence on Colonel Parker as a surrogate father was the main obstacle to our having a really satisfying relationship. Part of the problem must have stemmed from my own distrust of father figures. My experience had led me to believe that men who posed as fathers weren't to be trusted, and I saw Elvis's dependence on this advisor as dangerous, for him and for our relationship. I resented his open, trusting nature, and I was afraid for myself because I was moving through this treacherous show business world without any trusted companion or advisor. I was all alone, on my own, as I had always been, it seemed.

Elvis saw that I was upset. He talked sweetly to me and tried some words of comfort. But I was hurt. I turned away from him and stared at the wall for a long time. I couldn't hold back the tears. I wanted to tell Elvis to get out of my suite and out of my life and never come back. I wanted to tell him that he and Colonel Parker could hold hands until hell froze over and I would still be the biggest and most respected name in burlesque. I wanted to tell him that as long as people applauded, as long as they showered me with compliments and gifts, then, by God, I didn't need Elvis Presley or anyone else.

But I couldn't say these things. I really liked Elvis, and I wasn't ready to call it quits just because his beloved Colonel Parker was a dictatorial jackass. I wanted Elvis to stay another hour. I wanted to make love again, to talk about other things.

However, I made sure I didn't warm up to him too quickly. In a small way, I wanted him to pay for Colonel Parker's opinion of me. So I waited for him to put his arms around me and talk tenderly to me. I needed that. I needed closeness and affection. I could get all the sex I wanted. But I wanted Elvis Presley, the teen idol, to tell me that he liked me, even if he had to lie a little.

I also wanted the satisfaction of knowing that I was adored by America's hottest sex symbol. I wanted to climb to the roof of the highest hotel in Las Vegas and shout that I'd made love to Elvis Presley. Of course, I didn't. Colonel Parker wouldn't like that. I settled for the next-best thing—Elvis and I made love again. And it was good, even with Stormy still scratching at the door.

We alternated love and rest until four that afternoon, a marathon I'll never forget. We talked about everything, including marriage. But even though I enjoyed the conversation, I never believed we'd get serious about it. And I suspect that Elvis might have had second thoughts, too. My first thought was that I was just reaching my prime. I wanted to dance and make money, enjoy fame and riches, take cruises and wear the finest clothes.

And I didn't want to depend on others. I wanted to do it myself. So, even though I never said so to Elvis, my career was more important to me than our romance.

After Elvis left, I sat in a chair and looked out the patio door at the purple mountains in the distance, and I thought about who I was. What did it mean to have just made love with one of the most famous and desired men in the world, if I now sat alone and unsatisfied? What was it that I still needed, what part of me was still unfulfilled?

I was Tempest Storm, the superstar of burlesque.

I was making $3,500 a week.

Rich men showered me with diamonds and furs and cruises—some with romance on their minds, some just to be seen with me.

Waitresses, porters, and bellhops constantly tended to my every need.

A new red Cadillac convertible waited for me in the hotel's garage.

I'd partied with—and had been romanced by—some of the biggest names in the country. Mickey Rooney. Vic Damone. Senator John F. Kennedy. Nat King Cole.

On the surface, my life could not have been better. But underneath, I longed for a respectability that, by 1957, I knew was nothing more than a pipedream. Men wanted to go to bed with me. Those who would marry me for myself would want to change me after the wedding, would expect me to give up the glamor and riches, to settle down to domestic life and have babies.

Women envied the attention and pampering I got. Yes, they envied me on the one hand and disliked me on the other because they saw me as a threat. They didn't want their workaday husbands to be the ones paying attention to me. And they certainly didn't want to introduce me to their children.

To the average American housewife, the average anybody, I was pretty much what Colonel Tom Parker called me—a stripper.

A famous stripper.

A well-to-do stripper.

An envied and sought-after stripper.

But a stripper nonetheless.

The only way I could ever change the image was to quit, go into seclusion and let people's minds lose me in a distant past. But I wouldn't do that. I couldn't do that. I'd decided long ago to draw as much pleasure as I could from this life in the fast lane, and people could think what they pleased.

How did I wind up in this predicament? And how would I ever get out of it?

My name was also linked to Frank Sinatra's at one time. Why? I think it was because of an introduction he gave me the night he opened a new show at Caesar's Palace in Las Vegas in 1970.

I had first met Frank through Sara, a saleslady at Dorothy Beal's dress shop at the Sands Hotel. Before she introduced us, she filled me in on his reputation as rude and disrespectful to women. That was certainly Sara's impression of him. But I always found him otherwise. Without fail, he was respectful to me, treated me like a lady. I couldn't have asked for more polite and thoughtful behavior in an acquaintance.

On the evening of his 1970 opening, I showed up a little early for once and went backstage to see the star. When he came out of his dressing room, his necktie was crooked. I straightened it. "Frank," I said, "you need someone to look after you. You're a mess. And, darling, I hate to say it, but that suit just isn't you. You'd look much better in lighter blue."

He smiled about that and, being the showman that he is, he didn't miss a chance to capitalize on it. During his performance, I was seated at a front table, and, as he did for the other stars who attended that show, he introduced me. "Ladies and gentlemen," he said, "I'd like for you to meet a beautiful lady who taught me how to dress."

I stood up and took a bow to a thunderous round of applause. As I sat down, he added, "I'll bet you thought I was going to say that she's the lady who taught me how to undress."

Frank and I have maintained a friendship, and he has continued to introduce me to the audiences at his shows. The last time I saw him perform, at Caesar's Palace in Tahoe in

1981, he was as kind and warm toward me as always. I'm glad the Frank Sinatra I know is not the same man that Sara in Dorothy Beal's knew.

Michael Wilding, one of Elizabeth Taylor's ex-husbands, was rumored to have had a romance with me. It's true, but it was a very short romance. We met at the Copacabana in New York City, and I liked him instantly, partly for the stark contrast in our personalities, I think. Wherever I saw him, be it Palm Springs or New York, he was dressed the same way—casual but elegant. When he stood beside me in the fancy cocktail dresses that I most often wore for public appearances and at parties, we made a strange couple, for sure.

He had an intriguing accent and drew a lot of attention wherever he went. When he was with me, the odd-couple quality probably helped garner attention, but he also got his fair share of notice because he had a tendency to attract trouble. Find a scrape of any kind, any sort of difficulty, and chances are you'd find Michael. Trouble just seemed to follow him around, or maybe he followed trouble.

Even though our affair was short and never serious, partly because I didn't find him a very satisfying lover, I did think I could do him a big favor. I called my attorney, Nathan Cohn, and asked to come to my apartment. I didn't tell him what I needed because he had heard enough of my Michael Wilding stories to know what a difficult case the man could be. Once I got Nathan there, I called Michael and asked him to come over also, again not giving him a specific reason, but stressing that I needed to see him right away.

While we waited, I refused to tell Nathan the purpose of having Michael meet him at my apartment. Once Michael arrived, I introduced the two of them, asked Nathan for one of his business cards, and said very firmly to Michael, "Take this card, and remember Nathan's name. Please call him if you are ever in trouble and need a lawyer. There's nobody better."

I had had enough of troublesome men in my life, and I figured Nathan could handle them better than I could. At least he could handle them without their messing up my life. That's the way I said good-bye to Michael Wilding, fondly but efficiently.

Vince Edwards, who eventually became a television superstar as Ben Casey, was a dinner companion while I was appearing at the Dunes in Las Vegas in 1957. We enjoyed each other's company, and he escorted me back to my suite. He hugged me and kissed me, but I felt no real connection. I don't know why except that something was missing, the chemistry, the mysterious bond, that always made me feel that this one, this man, might be *the* man. It may be hard for someone who has lived a very different life to believe, but all my relationships with men sprang from that feeling. I eventually learned to enjoy the sheer pleasure of sensuality, but for me sensuality and romance could never be separated, and with Vince Edwards I did not sense the possibility for a great romance. Without that possibility, I wasn't interested in pursuing the hugs and kisses. Vince showed up at a very busy time for me, and I needed to concentrate on a new act that had been choreographed by Robert Sidney, who had perfected dance routines for the likes of Betty Grable and Mitzi Gaynor. My new act was drawing rave reviews in the Las Vegas press, Walter Winchell was flying in to see me perform, and the critics said I was on the edge of turning the room into a garage with my daring and provocative performance. I didn't want a man cluttering up my life right then. I was learning, from some painful experiences, that I had to be careful not to let my love life hinder my career.

Of course, I changed my mind when Elvis Presley came along. Even though I teased him unmercifully, I couldn't resist him. He was undeniably the most interesting younger man I ever knew. In addition to bringing that important spark of romance into my life, Elvis did one other important thing for me. He changed my body measurements for all

175

time, and in so doing he may have helped strengthen the career that I had realized was more important to me than Elvis himself was. He did all this with one crude phrase.

We'd had dinner at one of the hotels in Las Vegas in 1957, and we were returning to the Dunes for my evening performance. As we were walking out of the hotel, a hand suddenly landed on my backside and Elvis's voice said, "Fat ass."

"What?" I said, glancing around to see if anyone might have heard.

"I said you're a fat ass."

My mouth was hanging open in shock as he took me by the arm and guided me outside.

"Elvis! That's the crudest thing anyone ever said to me. I'm just exactly what every man wants to get his arms around."

"Maybe so, but you're still a . . ."

"It isn't true, damn it! Don't you dare say I'm a . . ."

"Fat ass? You are, honey. You just can't get around back and look like I can." And he laughed heartily.

At the Dunes, I went to my dressing room and took off my clothes so marks from undergarments would disappear before I performed. I put on a gown and while I worked to renew my makeup, I remembered what Elvis had said.

"A fat ass, huh?" I said to myself. Suddenly, I stripped the gown away and turned my bare backside toward the lighted mirror. I looked. I was a little heavy, but not fat. I had a tiny waist and an hourglass figure, and I was still holding at 135 pounds, my weight when I'd started performing nearly seven years before and the weight Lillian Hunt had persuaded me was ideal.

Elvis didn't enjoy any lovemaking that night. In fact, I didn't bother to go out after my last show. I knew that if I didn't go out, I wouldn't eat anything. And if I didn't eat anything, I would lose weight. Missing those first few late-night dinners sent hunger pangs through me, but in a few days I'd learned to survive on almost nothing. In two months, I lost twenty-four pounds. When I went back to eating, I was careful to stick to high protein foods. I still eat that way, and I've never put the weight back on.

I suppose I owe Elvis for motivating me to maintain the figure I have today. Like most people who diet successfully, I learned how to change my lifestyle, my eating and exercise habits. Since that casual observation by a very young man, I have thrived on such foods as poached eggs, fresh-squeezed orange juice, baked chicken, skimmed milk, and fresh fruit.

It seemed ironic many years later when I saw Elvis on TV and he looked fat and bloated. If I had seen him just before his death, I wouldn't have called him a fat ass. No matter how much motivation his comment gave me to do something that has proven good for me, it hurt. I still flinch when I remember it. I also wonder whether men suffer as much from the treacheries that befall the body itself. Would a man have been as changed by such a casual remark? For me the change was essential. Without having gotten in shape and stayed that way, I couldn't have survived as a dancer. Then again, Elvis didn't survive. I often wonder about the ironies of fate, and this is a perfect example of how fate has stepped in and shaped my destiny in the most surprising ways.

The last time I saw Elvis was in 1970. We were both attending a stage show performance by Perry Como at the International Hilton in Las Vegas. After the show, we were talking backstage when Perry admired my abundance of red hair and said, "Tempest, is all of that really yours? You know I'm a barber, and I'd like to get my shears on that."

I was in a good mood and felt like teasing Elvis again for old time's sake. I said seductively, "Perry, everything you see is mine. Just ask Presley."

Elvis, who had long been married by then, said, "Uh-oh, it's time for me to leave, folks."

But before he left, he caught me away from the others and asked, "Say, have you still got that goddamn barking dog?"

"No, she's been dead for years," I said. "But did you notice that I'm not a fat ass anymore?"

"You look great," he said, and he smiled the smile that had become so famous. "Did I really call you that?"

"You know you did. That's why I lost all that weight."

He looked almost embarrassed when I said that, and for a moment I remembered the fresh young guy I'd loved so long ago.

"Is it too late to apologize?" he asked.

"Of course not," I said. I had to struggle to keep from kissing him right there.

Vic Damone was another special love. I met him between my marriages to Johnny Del Mar and Herb Jeffries. He was appearing at Kiamesha Lake, New York, a resort in the Catskills, in 1957. I had gone there to study my lines in preparation for a summer stock version of *Bus Stop*. I'd landed Marilyn Monroe's part, and we were scheduled to open in a week at Memorial Hall in Dayton, Ohio. But once I'd met Vic, I couldn't leave him alone long enough to concentrate on my lines.

We turned each other on, even when we were ten feet apart. When we were closer, we sizzled. He was sexy and hot-blooded, and I called him my Italian Stallion—long before Sylvester Stallone took that nickname for himself.

We steamed up a few windows at the Concord. Then I left to do *Bus Stop*. This was a big opportunity for me to get into acting, serious acting, and I have often wondered what would have happened if I had not fallen madly in love, but had instead devoted myself to that play. This is another good example of those emotions that we can't control. They take on an amazing and a confusing power over us, and all the priorities we hold dear seem to fade away till nothing matters except the fierce grip of those mysterious passions.

Later, I left for Las Vegas to headline Minsky's Revue at the Dunes Hotel. A few weeks after I opened, Vic came to see the show. At the end of my act, I reclined on a chaise lounge wrapped in nothing but a long white fox. I closed out by running my hand around a tall light made like a candle, flicking the light out and darkening the stage.

I never thought about it until Vic came to see the show. He was hysterical with laughter after the show and said the candle closely resembled a certain part of the male anatomy and that I had done a wonderful job of turning out the light.

"Did you know I posed for that light to be made?" he joked.

The truth is, he could have. He was a lot of man, and he was a lot of fun. Fun was what I needed at the time. I didn't want to get caught up in a serious romance. I was playing the field and liking it, but I could have become very serious about Vic if we had met at a different time, under different circumstances.

We're still buddies today. I saw him as recently as July of 1985. We met at the Reno Hilton where I was headlining the stage show "Sugar Daddies," while he was starring in "Rhythm on Ice." I watched him rehearse and had lunch with him several times. Later, I met his fiancee, Diahann Carroll, and the three of us had breakfast in the hotel coffee shop. Later, I also had coffee with his three beautiful daughters. It made me feel good when one his daughters said, "My dad speaks very highly of you."

So there they are—the facts, my version of the stories people have told. As I look back, I feel lucky to have known so many exciting and wonderful men at various times in my life. But as I remember the things we shared and the problems we faced, I see a pattern emerging. One piece of the pattern has to do with my career. Certain men helped my career, either by boosting the public's recognition of my work through publicity or by being understanding and supportive of me as I pursued my profession. Other men may have felt slighted by my work, and it may be that some of the relationships would have turned out differently if I had been willing to abandon my career and sell short my dreams.

Another important piece of the pattern has to do with the gradual change in my feelings about sex. Some of the men I was with did a great deal to help me understand that sex could be a deeply satisfying exchange rather than a horrific or manipulative thing. Some led me to realize that sex can also be great fun, can be a release from the pressures of the professional world, especially in a high-powered profession like show business. I've also learned the hard way that society still tends to have one set of sexual rules for women and another for men. I'm still trying to figure out how to deal with that difference, in terms of both having a good, lasting relationship and asserting an accurate image of myself in a world still willing to mark me with the stripper's stigma.

Finally, I see in this pattern of my relationships with men evidence of a great emptiness inside me, one that I'm now sure dates back to the earliest days of my childhood and my discovery that I had been abandoned by my natural father and subsequently "captured" by my stepfather. Therefore, I grew to puberty without an adequate male role model to help me make good choices in my own relationships. When I couple this phenomenon, which my psychologists have assured me is almost universal among women who have never known a loving father, with the unavoidable psychological damage of the rape experience, I sometimes wonder that I have ever felt any joy in love at all.

But I have. And that is the most important piece of the pattern. I still dream. I still believe in the possibilities of love. In fact, Vic Damone didn't really turn my head the last time I saw him, in 1985. At that time I was in love again, still believing with all my might that something would make it right, this time, for sure.

With Harry James in Las Vegas, 1970

Hugs for Sterling Hayden . . .            . . . and Red Buttons

Billy Hufsey of the television series *Fame*

To Engelbert
You're looking as
lonely as ever
lots of love
Engelbert xxx

Engelbert, one of the sexiest men alive

Jack Lemon, a real charmer

Dancing with Walter Cronkite at a *People* magazine party

Vic Damone, always a friend

Singer Gary Puckett in Reno

Marty Caplan, a source of joy and pain

With my mother on her birthday, 1981

My daughter Patty, a reason for living

# *Eight*

Herb Jeffries was an incredibly handsome and deeply mysterious man to me. Even before I went to Hollywood, I'd read about him in gossip magazines where he was famous for two things. First, his song "Flamingo" went to the top of the pop charts and made him a very popular singer in the late 1940s. He'd once been lead singer with Duke Ellington's band, and, according to accounts I'd read, he was black. Second, a scar on his light-skinned face was something of a legend in itself. *Confidential* magazine said it had been put there by an angry, jealous woman, Ronnie Quillen.

Soon after Jim Crowley, the man who brought me to California originally, and I parted company, I went riding around Hollywood with some friends, and I asked if we could drive past Herb Jeffries's house. I was curious. Of course, I never would have believed on the afternoon of that ride that I would one day marry the man. Later on, if someone had asked if I might marry a black man, I would have answered: Yes, Nat King Cole. But Herb Jeffries wouldn't have crossed my mind as a potential husband.

Herb came into my life in 1957 at a time when I could have given up burlesque for the right man and a comfortable lifestyle. I had considered getting out of the business and had tried several things in the late 1950s:

1. I'd given up—for all time—any chance of a career in modeling. Only a severe breast-reduction operation would have permitted me to get into big-time modeling.

2. I'd tried to get into acting, but the closest I ever came was playing that part in a road edition of *Bus Stop*. My only real offer in movies was to portray a burlesque queen. I turned it down because I wanted to do serious acting.

3. I'd taken voice lessons in New York to try to become a pop singer. I even cut a demo record. I also fired an agent who wanted to bill me as "The Singing Stripper."

Singing was perhaps my best chance for a change in professions. I had a contract with Roulette Records and Maurice Levy and an album in rehearsal. The concept was to be built around a "Stormy Weather" atmosphere, with all the songs fitting that mood. I was working with Arnold Goldand, who wrote songs for Paul Anka, among others. So singing was a serious consideration. Then I met Herb.

In 1958, I left Las Vegas for an engagement at the New Burbank Theater in Los Angeles. I rented an apartment not far from the theater. California had been home to me in my mind for a long time, and I saw this move as a return to my home base.

One hot night I returned to my apartment, took a shower, washed off all my makeup, and shampooed my hair. That's when Bobby Lucas, a singer, called to say that he wanted to drop by for a visit.

Bobby was like a brother to me, and I didn't mind his seeing me without makeup, dressed in short shorts and a shirt tied at the midriff. However, when the doorbell rang,

Bobby was standing there with a tall, handsome man at his side.

"Bobby! What the hell do you think you're doing, bringing a stranger up here? Look at me! I just got out of the shower!" I could feel my still-wet hair dripping onto the shoulders of my blouse, and I wondered what it looked like to this stranger to see a woman with her hair wringing wet.

"Hey, calm down," he said. "This guy is just like family. Tempest Storm, meet Herb Jeffries." I nearly fainted.

This knockout of a man—who'd once appeared on the cover of *Life* magazine—was standing at my door. I felt almost naked standing there without my eyelashes or makeup. Later, I would tease Herb about his marrying a woman from whom there could be no surprises. He saw the natural, unadorned Tempest Storm on that first night. I still remember his telling me that my eyes were beautiful without makeup.

"Bobby, I'm going to kill you for this."

"No, honey, you're going to thank me for doing this because Herb's just dying to meet you."

I was so flabbergasted by this surprise I could hardly carry on a decent conversation. When they finally left, the only thing I could remember was that I'd accepted a date with Herb. He really put the rush on me. We dated almost every night. His own career wasn't going so well at the time, and I didn't mind helping out with the expenses as long as we were having a good time. Perhaps the lagging career and the financial problems should have sounded a warning. But I was too enchanted by Herb Jeffries to think very much about his career.

It turned out, of course, that Herb didn't consider himself black. Not long after we started dating, I met his mother. She was fair, red-haired, and Irish. His father, who was deceased, was described to me as a dark-skinned Latin. Herb's mother explained—in one simple sentence—why many people thought Herb Jeffries was black.

"He sang with Duke Ellington's band," she said.

"Is that the only reason?" I asked.

"Yes," she said, "I begged him not to join that band. I told him that he would be branded a black man. He has just enough of his father's looks that some people might think he's a light-skinned black."

"That's incredible," I said. "Just because he sang with Duke Ellington?"

"Well, like I said, I begged him not to do that, but he wouldn't listen."

Herb used to brag that he had a great-grandparent who was black and that he was one-eighth black, but that never was confirmed to me. Besides, I was in love with him.

Herb and I dated for more than a year, and I was loyal to him except for one sentimental and very sweet reunion with Nat King Cole. I went back to Las Vegas in late 1958 for an engagement at the Dunes. Nat was appearing at the Sands. He called and wanted to see me, so after the last show I went to his suite to talk. More than anything else, I think I went there to test Nat's affection for me. I wanted him to tell me that he still wanted me, that he didn't want me to get married. But he'd heard about my relationship with Herb.

"Don't you want me anymore, Nat?" I finally asked when he didn't respond to my affection.

He stared at me for a long moment and then said, "I want you more than anything else in the world. I want to make love to you at this moment." He stopped and regarded me for a moment, then said, "How could you do this to me, Tempest?"

"Nat, you're married, and there's no future for us. I need something more solid than an affair."

We did make love again, a long and passionate session that lasted for more than two hours. But it was the good-bye of star-crossed lovers who had finally realized that they must go on with separate lives.

I left with tears in my eyes and never knew another tender moment with Nat King Cole. I regretted that in many ways because, even now, I believe I loved the man as much as I have ever loved anyone. To this day, I have a special place in my heart for the feelings we shared. We remained friends till the day he died.

Herb kept calling and asking me to marry him. I told him I was more interested in my career at the moment, and we'd talk about it later. In addition to wanting to concentrate on my career, deep inside I knew I was madly in love with Nat and not ready for another love . . . not right then.

Many of my friends knew about our romance, and every one of them urged me not even to consider marrying Herb.

"You've got the world in the palm of your hand," they'd say, "but if you marry this guy, it could all go right down the drain." The more I heard that, the more I was determined to marry whomever I wanted without its reflecting on my career. I thought my contracts should be based on my ability to draw—and please—audiences, not on who my husband happened to be.

I really hated for people to tell me not to do something, and I could feel that old stubbornness rising up and making me rebel against what others thought was good and right for Tempest Storm.

When I returned to Los Angeles, Herb took me to out-of-the-way restaurants and nightclubs in an effort to protect my show business reputation. But it did little good. Columnist Dorothy Kilgallen first broke the news that Herb and I planned to marry. As soon as that word was out, one of the tabloids carried a story with a big headline that said, "Tempest Storm Will Marry Negro Singer."

Herb and I were performing in San Francisco as the date approached. When we went to the courthouse in San Francisco to apply for a marriage license, we were not alone. A small army of press people was waiting for us. We joked with them, and finally, we started filling out the paperwork for the application. When Herb reached the block that asked for his race, color, or creed, he smiled at me, kissed me on the cheek, and said, "Well, honey, here goes."

He wrote, "Caucasian."

This was not the story the press had come to cover. Two people in love and about to start out on a life together, even if those two people are in show business and regular grist for the gossip mill, is not nearly the eyebrow-raising material that an interracial marriage would have been. Of course, the wedding was properly noted. But many reporters probably had to revise the sensational stories they had roughed out ahead of time.

Almost immediately after the wedding on May 21, 1959, I noted several areas in which Herb and I would have trouble throughout our ten-year marriage.

First, he was insanely jealous.

Second, he didn't like to work at keeping his career going.

Third, he didn't want me to pursue my singing career, which I viewed as my best possible route out of burlesque with a decent living still possible.

None of these factors, in isolation, suggests a positive environment for working out family matters, for maintaining a placid domestic life. In combination, they were deadly. Perhaps I should have looked more closely at the man I was marrying, asked more questions, demanded more answers. But I didn't.

At first, I was very committed to the marriage. I came from the old school where the wife always gave in to the husband's wishes. For instance, when I mentioned a possible move into the music field for me and he said, "One singer in the family is enough," I gave in without a fight. I have regretted that decision many times since. In the beginning, we could have gotten an act together. In fact, we did work several nightclubs together. But things got steadily worse.

Every time I returned from an out-of-town engagement, Herb was extremely watchful and nervous. He would look through my things as I unpacked, and I always had the feeling he was half watching for something to use against me in some way. Of course, he never found anything, but that didn't stop him from making accusations. I felt he was being overprotective and interfering. After all, I had been a performer for long enough to know how to deal with life on the road, how to conduct myself and avoid the kinds of problems Herb seemed to think I had no control over. Now I understand that he must have felt insecure and afraid of losing me, but then I was sure he was trying to imprison me, trying to keep me from being myself and pursuing my career.

I picked my share of the fights, too, though. The arguments I started usually concerned his continuing lack of interest in his career. Even though he was seldom sick, he copped out of more engagements than many singers are ever offered. I was convinced, and still am, that a powerful career drive is necessary to keeping yourself successful, and it concerned me that a man of Herb's talents had little or no such drive.

For example, through my connections in Las Vegas, I got Herb booked into the Frontier Hotel at $2,000 a week. Then, quite suddenly, he came down with laryngitis. After he had taken a week off to recuperate, the management at the hotel kept calling, wondering when he would be able to come back. He'd fake laryngitis on the telephone and laugh sarcastically after he'd hung up and talk in a normal voice. The laryngistis got him out of the contract, which turned out to be a good thing, as he got an important offer to appear in Sydney, Australia. Of course, he didn't want to fly to Sydney. Luckily, in this case the Australians provided cruise passage for both of us. There was always something that made going after professional opportunities too hard or too uncomfortable for Herb.

Herb had often told me the story of how he helped Tony Bennett get the first recording contract Tony ever signed. I know that Tony thought a lot of Herb, and he tried to repay the old debt by getting Herb an engagement at the Playboy Club in Los Angeles. Herb sang beautifully through each week, and on the weekend Tony would come in and join him to boost the box office. It seemed like a great chance for Herb to get his career going again, and it gave Tony the opportunity he had been waiting for to return a professional favor.

I went to the show one night and raved about Tony after he'd finished singing "September of My Years," one of my favorite songs. Herb flew into a rage and said, "Well, you sure as hell never bragged like that on my singing."

I said, "Of course I have. I just don't hear Tony sing as often as I hear you."

This incident really upset him, and he decided not to continue on the Playboy circuit, as had been the original plan. This is just another example of the terrible insecurity in Herb that plagued our relationship. I was disappointed that he would miss such important exposure, but there was nothing I could do if he wasn't going to work. Still, as long as I was having to pay the bills, I couldn't help being resentful. I put everything into keeping my career going and trying to keep our marriage together. I really believed that this was the relationship that I had always wanted and that it would last forever because I loved him and was happy and content in the attention and devotion he showed me. Those are qualities every woman needs in the man she loves, and in those ways Herb was a wonderful husband. But a woman also needs a good helpmate. Because Herb seemed sworn to neglecting his career, the pressure on me as the sole provider was intense.

Few things I did ever seemed to please Herb.

I remember when we were going to the inaugural of Los Angeles Mayor Sam Yorty. I wanted to leave an impression with the elite of Los Angeles that would never be forgotten, so I dressed in a Trivilla gown of cut black velvet. Its plunging neckline was revealing but not vulgar. My hairstyle had taken the hairdresser two hours. It was one of the most stunning hairdos I ever wore. I will never forget Herb's first glimpse of me when I came out of the bedroom. He was stunned.

He looked at me and said, "You're not going like that, are you? God, your hair! And that gown! You're going to spill out of it."

I'd spent the entire day getting ready and his remarks really hurt. It was the old stigma again. I knew there would be other celebrities there in gowns cut as low or lower, with hairdos that were dramatic and special, but neither Herb nor anyone else would think to chastize them. They would look elegant. Because I was a stripper, I looked vulgar. At least that's the way Herb's reaction made me feel. I'm sure his own insecurity and jealousy made him react this way.

When we arrived at the inaugural, Mr. Blackwell, the designer, approached us and said, "Tempest, you look absolutely gorgeous. Even though that is not my dress, it is perfect for you. Your hair, your makeup . . . yes, everything about you is perfect."

Coming from him, I took it as the ultimate compliment. When that gentleman made up a list of best-dressed—or worst-dressed—people in Hollywood, it was taken as gospel. Still, it would have been nice to have my husband compliment me as nicely as this casual acquaintance had.

After we sat down, Herb leaned over and said, "Darling, you look absolutely gorgeous tonight." I wasn't sure whether he was mimicking Mr. Blackwell or really trying to pass along a belated compliment. But under the circumstances I took it as far too little far too late. I kicked him so hard under the table that his shin was black and blue for a week.

We had many good times, including cruises to Australia, Hawaii, Paris, Monte Carlo and the South of France. But this marriage I often called "The Rocky Road Romance" never smoothed out. I traveled and worked. Sometimes Herb went with me, but mostly he played golf. In fact, I often played with him, and we both enjoyed it. I felt that it was one way for us to be closer, if we could share an interest. I was especially happy when Herb played in a big tournament because he seemed to enjoy it so much, and I loved watching him compete. I continued trying to understand his neglecting his career because I loved him dearly. However, the longer we were married, the more the neglect increased.

I did everything I knew to try to please him. Then, just before Christmas of 1960, he flew into a jealous rage over a simple thing like a shopping trip. He often badgered me about the money I spent on clothes, but this time he didn't even have that to vent his anger on.

Herb had two children by a previous marriage, and I had always been concerned about them, looked after them, and wanted to do things for them as a way of doing something special for Herb. I felt the same way about his mother, who was a wonderful woman who had taken the time to teach me how to cook. She'd also been wise enough to know that as newlyweds we didn't need to live with a ready-made family. I told Herb we really ought to get the kids and his mother something for Christmas. As usual, I had put off Christmas shopping until Christmas Eve. I asked if he wanted to go with me, but he said, "No, you go ahead and take care of everything." I was happy to do that because I loved him and I loved them. It was the holiday season, and I was overflowing with good will and a warm heart.

It was a busy, tiring day, the stores filled with all the other last-minute shoppers and the usual Christmas Eve frenzy of activity. Besides the holiday shopping, I needed to stop at the furrier to get my furs out of storage since we were leaving for Australia a couple of days later. Herb was scheduled for an engagement there, after which I would have to fly directly from Australia to London for an engagement of my own. It would be summer while we were down under, but I would need the furs for London's chilly winter.

When I returned home from shopping, I was worn to a frazzle. Herb was standing in the doorway, looking at me with a frown on his face.

I said, "Here, honey, help me with these packages."

He didn't offer to help or answer me until I had carried an armload of packages into the house. Then he asked, "Well, who did you sleep with today?"

I decided to ignore that remark. I put the packages down and went back to get the rest. He ranted and raved at me all the way out of the house and back in again, without lifting the first package himself. I made a third trip to the car for my furs. Again he followed, harassing and accusing me. My temper was beginning to flare. I had had enough.

When I got the furs safely in the house, I turned on him and asked angrily, "OK, Herb, what's the problem?"

"I think you've been in bed with someone."

"Well, I don't really care what you think. I've been all over this town, shopping for *your* children and *your* mother. I've carried packages. I've waited in every line in town. And you think I've had time to go to bed with someone? You're insane. Why are you spoiling our holidays. This is supposed to be a family time, a happy time. Just drop it because I don't feel like an argument."

But he wouldn't leave me alone. He followed me into the dining room where I was putting Christmas presents on the table. His words became harsher, more accusatory. Finally, I exploded.

"Damn you, Herb. I've had it! Do you hear me? I've had all I can take!"

I turned away from him as tears began to flow. And that's when I saw the twelve beautiful long-stemmed, cut-glass wine glasses that had been a wedding gift. I remembered Herb's supposed fear of broken glass. That scar on his face came from broken glass, the stories said. Even though he had never talked about the fear, I remembered a time when he almost stepped on a piece of glass while we were walking on the beach and how he drew back, his face as white as a sheet.

With my anger at the boiling point, I grabbed one of the expensive glasses and said, "You'd better be careful, Herb, or I'm going to make this side of your face match the other side."

I hurled the glass at him. Before he dodged that one, I sent another hurtling at him. Glass smashed on the walls around him and littered the carpet at his feet. I kept yelling "Damn you, Herb," each time I threw another glass. Finally, they were gone, all broken, scattered about the room. I ran into another room. I wanted to finish crying and calm my nerves.

Herb cleaned up the mess, so I wondered later just how frightened of broken glass he really was. However, he started ranting again just before bedtime. I had already changed into my negligee, but there was no peace, no silent night to found in our home on this Christmas Eve. I finally got up, slipped on my long mink coat, and headed outside. I didn't know where I was going, but I had to get out of the house. My temper was on edge again, and my nerves were shot. I decided to go for a ride.

Herb followed me outside, trying to question me about where I intended to go. I heard him shout, "Are you going back to see your boyfriend again?" When he said that, I tried to run over him. I didn't hit him, but I came very close. At that point, I was ready to kill him, I think. I went to a movie. In just my negligee and fur coat, I watched *Suddenly Last Summer* from beginning to end, sitting alone in a deserted theater on Christmas Eve.

In an effort to get Herb to pick up his career, I tried booking engagements with us on the same bill, but it didn't work out. We always wound up arguing about top billing and the details of the show. None of this mattered that much to me. I just wanted us to be happy and for both of us to attend to our professions. But Herb was jealous of everything and anyone.

One escapade in particular made me worry about Herb's jealous fits. I was appearing in Boston when a rich Englishman decided he wanted to have dinner with me. I told him, "I'm married, and I don't go out on my husband. He'd kill us both."

But this gentleman, who drove a Rolls Royce and spent money like it was water, wasn't going to be easily put off. He begged me to have dinner with him, promising that nothing would ever be said about it. "Just this once," he begged.

I gave him my flattest "No!"

When I returned to my hotel suite, the rooms were literally overflowing with flowers. An hour later, someone knocked on the door of my suite. It was a delivery boy with a dozen beautiful roses, and I immediately began to wonder where on earth I would put them. The card asked me one more time to meet him in the restaurant of the Sommerset Hotel. I admired the roses and ignored the message.

An hour later, another knock. This time, it was a dozen carnations. Beautiful. The card said my admirer was still waiting in the restaurant. I put the flowers on the opposite end of the dresser from the roses, tore up the card and dropped it in the waste basket with the other one.

The persistent Englishman began to call my room, reiterating his invitation and embellishing his plea. I told him as firmly as I could that my answer was final and that he must stop sending the flowers immediately. I was expecting Herb that night or early the next morning, and I could imagine his reaction to a suite covered with floral tributes.

Another hour passed and another bouquet of flowers arrived. I didn't bother reading the card. I decided the only thing for me to do was to get out of the hotel room for a while. So I went to a movie. While I was out, I dined in an elegant little café on a side street. Four hours later, I returned to find ten more bouquets of flowers in my room.

It was entirely possible that Herb was already in town. I frantically called the maid. "Is there any way you can get these flowers out of my room?" I asked her. "Please, can you help me?"

As she was carrying them to the hallway and placing them on a cart, still another box of flowers arrived. "Listen, my dear," I said. "All of these flowers are yours. Just make sure no more flowers are delivered here. Can you take care of that?"

She smiled and pushed the cart down the hallway. I have no idea how many bouquets were sent to Tempest Storm that day. I never asked the maid. And, thankfully, I never saw the persistent suitor again . . . although I remain fascinated by the lengths to which he was willing to go to get my attention.

In fact, my fascination led me down to the bar, partly because I thought it would be nice to have a quiet glass of wine and relax a little, congratulate myself on averting potential disaster. To my surprise, there was Herb. He has already checked in. He said he wanted to surprise me, but I knew that he also had not let me know he was there because of his suspicions. He thought he might catch me doing something, anything, that would justify his obsessions.

I thanked my guardian angels that I had come to the bar alone, and then I remembered all the torn and discarded notes from the flowers. They were in the trashcan in the suite. I removed them and threw them out the window just minutes before Herb got his luggage out of storage and came up. Knowing my jealous husband, he would have searched the waste basket, pieced the cards together, and accused me of everything under the sun.

Herb's jealousy once drove me to share my troubles with a priest in Colorado. The priest suggested that I give up my burlesque career for a year or two to see if that would save my marriage. I had to tell him we would starve to death in less than a year if I quit performing. Besides, I knew by then that I'd become a victim of my own success. I had established a lifestyle of minks, diamonds, cruises, and first-class living. I wasn't willing to give that lifestyle up, and the only way I could maintain it was to keep working.

I am convinced that jealousy can destroy a relationship, not matter how much the people involved care for each other. There is too much constant tension, too little trust and support. In 1962, I filed for divorce, but before my petition came up in court—in fact, before the newspaper clipping was pasted down flat—Herb and I had reconciled. Frequently reporters, business associates, and acquaintances asked if we were still married.

About two months after the reconciliation, I was appearing in Philadelphia and staying at the Warwick Hotel where Nat King Cole and I used to rendezvous. While in this place of many fond memories, I became very ill. I thought I had the flu. I flew back to Los Angeles and went to the doctor. After the examination, he sat down next to me and said, "My dear, you are pregnant!"

I couldn't believe it. I screamed at him, "You've got to be kidding!" But he assured me that it was no joke.

"It can't be. I've been told by half a dozen doctors that I can never have children," I said.

"Well, those half a dozen doctors are wrong, and this doctor is right," he said. "I've told women that they would probably never have children and they did. But I've never been wrong about this. When I say a woman is pregnant, she's pregnant!"

As I left his office, I was in turmoil. Because I had spent years believing I'd never be a mother, I had no emotional preparation for this announcement. I had shut off what instincts in that direction I might have had over the years so that I wouldn't feel disappointment and loss over something it was impossible for me to have. In addition to having this news come as an emotional shock, I was immediately concerned about the effect of a pregnancy on my career. I just knew that my figure would be ruined forever and that I would never perform again. But I didn't consider abortion for even one moment. All I had to do was recall my last abortion and how I nearly died. I would have borne a dozen children before I would have had another abortion.

Herb and I shared some of our happiest times during the months before our daughter's birth. We lived for part of that time in Hawaii at the estate of Henry J. Kaiser, the steel magnate. It was a beautiful, romantic setting, and our time there filled me with hope for our future. My last engagement before the baby came was in Hawaii while I was four months pregnant. After that, I showed too much to continue performing.

The pregnancy cost me what could have been the most financially rewarding and productive six months of my life. I'd landed a four-month contract to appear at the Mikado Club in Tokyo for $6,000 a week. The Honolulu press did some arithmetic and told their readers how much this baby was going to cost Tempest Storm. But I'd already figured that out. I called her my $100,000 baby.

My Japanese friend Kaku had been working on the contract for about a year, and he and the club were just about ready to start the publicity rolling when I called him and told him I was pregnant. At first there was dead silence on the phone. He finally asked, almost tearfully, "How can you do this to me?"

I had no answer for him because I, too, was wondering how Lady Luck could do this.

One of my biggest fears about the pregnancy was my fear that I would wind up with scars that would prevent my ever returning to the stage as a performer. My body was the instrument of the art, and I could not imagine what would happen if that instrument were irreparably damaged. Fortunately, I found good doctors, the best doctors, and they understood my concerns and assured me that such a thing wouldn't happen.

During the time I was carrying the baby, I made it a point to be the best-dressed pregnant lady anyone had ever seen. I knew how important image was to my career, and even though I couldn't perform, I was determined to be the woman my fans expected to see when I was out in public, pregnant or not. Toward the end of my term, in the eighth month, I went to see Herb sing one night, and some friends at the club complimented me on how great I looked and inquired about where I would be appearing next. I laughed and told them my next engagement was at the hospital, that I was having a baby in four weeks. Their surprised expressions let me know that I had remained the woman others had been accustomed to seeing. That encounter was a terrific ego boost for those last few hard weeks of pregnancy.

When the nurses first brought my baby to me, I didn't know what to do with her. I had hardly touched a baby in twenty years. I was afraid to hold her, afraid I might break her. She was so tiny and beautiful, so fragile. I didn't know whether to give her a bottle or not. Then the nurse came in and jammed the bottle in her mouth. That helped. I suddenly realized that tenderness and concern can do a lot to make up for insecurities. I could do a better job than the brusk nurse had done. Gradually, I became more confident.

I named her Patricia Ann, and as I held her, I grew prouder and prouder to be her mother. Tempest Storm was becoming more domesticated than she had ever thought she would be. Just as I was settling into being a parent and enjoying it, when Patty was two months old, Herb said one of the most hurtful things anyone had ever said to me. He was sitting in bed one morning with his arms folded across his chest. He asked me when we'd gotten back together. I told him. Then he said, "When was Patty born?" The insinuating way he asked the question and the expression on his face said the baby wasn't his.

At that moment I saw no way to go on. If we couldn't be happy and share the joy of having this precious child together, if his jealousy had to taint even this experience, how could we live together? What kind of life would Patty have in that atmosphere of distrust and insecurity?

I went back to work almost exactly two months after Patty was born. My first engagement was at the Tropics nightclub in Denver. The papers had announced Patty's birth, but no one believed I had had a baby. When I opened, I was back at my regular weight—116 pounds—and even in my revealing profession, I didn't show any signs of having delivered a baby. The doctors had come through on their promises. Even though Patty's was a Caesarean birth, plastic surgery removed all traces of scarring.

"You didn't really have that baby, did you?" one woman asked. "You went out and adopted her."

I took that as a compliment.

Somewhat to my surprise, I loved being a mother. I got so involved with Patty and with wanting the absolute best of everything for her that I wound up dissatisfied with all the nannies and other helpers I had. I worked it out so that my dressing rooms would be equipped with whatever I needed to care for Patty, and she traveled with me. I was so proud of her, and everyone who visited the dressing room exclaimed over how beautiful and smart and well-behaved she was.

Today, the press is full of stories about the conflicts and difficulties of women who want to have it all—marriage, career, parenthood. But I was trying to have it all back before anybody realized that doing so was possible, much less before anybody considered the toll that effort took on everyone involved. Many times I would be racing for a plane in the high heels and long furs people would expect Tempest Storm to be wearing. But I would also have a diaper bag hanging off one shoulder and Patty on the opposite hip, her arms tight around my neck. Those additional features may not have been associated with my image, but for six years that was the way I lived.

And I loved it. Patty seemed to thrive, too. Once, when she was no more than two or three, I was onstage and doing well, but there was nothing at this particular place in my act that would draw the spontaneous and deafening applause that erupted. At least other audiences hadn't gone wild at this spot. Then, as I was turning, I saw my tiny daughter. She had wandered onto the stage, and the audience was going wild over her, not her mother. It's a wonder she wasn't bitten by the show business bug right then. Few performers have ever had a warmer reception to their first stage appearance.

Patty stayed with me through her pre-school years. We truly shared our lives, and even though it was not easy flying a child around the country and caring for her in hotel rooms, we had many good times. She loved going to my dressing room, playing with the makeup and charming everyone backstage. She was an incredibly beautiful child who never met a stranger. Because of that, there never was a shortage of volunteers to look after her while I was onstage.

Sometimes, Herb traveled with us, too, and he was a big help in looking after Patty. Herb and I even shared many beautiful romantic times together, and I felt that we had a chance to be a real family, even if we were an unconventional one. But then Herb would manage to undercut the good times by being completely oblivious to my feelings. How many wives come against that old cliché that their husbands just don't understand them? I know that I did.

During one of our trips in 1964 Herb walked into my dressing room one evening in Philadelphia and said without the slightest display of compassion, "I guess you heard the news about your old boyfriend?"

"Which old boyfriend?"

"Nat King Cole."

"No." My heart skipped a beat. "I haven't heard anything. What about him?"

"He died today. I just heard it on the radio."

Herb turned and closed the door without a single word of comfort, leaving me alone with my thoughts. I suppose he figured this was one less rival to concern himself with. But I didn't take much time thinking about his thoughts. It was only later that I realized how cruel his announcement had been. At the time, I could only cry, mourning the loss of one of the greatest loves of my life.

I was probably crying for the loss of two great loves, for slowly and reluctantly I was concluding that my marriage would not work.

Herb and I divorced in 1969 after our third separation in ten years of marriage. Patty turned six that year, and I could feel my life with her growing more complicated. Two things worried me. First, she would soon have to enter school, and she could hardly do that and keep traveling with me. I thought about hiring a tutor, but a traveling tutor meant she wouldn't have playmates or enjoy the simple pleasures of going to a regular school. Second, she was getting old enough to begin understanding that her mother's profession was not one she could brag about to her friends. A playmate once said, "Patty, your mother is a stripper." Patty responded by contradicting her friend and saying, "No, my mother is a beautiful exotic dancer."

But the stripper's stigma had struck again, tearing the heart out of me and making me feel empty and lost. There would come a time when she wouldn't want or be able to deny that statement. This time, there was no way for me to strike back. I knew I had to let her go.

Early in the summer of 1970, Patty went to visit her father in Los Angeles while I performed at the Aladdin Hotel in Las Vegas. I anguished over the decision I would soon have to make, and there were nights I didn't sleep as my mind searched for an answer. Patty solved the problem for me.

She idolized Herb, and despite his shortcomings as a provider, he certainly was a wonderful father. On the phone, she told me that she had a yard to play in (something that even the fanciest hotels don't offer), plenty of dolls and toys (with me, she could carry very little), young friends with whom to play (another shortcoming at the posh hotels), and a school right down the street. She said she wanted to stay with her father. Under the circumstances, I conceded that, even though I had custody of her, she was better off with her father.

After I agreed to the arrangements and Herb and I had talked at length, I hung up the phone. I sat there a long time, staring at the wall. What could I do? I could leave burlesque. As far I could see that was the only way I could keep Patty with me. But, if that was my decision, how would I earn a living, how would I pay the bills, buy the dolls and the nice clothes and all the other things I wanted my daughter to have? I had considered leaving my profession before, but my own needs and desires held me back. I wanted to live in the manner to which I had become accustomed. Now, my needs were secondary, but for my daughter to have all that I wanted her to have, all that she deserved, I had to keep performing. I was trapped away from her, with no other way to make a comfortable living.

I cried myself to sleep thinking about Patty and praying that my decision was the right one.

I visited Patty at every opportunity. I took her shopping for all of the things little girls want, and we enjoyed each other's company. She still loved me, had always loved me, and I knew that. But she had her new friends and school and all sorts of things to occupy her time. She seemed happy and well-adjusted, but like all young women she began to grow away from her mother and become more involved in her own life. She never asked questions about my work. I suppose Herb provided the answers to any questions that came up in my absence.

The connection between Herb and Patty was strong and important, and it served to keep me connected to him, too. I thought he was doing a beautiful job with our daughter, and on several occasions we tried to get back together so that we could be a family once again. Regardless of whatever problems we had had, I felt lost without Herb and Patty. She loved both of her parents very much, so why should she have to live without either of them? We tried to make a go of our relationship for the sake of our daughter.

We had a chance to work in Europe, where the atmosphere would have been ideal for our family. There, we wouldn't have had to struggle with the issue of whether ours was a mixed marriage. We and our child would have been accepted for who we were, without questions or whispered rumors, which remained a problem for us in the United States. But we considered Patty's future. We wanted the best education for her, the best of everything, and there was no doubt that, economically, we'd be better off in this country. So we passed up that chance. Had we made the move, we might still be together, and much of the subsequent pain we all went through might have be avoided.

We did move to Hawaii for a while, and we were happy. Some of the peace and beauty of that time when we lived there awaiting Patty's birth returned, and I knew a joy I had thought was gone forever from my life. We made a romantic return to the scenes of our honeymoon in Paris. We did all sorts of things in an effort to get it right. But, still, I was in conflict, turmoil, inside myself. I grew restless and felt torn between the need for stability and security and the old longing for adventure and new challenges.

I accepted an engagement in Orlando, Florida, and while I was there that restlessness led me to forget what we had been trying to do, be a family. I truly believe that, if everything had been fine in the marriage, I wouldn't have had such feelings. But I'm equally sure that I wouldn't have begun to have serious health problems, both physical and emotional, if I had felt completely secure in being away from my family.

As my nerves and my health got worse and worse, the doctors I saw kept prescribing medication, which I, of course, took faithfully according to their instructions. But I didn't feel better. I felt worse. I decided that I needed my family, my daughter and my husband. I still thought of Herb that way, even though we had never remarried. Yet I was terrified that they wouldn't accept me, that Herb would refuse to let me return to them.

I found myself alone in New York, terribly unhappy, and dependent upon these pills the doctors kept prescribing to keep myself going. As afraid as I was of Herb's rejection, I was more afraid of being away from them, of sinking deeper into the depression and illness that had taken hold of me. So I called them. I called my family.

I am convinced that Herb's understanding at this moment saved my life. He didn't reject me. He said of course I should come home to them if that is what I wanted, what I needed. They were there for me. No words have ever been more joyfully or gratefully received. I immediately made reservations to fly from New York to Hawaii.

I have become convinced that the pills I was taking were hurting rather than helping me, so before I left, I destroyed what were left and packed for the flight, determined to start this reunion with a clean slate. I didn't want Patty to see me as a sick person, having to take medicine every day.

This all took place before the dangers of prescription drugs became common knowledge. I had followed my doctor's instructions, but he hadn't told me anything about the possible consequences of my discontinuing the medication entirely. I boarded the plane for the ten-hour flight full of longing for my family. All I wanted was to land safely and hold them in my arms. I wanted to touch Patty, to know that she was all right, that she was real, and that she loved me. I wanted to know that Herb was being truthful when he said that they were there for me. If I could just get through this flight, I thought, it will all be fine.

Shortly after take-off, I began to feel violently ill. The flight attendant noticed that my color had faded and became concerned. She offered what assistance and comfort she could, but I was so sick that I was sure I would die before the plane landed. My daughter would be there expecting to see her mother, and I would be dead. I would let her down again. They would do an autopsy, and someone would tell Herb that I was dependent on drugs, that I had died in withdrawal, and I would be dead and couldn't explain that it was all because I missed them so much and had been doing what the doctors said would make me better when all I needed was them. What a cruel irony, I thought, to die this way. It was the most horrible flight I've ever made.

But I didn't die. I landed, and my family was there, just as they promised they would be. I had what I wanted and needed, and I will never understand how the pain and the horror of that flight and the weeks and months that led up to it didn't keep me with them forever. I will never understand why my happiness and satisfaction wore away so quickly, why I went away again. It was a terrible, terrible mistake.

I left my family again on March 3, 1975, headed for Miami Beach. I will regret that departure for the rest of my life. I will spend the rest of my days seeing my daughter's face full of uncertainty and fear and hearing her say, "Mommy, are you coming back this time?" I will always wish she had been spared that pain. I can only pray that she has forgiven me.

# Nine

During the time just after my divorce from Herb and my separation from Patty, I dated several men. I was feeling down, and the trauma of a failed marriage, bad enough on its own, was compounded by the terrible anxiety I felt about not being with my daughter. One of the first men I went out with was Trini Lopez, a good-time Charlie who helped me to have some fun again and eased the pain of what I'd been through.

Trini was appearing at the Landmark Hotel in Las Vegas at the same time I was performing at the Aladdin. He invited me to see his show, and I accepted. We met him afterwards and spent some time with mutual acquaintances. My marriage to Herb had just ended, and Trini felt like the cure I needed. He liked to stay out all night, partying wherever there was a party, making one if there wasn't one. We laughed a lot, and considering my state of mind, that helped.

Trini was always exciting. We often went dancing at the club on top of the Desert Inn. He was fun to be with, and

215

without a doubt, he knew how to make lovemaking fun and adventurous, which was a pleasant change from all the feelings of responsibility and obligation that come with any marriage and take their toll on romance and pleasure.

For instance, he wanted me to dress in black stockings, black garter belt, and black high heels while we made love in his mirrored suite. If his penchant for experimentation went beyond that, I never found out. But these elements of fancy and invention made him an exciting partner and helped boost my spirits during this rough time. I learned to remember that sex could be fun. Once, in our passion, my high heels destroyed some really beautiful satin bedsheets, and they also left their mark on Trini's bare skin at times.

Perhaps our most domesticated evening came in December of 1969 when he helped me decorate a Christmas tree in my suite. I was getting ready for Patty's arrival for the holidays, and Trini was helping me make sure everything was ready before I flew to L.A. to pick her up. While Patty was visiting, she and I watched Trini perform on television, and he and I continued to be good friends. But my romantic interest in him ended not long after that holiday season, and soon afterward I met Engelbert Humperdinck.

Engelbert, an unusual name that stirs fond memories. Most women will meet a man somewhere along the way that they absolutely can't resist. You may be thinking, "What's with Tempest Storm? Can't she resist anybody?"

I have found that there are many different temptations to resist:

attractions that melt the heart—like the one I had for Nat King Cole;

intense physical attractions—like those I felt for Elvis Presley and Jack Kennedy;

comfortable relationships that come right after a divorce or other personal trauma—like those I shared with Hugh O'Brien and Trini Lopez;

genuine friendships that wind up in the bedroom—like my early relationship with Sammy Davis, Jr.

But Engelbert was different from any of the others. He was neither as gentle nor as thoughtful as Nat King Cole, nor was he as physically demanding as Jack Kennedy. Our relationship was, I suppose, based on some of the best of all the others but an exact copy of none of them.

We met in 1970. I had just finished an engagement as the headliner in Minsky's Revue at the Aladdin Hotel in Las Vegas and was taking a few weeks off before going to San Francisco. Engelbert was appearing at the Riviera. I went to dinner with a friend that evening, and afterwards we decided to take in a show. We went to see Engelbert.

He was a beautiful sight up there on the stage. He looked strong and sexy, and his voice came across the same way. Closing my eyes as I listened to his medley of songs, I knew emotions ran deep in this man.

At that moment, mine did, too.

I didn't wonder about his marital status or whether he might reject me. After the show, I simply excused myself and went looking for a house phone. It never occurred to me that he might not answer. A man answered my call.

"Hello? Engelbert?"

"No, this isn't Engelbert. May I tell him who's calling?"

"Yes, this is Tempest Storm."

In a moment, I heard his unmistakeable voice. "Yes, dahling."

"This is Tempest Storm."

"Yes, I know. My manager told me. It's so nice of you to call."

"Well, thank you, dahling, and you were great," I said, mimicking his heavy English accent.

"Where are you?"

"In the casino."

"Please come backstage for a visit."

Then I said, "I'm with someone right at this moment, but won't you call me later?"

We chatted a few more minutes, then I returned to my friends. I felt sure he would call.

He did, the next day, and we set a date for dinner that evening. I still didn't ask about his marital status, and he didn't mention it, either. In the next few days, we attended a couple of parties together. In the meantime, I picked up on the fact that he was married but unhappy. In fact, Buddy Greco, one of Engelbert's closest friends, said Engelbert and his wife were close to a divorce and that Engelbert might be a good catch for me. I didn't bother to tell him that I wasn't interested in a lasting relationship at the time.

Engelbert was one of the most flattering people I ever knew. When two stars are together, one often gets more attention than the other, and such a situation can sometimes turn bitter. But Engelbert is one of those rare people who obviously enjoys putting others in the spotlight. A dozen big stars showed up at one of the parties we attended together. I was dressed in a white-and-gray slinky evening gown cut down to my navel and glued to my body. I could feel eyes fixed on me every time I moved. Then Engelbert asked me to fix him a drink. He always asked me to mix his drinks. He said they tasted better if I mixed them.

Engelbert also liked to watch me walk. As I walked to a bar at the far side of the room, he said, "Look at her. Nobody has a walk like hers. My God, she doesn't walk; she just glides. Now that is the mark of a great dancer!" Flattery at a time and place like that does great things for a woman's ego, and Engelbert's admiration came at a time when my ego was ready for a boost. Our becoming lovers was another step in the healing process I was working through.

It turned out that Engelbert had his own insecurities as well. He doubted his prowess as a lover. Once, in a joking way, he asked if I thought he needed a transplant. I'd never heard a more ridiculous question, and I decided to keep the

tone light and playful. I told him that his idea was absurd—
he had all the right equipment; it was just a matter of learning to use it.

Some men might not have understood this kind of romantic play, but Engelbert did. We both found the lighthearted
fun stimulating, and our romance sizzled for about six
months—whenever and wherever we could get together.
When both of us were playing the same city, the romance
and the lovemaking were so exciting, so refreshing, that
we'd find ways to be in the same place even when we
weren't supposed to. We juggled schedules and rearranged
commitments with that breathtaking energy that comes with
real passion.

I was performing in San Francisco and he was singing in
Las Vegas when he called and suggested that I fly to meet
him. Every such reunion was well worth the effort we both
made, and those suggestions from him made me feel special
and desired in just the way I loved.

"Dahling, it has been such a long time."

"I know. But we can make up for lost time, can't we?"

He was sitting up in bed the next morning, ignoring his
breakfast tray as I dressed for the flight back to San Francisco.

"Wait, dahling," he said. "Let me look at you just a
moment."

I stood motionless. Finally, he said, "What a body, dahling. I just wanted that picture in my mind."

I kept his picture in my mind for many years, too, and
even though we didn't get together for eight years after my
return to San Francisco, my desire for him was as intense as
ever.

In 1978, I opened at the Twentieth Century Hotel. One
night after the show, the hotel owner asked if I'd like to go to
the MGM and see Engelbert. The first thing I noticed was
that both of us had changed hair color since our first meeting. I'd been a brunette when we first met, but I had gone

back to my red hair. Engelbert, on the other hand, had lightened his hair from a very dark color to blond.

After watching the show, my date and I went backstage, and Engelbert grabbed me and hugged me like there had never been an end to our relationship.

"So, you've come back into my life after eight years?" he asked. "I can't believe it!" and he hugged and kissed me right there as if he'd never received a nicer gift than my return.

After that greeting, half a dozen of us—the hotel owner, several of Engelbert's friends, including his karate instructor, and me—sat around his dressing room with him and talked. Suddenly he said, "Dahling, fix me a drink. I want to see if you still glide the way you used to."

As I mixed the drink, I said, "You've changed the color of your hair."

He said, "So have you, dahling."

"And you've lost weight."

"Yes, dahling, but not down there." His eyes twinkled mischievously at our private joke.

"That's wonderful," I said, "but have you learned how to use it?" I hoped that our old playful romantic style would still work and that he would understand my tone.

"You'll never let me live that down, will you?"

"Of course not, dahling. But you really did use it right."

Engelbert and I had one more reunion a year later. I had broken up with my boyfriend, Marty Caplan, and I went to Lake Tahoe to spend a couple of weeks with Engelbert and get some rest, I hoped. But there was little rest to be had.

When he came off the stage that first night, he said, "Come to my dressing room."

"Are you crazy?" I asked.

"But, dahling, it's been a whole year."

"I know, but this is not the time or place."

His dressing room was gorgeously appointed—two rooms, a bar, and a bath, all tastefully furnished and quite beautiful.

The suite was filled with friends and well-wishers, and as much as I was intrigued by his suggestion and complimented by his urgency, I knew that his idea was crazy. Suddenly, he said, "Come here!" and pulled me into a room alone. "I've always wanted to make love to you right after a performance."

"Hey, lover, there are a lot of people out there."

He looked at me in a black jersey gown with a low-cut neckline and reached to lock the door. "You look like a million dollars, so what do they matter? I have to have you."

"Dahling," I said, using his favorite term of endearment and imitating him in hopes of turning the moment to joking, a lighter mood, "you have lost your mind if you're thinking what I think you're thinking."

"I haven't lost my mind, just my heart," he said. "I've just got to make love to you right now."

"Yes, you have lost your mind," I said. "A dozen people are sitting out there. And you're going to make love to me? Here?"

"Yes, dahling. Here. Now!"

"Engelbert, for God's sake . . ."

But the man's appetite for sex knew no bounds, and my reasonable arguments had absolutely no effect on him. I was trying to be a lady, to be a mature, responsible person, but Engelbert was having no part of such sensible behavior. His passion was running too high. I have yet to decide which shook me up the most—the possibility of someone's knocking on the door or his penchant for raw passion on a dressing room table. It was a wild night, and I did find it romantic in an oddly disconcerting way. But at the same time I was embarrassed at what the others who'd been in the suite must think. Engelbert kept saying he could think of nothing but me.

Finally, at my insistence, he went out one door, and I waited a few minutes, then left by the other. It was all I could think of to save appearances at that late point in the evening.

Once we were both back in the main room, we sat around and talked as if nothing had happened. That part of the evening was good training for any acting I might ever do. I'm still not sure that I wasn't blushing furiously.

I shall never forget this sexy Englishman—not just for his wonderful lovemaking or even his classic singing style, but also for his personal warmth and the way he treated me. No man has ever made me feel more desirable. Along with all his other traits, Engelbert is blessed with a magnificent body. Clothed or unclothed, he has a grace and a way of carrying himself that I can't help but admire. The truly special thing about him, though, is that the inner man, the person I knew, is every bit as breathtaking as his body. The contents are as lovely as their package.

The early 1970s marked some important milestones in my career as well as in my personal life.

I had never given up on my quest to battle the stigma of the stripper until I changed the way the public looked at those of us who performed as dancers in the classic burlesque tradition. I had no interest in battling for the porn theaters and clubs that had sprung up. What I was concerned with was correcting the misperceptions about the art that I practiced with taste and class, I believed. Many critics and fans agreed with me, and I remained tired of being misunderstood and unfairly labeled. In 1971, topless dancing was forbidden in Orlando, Florida, where I was appearing at the Luv Theater.

Usually, if exotic dancers wore a flesh-colored net bra—even if was a transparent garment—the authorities wouldn't interfere. But I wanted to dance without a bra, to illustrate the hypocrisy of the current practice. It was a matter of principle to me. I had my attorney to check out the local law ahead of time so that we were sure of what it actually said, and he concluded that pasties would suffice to satisfy the local statutes. Apparently, the police didn't interpret the law in the same way because I was detained on misdemeanor charges and held, but not incarcerated, until my lawyer posted bond. The charges of indecent exposure caught my attorney by surprise, and I spent a couple of hours at the precinct before he could make the necessary arrangements. The police officers there treated me very well, and I was convinced that my challenge of the archaic laws was an important thing to do. Still, it was intimidating to be in police custody, no matter how kind the officers were or how firmly convinced I was that I was really in the right.

When I was released, the attorney and I went over the law again, and we still felt that his interpretation was accurate. So I danced again the following night with my flesh-colored pasties in place.

Again the cops hauled me away. But this time my lawyer was better prepared, and I was released much quicker. He maintained that I was within the law, so I tried it again the next night. Same result. I finally cried "Uncle!" and danced in the net bra while waiting for the date of my court appearance. I felt sure that the judge would agree with our interpretation, and I had been detained enough times to establish the point in the minds of the public.

I was right. Two weeks later, I appeared in court, and the judge dismissed all charges. I had achieved a small but a significant victory. An archaic law was taken off the books, and, because of my efforts, topless dancers were at last acceptable in Orlando. I danced that night without police interference—or pasties—and my act made the society page of the Orlando newspapers.

The other milestone—one that I'll always cherish—came in 1973.

Mike Belkin, a promoter who worked out of Cleveland, Ohio, put together a college tour for my act and a rock band called the James Gang. I still don't know whether Mike did a great selling job with a little deception or some college officials just weren't paying attention. One administrator said he thought I was a singer, but the minute I hit the stage he found out otherwise.

We had been booked into some of the most noted colleges in the country, including Seton Hall, William and Mary, Purdue, and Hofstra, but as word about my act spread, at least one college— Valparaiso in Indiana—banned me from performing. It brought back memories of my earlier experience with the students at the University of Colorado. A disc jockey called and questioned me about the cancellation on the air and let me know that the students were really upset about the situation. Officials at most schools just closed their eyes and hoped for my early exit.

But the college kids were great. I was used to playing nightclubs filled with cigarette smoke, but I did notice that the marijuana smoke that sometimes filled the halls where I performed on the campuses was stronger stuff. You could get a contact high in those places.

After the shows, I often fielded questions for an hour or more for a crowd of college girls who wanted to know everything from where I got my negligees to what kind of cosmetics I used. Some of the guys would say, "My father saw you dance." But one starry-eyed boy about nineteen years old left me speechless when he looked at me with big, admiring eyes and said, "Gee, I wish I had a mother like you."

For six or seven weeks, we performed one-nighters at colleges and civic arenas in such places as Toledo and Dayton, Ohio, Providence, Rhode Island, and Massey Hall in Toronto, Canada. Finally, on March 23, 1973, I became the first—and I am still the only—stripper ever to perform in Carnegie Hall in New York City.

It turned out to be the most prestigious performance in my career, but it's a miracle that there was a performance at all. Just before I arrived in town, the executives at Carnegie learned that I was a stripper, not a singer. They wanted to cancel my appearance. Again, the stigma raised its ugly head, and again I was determined not to surrender. Not performing on a college campus was one thing, but I felt quite strongly about being the first exotic dancer to perform at this prestigious landmark of American culture. I wanted the recognition, the acknowledgment that mine was a class act, and where better to get such recognition than Carnegie Hall?

We finally compromised: I could perform if I did not give any pre-performance interviews to the press. At first, I told Mike Belkin that I just wanted to forget it. Who did they think they were? Strippers couldn't practice free speech if they wanted to perform on the great Carnegie stage? It was all turning into too much hassle.

But Mike said, "No, we're not going to forget it. You're going to perform. You're going to be the first exotic dancer to dance on that stage. I want it, and you should want it too. You'll always be able to say you performed here."

Far from it. A notice slipped by the executives who negotiated the compromise and appeared in the Carnegie Hall magazine, and even many of the stuffed shirts in New York knew Tempest Storm was not a singer. We played before a sold-out house.

The applause in Carnegie Hall sounded different from anywhere else I've ever performed. Maybe it was just knowing where I was that made the difference, but I soaked up the thunder as it rolled toward me. I loved it, and it turned out that Mike was right. It's something to remember and hold on to and be proud of. It's another blow to the seemingly invincible stigma.

I also felt that the audience here, accustomed as they were to seeing great artists perform — ballet dancers, musicians, singers, truly appreciated the art of my performance. They knew enough about traditional dance to recognize that my work was made up of the same elements, that what I did required the same meticulous choreography and rehearsal. When they applauded me, they were applauding my talent.

They were acknowledging the class of my act, and I reveled in their appreciation.

After the show that night, the Carnegie Hall executives who had opposed my appearance sent an usher backstage to ask me for autographed pictures. I was stunned because their interest meant that my performance had changed their attitude. They did actually see me differently than they had when they knew nothing about me except that, in their eyes, I was a stripper. If I could earn their respect with my work, then maybe it was possible that I could make a significant contribution to lessening the stigma's power over women who wanted to continue in the great burlesque tradition.

I politely refused to give the messenger the pictures that he was requesting, although I made sure he didn't take the refusal personally. To me, it was a matter of principle, and I was feeling invincible right then. My principles had been confirmed in one of the world's greatest centers of art. People understood that I was an artist. That was more important than handing out publicity photos to those I was having to pull out of their ignorance and misinformation.

That performance at Carnegie Hall merited notice in *Time* magazine. Who would have thought that agreeing to do a college tour would have resulted in such triumph?

After that tour, everywhere I went, people mentioned my verbal battles with the prudes who'd banned me from performing and those who'd tried to block my performance at Carnegie Hall. The tour had raised the issue, and people were talking about it. Their consciousness had been raised.

But despite the attention and the success at something very important to me, things didn't feel right inside myself. I longed for the respectability that had eluded me as a stripper. I wanted more time to spend with my family in our beautiful home and wanted to be free to take pleasure in the comforts of everyday life. My crusading had been successful, but it had taken its toll on me. Having won a battle, I knew that the war was still ahead, but I just didn't know if it was worth the cost to my family.

All the hard work it took to become a star, to have gotten to this place in my career, led only to harder work to stay on top. After dancing at Carnegie Hall and after changing some important minds about my profession, I felt enormous pressure for my work to get better and better. The more successful I was, the larger the demand for my appearances and the higher the expectations of my audiences.

I became increasingly unhappy with life on the road. I was longing for extended time with my family. I was longing for what I didn't have, ordinary life.

Yes, I was earning up to $4,500 a week. I had lived the good life. I remember once winning $20,000 on one roll of the dice for a Saudi Arabian prince. I'd owned as many as seven fur coats at one time and joked about having one for each day of the week and the jewels to go with them. I had to work harder and harder to maintain what I had come to accept as the norm. Forecasters in the entertainment world had predicted that the explosion of porno movies, bars with totally nude go-go girls, and live sex shows would deal a death blow to my profession. Even though my performance at Carnegie did much to make me personally exempt from that trend, it still meant fewer places to perform and more travel, more being away from home and Herb and Patty.

On several occasions, I looked at the possibility of getting into movies or TV. Acting was still my first love, if I could have chosen my profession instead of having my profession choose me. I thought that perhaps I might land a part in a soap opera. I'm sure I could be every bit as good as most actresses on many of the TV soaps.

Then I fell in love with Marty Caplan, and my plans were drastically changed.

# *Ten*

Marty Caplan's name first came to my attention in 1964 while I was appearing at the Paris Theater in Miami Beach, Florida. Herb and I were house guests of Leroy Griffith, a theater owner. Leroy's wife, Joy, asked me if I knew Marty Caplan. I hadn't heard of him. She told me that he owned several burlesque and porno theaters that reached from Los Angeles to Pittsburgh to Miami. She seemed to be quite taken with him.

Her praise stirred my curiosity, but I was mainly interested in our differences. From what Joy said, Marty Caplan had made his money by capitalizing on the trend to move away from burlesque and into porno theaters. That was the trend that my career was in opposition to; my performances were one of the things keeping burlesque alive. In that sense, this man she was telling me about was the enemy. For a number of years, Marty Caplan was nothing more to me than a name in the business. Yet, for some reason, it was a name that stuck in my mind.

229

In 1971, I was experiencing the difficulties that led to the breakdown of my reconciliation with Herb. The pressures of the road, the feeling of emptiness that I could neither explain nor shake off, all the headaches of being in the profession— these forces led me into a relationship that eventually led me to Marty. I was appearing at the Luv Theater in Orlando, Florida. During my engagement there, I became intimately involved with Richard Rodan, who became my manager. Before the Orlando contract expired, he started putting together a new show and suggested we go to Miami Beach to talk in person with Marty Caplan about booking it into his theater in Pittsburgh.

At his office on 41st Street in Miami Beach, I first met Marty face to face. He was a stocky man with salt-and-pepper hair, certainly attractive, but he was too heavy for me. I liked my men lean . . . and rich, of course. I thought that if he were thinner, he would be a knockout. From what I'd heard, he was worth a fortune. I was in a dangerous state of mind, and no possibility seemed too farfetched to consider.

Richard booked me into Marty Caplan's new Casino Theater in Pittsburgh, and Marty and I didn't meet again until 1975. I talked to him on the telephone in 1972 on behalf of Richard, who had run into legal problems as a result of shady deals and bad checks. After making that phone call, I washed my hands of Rodan and chalked up the lessons I'd learned to experience, bad experience, both personally and professionally. While we were talking, Marty said he owned a home in California, and he suggested that perhaps we could have dinner the next time he traveled to the West Coast.

I told him that was impossible because I was flying to Hawaii to spend some time with Herb and Patty. Although I didn't go into detail with him—he was, after all, a relative stranger—I had hopes that the visit would bring us back together as a family. My prayers were answered. Herb and I got back together, and everything was fine between me and the two people who meant the most to me. Having dinner with Marty Caplan was certainly not very high on my list of priorities.

Herb was booked into Harold's Club in Reno, a career opportunity that made me very happy for him. The three of us moved to Reno and lived there until the contract expired. After that we moved to Coronado Cay, California, and purchased a beautiful home. This was a happy, peaceful period in our lives, and I loved every minute of that time. The house was a dream come true for us, Patty was wonderful, and Herb and I got along well.

In March of 1975, I returned to Miami Beach for an engagement at the Gayety Theater. I had left California reluctantly because we were so happy, but I did have to consider my career. That pressure never left me. One night, the theater manager said Marty Caplan had been looking for me while I was out having dinner. I wondered why this man's name kept cropping up in my life. I told the manager to tell him if he called back that I'd see him as soon as the eight P.M. show was over. After that show, Marty came to pick me up, but I didn't recognize him. Two other people were in the car—his sister, Louise, and a nephew, Larry Carr.

"Where's Marty?" I said.

"I'm Marty," said a slender guy in the back seat. I was surprised because he wasn't the heavyset man I'd met four years previously. Although I knew how excess weight can change a person's appearance, Marty looked so streamlined and healthy that I couldn't believe he was the same person. Not only had he slimmed down, but his hair was no longer salt-and-pepper gray. It was an eye-catching streaked blond.

When I commented on the change in his hair, he teased me by saying, "Well, I thought you were a brunette." A kind of excitement was generated by our being so surprised about each other's appearance, I think.

We went to Junior's Restaurant on Collins Avenue in Miami Beach for coffee and dessert. Marty told me that night that he wanted to discuss my appearing at another of his theaters in Florida. I said I'd be glad to listen.

Two days later, he called me and asked me to meet with him at his office. He wanted me to appear at the Sun Art in St. Petersburg. After we went over all the details, we signed a contract for my appearance there. Then we talked for a long time.

After that, he started picking me up after my afternoon show each day, and we'd have dinner together. At dinner on that first evening, he said he wanted to stop by his house so that I could see a forty-by-sixty-inch picture of me hanging on the door of his bedroom. It was nothing unusual for a man to tell me such a thing. After all, thousands of my posters had been sold in the cities where I appeared. But this wasn't a run-of-the-mill poster, he assured me. It was a picture he'd had enlarged to life-size.

At his house, we stood looking at the huge picture together. It crossed my mind that any number of women had probably asked him to remove it, but I didn't bring that up. Then we walked back out into the living room and stood before the fireplace. I'd become increasingly fond of Marty, and I loved the attention he showered on me. In that moment, I could feel the electricity between us, and I knew what was coming.

He kissed me, a long and passionate kiss that left us as breathless and wide-eyed as a couple of kids. I wasn't prepared for the way the kiss affected me. My reaction was a complicated one, fueled by a powerful, irrational attraction as well as a strong measure of guilt. What was I doing? I tried to block out everything but the picture of my family in our home in California. I tried to focus on that. But it was as if a part of my mind was determined to block out the very thing I was trying to focus on. I was out of control. I couldn't say what I should have said, do what I knew was the right thing to do.

"God, I've wanted to do that for so long," he said.

"What took you so long to get around to it?"

"I wasn't sure how you felt."

"Now you know," I said, and we kissed again.

The warning bell in the back of my mind rang louder and louder, but I might as well have been deaf. My attraction for Marty was too strong. It bothered me that I could feel so helpless in his arms, but I simply couldn't resist. He took me by the hand and started to lead me back toward the bedroom.

"No, Marty, I can't. I've got a show to do."

"Oh, don't let that worry you."

I drew on all of the resolve in me to say, "Sorry, Marty, I've got to get back to the theater. Maybe . . ."

He relaxed and said, "Later? OK? I'll pick you up after the last show."

Throughout that evening, I danced while my mind dwelled on Marty and the relationship he so obviously wanted. Marty was an irresistible man. The chemistry was strong between us, and my desire for him was rapidly over-riding my common sense. The electricity that seemed to surge through my body when he was near or even when I thought about him frightened me. I had never felt this way before, partly, I guess, because I had never had so much to lose before. Certainly other men had been attractive to me. But with Marty there was an element of danger—I could lose my family, I kept thinking, my family—that attracted me at the same time it horrified me. Marty was a doting and sensitive man who made a change in lifestyles seem very attractive. Of course, I thought I had found the lifestyle I wanted. It was waiting for me back in California.

Before he picked me up that night in Miami Beach, I'd made a promise to myself that I would go very slowly, not let my emotions run away with me. It was a promise I would not be able to keep.

Marty was waiting for me after the 2:30 show, and we drove back to his place. I think he sensed my desire to go slowly. We sat on the couch and talked between gentle kisses. He told me he had to fly to Los Angeles for a couple of days and that he would miss me. He made one move to suggest that we move beyond the kisses and the talk, but I wasn't ready and he didn't argue with my resistance. We talked for a long time, and he finally took me to my hotel suite. He kissed me good night with a fervor that almost made me invite him inside, but I didn't. I needed time to think.

Why was I feeling so strongly about Marty? After all, I was back living with my husband and daughter, and I was happy. I had everything I wanted—money, a beautiful $150,000 home in Coronado Cay, my career was going well. I certainly didn't need Marty's money or his help to promote my career. I must have asked myself a million times while he was gone: Why? Why? Why? But even now I have no answer. No answer.

When he returned to Florida, he called and said he'd like to see me after the show. We went to dinner, I returned to do the two final shows of the evening, and then we went to his home. As soon as the door was closed, he kissed me long and passionately. Whatever was happening, my feelings were getting stronger and stronger. I knew I was out of control, which was always an uncomfortable feeling for me. I liked being the one in charge, the one who could take or leave the involvement if I needed to. But right now I was feeling powerless to change the course of events.

I still didn't understand why Marty Caplan had this unexplainable effect on me. I'd been romantically involved with some very powerful and immensely handsome men—movie stars, politicians, even a sheik. Why did Marty Caplan, whose name not many people would recognize, exert such a hold on me?

"I need you, baby," he said, "I need you right now." And he kissed me again. I felt my resistance melting. Very soon, we were making love, madly, with great passion. It was every bit as exciting as I had thought it would be, and when it finally ended, we lay in each other's arms cradled in a sea of dreams for the future. From that very first encounter, we had a wonderful intimacy. We confided in each other, talked, touched, grew closer than I could have imagined I would ever feel with another person.

"It was hard for you to make this decision, wasn't it?" he asked.

"What did you think? That I was easy?"

"No, of course not. I'm just used to having my way with women. They don't usually put up any resistance. But I know you have other people to think about."

It was a kind thing for him to say, but it also hurt to think about those other people. I must have looked too sad for the moment. He tried to lighten the mood.

"Do you know how much I wanted you just before I left for L.A.?"

"No, tell me," I said. It was important to know that he really wanted me.

"I wanted you so bad that I almost canceled the trip."

At the time it sounded right, like music to my ears. Later, I thought about what he was really saying. After all, he didn't cancel the trip. For ten years, I would waver, never knowing exactly where we stood. But at the outset I had no choice but to believe we stood exactly where I wanted us to stand— together. I had made my decision, or I wouldn't have been in his bed that first time.

Our relationship was always full of turmoil for me. First, it intensified so that I didn't want to go back to California and leave Marty in Florida. So, against my better judgment, because I knew it would finalize the rupture with my family,

I rented an apartment in Miami Beach. Marty went away on business, and by then I realized that he wasn't ready for the relationship I needed and wanted. I don't even remember what caused the breakup, but we remained apart for nearly five months. Almost from the beginning I understood that Marty wasn't ready for a wholehearted commitment. I also knew he had always been known as a womanizer. Still, I was committed, and I was willing to wait for him to feel the same way. Nonetheless, I wasn't ready to be stepped on or abused, and the volatile atmosphere of uncommitted love produced some difficult situations.

I had too much pride to ask Herb to take me back again, so I found myself alone after Marty and I parted. Finally, in October of 1975, he called from Dallas and said he wanted to see me. This is how deeply absorbed in the relationship I was: the sound of his voice over the phone rekindled every passion and desire a grown woman could muster. I could not get over how all-encompassing his hold on me was. He flew back to Florida a few days later, and we picked up our romance just as though we'd never been apart for more than a few hours. It's strange how one deludes one's self at such times. For some, it is fate or lack of discipline or just plain lust. For me, it was love, pure and simple. It was scary. I couldn't control my emotions, and such a discovery is frightening.

In Florida, I met three members of Marty's family—a sister, a cousin and a nephew. Altogether he had nine brothers and sisters. I finally met most of them in September of 1976. I flew to California between engagements in Pittsburgh and Kansas City. Marty met me at L.A. International Airport and took me to his home in Truesdale Estates in Beverly Hills.

I was looking forward to the time we had to share. I'd taken a month off just to be with Marty, and I was anxious for us to have a good visit, to grow closer. Imagine the shock I felt when we walked into his house. His family looked like a group of refugees from a sixties commune. They sat around the house like a bunch of zombies—unkempt hair, shabby clothes, and blank stares. But, despite their lack of drive and energy, they also conveyed an air of arrogance and superiority. They clearly did not want an outsider around, and I was definitely an outsider in their eyes. I began to suspect that one reason for Marty's womanizing was these relatives. They probably drove women away. Staying among these strange relatives of the man I loved, I soon found that the old saying is true: Just because you have money, it doesn't mean you have class.

There was definitely a lack of class here, and I was soon to face a cruel hypocrisy as well. When Marty was around and even when he wasn't, the entourage would be as nice as could be to my face, but let them get together when I wasn't around, or when they thought I couldn't hear, and then their true colors showed. I began to see through the facade fairly quickly, but it took me a long time to become distrustful enough to convince myself thoroughly that they were doing everything they could to undermine me in Marty's eyes. After all, they were his family, and he was devoted to them. I tried to see their redeeming qualities. They had none. When I heard them gleefully exclaiming about their success in "getting rid of" Marty's first wife, I knew I was in trouble. I said to myself, "I guess I'm next," and I wondered how they could be so cruel about the mother of Marty's only child, their nephew.

All their efforts to be civil—the peaches-and-cream conversations, the sweet-talking, and the polite conduct soon became transparent. They resented me. Marty was the brains and the manager behind a multi-million dollar business, and they were obviously afraid they might lose the "godfather" of the family to me. From the minute they decided I was the enemy, they were like an American Express card—we couldn't leave home without them. I began to find out about all of the undercurrents within this clannish, jealous family.

Once I overheard a conversation between one brother and the maid. They were so desperate to destroy my relationship with Marty that they tried to draw the servants into the conflict. He said to her, "We've got to get rid of Tempest."

Her response made me feel a little better. She said, "Why? She and Mr. Caplan love each other. They are good for each other, and they're very happy together."

"She's just not right for him," he said. "We've got to get her out of here, out of his life, before our brother's stuck with her."

You can imagine what it was like to try to have a relationship in that atmosphere. One of his brothers told me point-blank not to count on marrying Marty. I told him that he should leave that up to Marty to say. When I spoke to Marty about it, he brushed the comment aside by saying that that particular brother had always been sour on women. They were all hostile to me and did everything they could to make my life miserable.

Marty's sisters always seemed ashamed of the family business, although they certainly didn't refuse to enjoy the benefits that came from its profits. They seemed to have forgotten that two of the sisters had been strippers themselves. Once on a trip to London, Marty became interested in acquiring the American distribution rights to the Joan Collins film *The Bitch*. This was just before Joan Collins became a big star in this country. Her previous film, *The Stud*, had not done well in American release, and I thought Marty was making a mistake to get involved with the second film.

But he was a stubborn man, and once he got his mind set on a project, he didn't give up. After we got back to America, Marty asked me to help promote the film. I decided to give him all the support I could to get it released in this country, even though I had my doubts about the project's potential for success. As proud as he was, Marty was not above asking me to use my connections with Greg Bautzer, a

238

Beverly Hills attorney with many famous show business clients and one of my former lovers. I hadn't spoken with Greg in several years, and it felt a little funny to be calling on him for help. But I did get in touch with him.

He agreed to meet with Marty and to see what he could do to arrange a meeting with the proper people at Twentieth Century Fox. However, he said that since *The Stud* was not doing well in American release and was headed toward cable TV, a sure sign of commercial failure, the chances of the studio's wanting to get involved with *The Bitch* were not good. In Hollywood, you're always only as good as your last project. Joan Collins might have been big in Great Britain at that time, but, according to Greg, in the United States, she was box office poison.

I also called my friend Frank Sinatra and asked his opinion about Marty's plans. Frank agreed completely with Greg. This good advice didn't deter Marty from doing promotion for the film and spending $10,000 for a billboard at the Los Angeles airport. The billboard featured Collins in a merry widow and said, "*The Bitch* is coming for Christmas." When his family found out that he had a meeting set up with the Fox studios, they were thrilled — until they realized that it was through my connections, because of my help, that the arrangements were made. They could never appreciate my ideas or contributions.

Even with all the money Marty spent on posters, ads, and getting Joan Collins on the Dinah Shore show, the deal for *The Bitch* never panned out, and eventually Marty lost his option and a few hundred thousand dollars. But the incident sticks in my mind because of his family's reaction to my help. One of Marty's sisters complained, after she realized what I had done, that nothing I could help him with had any prestige to it. Did she think the family had a lot of prestige from being in the porno business? The whole thing made no sense to me, and when I complained to Marty about what a jealous shrew she was, it was obvious that he had taken an objective look at his family and didn't like what he saw. He asked me, "Do you think I could tolerate them if they weren't my family?"

The irony of Joan Collins's having become a huge star in this country only a few months after Marty's deal fell through is no greater to me than the irony of my being completely unable to please his family in any way. I wanted to pull out of that zoo and take Marty with me, but I knew he wouldn't give up the family business empire, nor could he leave without it. So he tolerated the situation, and realizing how much I loved the guy, I couldn't bring myself to leave either.

Gradually, I began to feel like I was in prison. There was no one to whom I could talk freely. It was like living in a commune, but without the love and peace and brotherhood and sisterhood that I thought came along with that sort of living. It soon became clear to me that Marty didn't trust his relatives. He had a tape recorder hooked up to the telephone in his Beverly Hills home that would activate to record all incoming and outgoing calls. The first thing every morning, he'd put on a pair of headphones and monitor all of the calls. I found it very puzzling that someone would tape family conversations, and it made me wary about what else might be going on.

Marty thought that I was so naive that I didn't know that the conversations were being taped, but I did, of course. My curiosity finally got the better of me, as I think it would have for anyone. After he left the room, I started listening to the tapes. I found out three things.

First, his family members were saying all sorts of things about me to undermine me and alienate me from Marty. They called me a gold digger and said I was just after Marty's money. When I tried to discuss these accusations with Marty, without revealing where I got the information, I learned that they also eavesdropped because his brother burst into the room, accusing me of lying.

Second, they were going through my closets when we were gone. I knew they were looking for something to use to turn Marty against me, but they didn't find it because there wasn't anything. Even though they were disappointed in their snooping, that didn't stop them from talking over the phone about my clothes and my other personal belongings. If I had been able to maintain a sense of humor, I would have laughed at the thought of their thinking about borrowing my clothes. How could you squeeze a size 14 into a size 6?

Third, I learned that my lover still was not committed to our relationship. Several of the calls on the tapes were from women that he was apparently still seeing. This was a crushing blow, but I tried to rationalize it. He was under so much pressure from the family. He might think differently than I did about commitment. I grasped at any straw. I didn't like it, but those were the conditions.

I'd really gotten myself into an unbearable situation, yet there were those moments, although rare, when Marty and I were completely alone, in our room, when he made me feel as if none of the rest of it mattered. Those moments were islands of happiness, a paradise unfortunately situated right in the middle of a dangerous, murky swamp.

Not long before Christmas of 1976, I was back in Miami and so was Marty. A few of his family members were always nearby, but it wasn't the Grand Central Station atmosphere of Los Angeles. When things had settled down in Miami and Marty and I had found a little peace, I wanted very much for Patty to join us, at least for a visit. But mentioning that to Patty was a mistake. She remembered her question to me as I was leaving the airport to go to Florida as well as I did. Now that she had my answer—I wasn't coming back—she was understandably hurt and resentful toward Marty. After all, he was the reason I wasn't there with her.

She was growing up and was quite capable of expressing herself explicitly. When I asked her if she wanted to come to

Miami, she said, "No, I love you, Mommy, but I want to stay right here with Daddy." She adored her father, and I should have known better than to press the subject. But I also knew that she loved and needed me, and I certainly loved and needed her. When I mentioned the fact that I did have custody of her, she said bitterly, "If you make me live with you, I'll hate you even more." I knew that it wasn't me she hated. It was Marty, the man who had taken her mother away.

I realize she was only ten years old, but I used to say she was ten going on thirty. That comment certainly had an adult sting to it. It hurt. I knew Herb had not told her to say any such thing. It came straight from her heart, the heart of my own bright little girl. There was nothing I could do except drop the subject, and we were able to talk fairly well about other things.

I had always respected Patty's intelligence and her maturity. I had always treated her like an adult in that I let her make her own decisions and encouraged her natural sense of independence. I knew how important it was for a young girl to grow up feeling that independence. Without it, she would be in too much danger of being exploited and manipulated. I certainly didn't want that for my daughter. But now that decision about how to deal with my child was painful because she was using her maturity and her independence to separate herself from me. I know that she had been hurt, I understood the defense mechanisms she felt forced to resort to, but I still grieved for the closeness that I had sacrificed to my great passion for Marty.

I went shopping the next day and bought her some very beautiful clothes and some other presents that I thought she would love. Marty bought her a gold necklace with a gold coin for a pendant. We wrapped them and shipped them to arrive in time for Christmas. The phone call I expected when the presents arrived didn't come. I waited, not wanting to push, not wanting to hurt her or myself anymore than we already had been.

A couple of months later, I called her.

"Did you get the presents?" I asked.

"Yes," she said and fell silent for a moment. Then she asked, "Is that all you could afford?"

Her question cut through me like a knife. I was speechless for a moment. I knew that she was really asking something else, lashing out in anger and frustration at losing her mother. So I decided to let the remark pass and change the subject. I made a bad choice, though, for my next question. I asked, "How did you like Marty's gift?"

"It's cheap, really cheap. You don't really care about me. You're just trying to buy my love."

Obviously, she was deeply hurt by my association with Marty and simply wanted me to come home to her. She blamed him for everything that had happened to our family, and she couldn't get directly back at him. I was the available target. But I had my own feelings, too, and I was not in the best of shape. What she said hurt. My face began to burn with embarrassment and anger, and I followed her example, dumping all my hostile emotions, none of which were her fault, on her, the available target.

"Well, Patty, I waited two months for you to say, 'Thank you.' Then I wondered if the presents had gotten lost in the mail. It was the saddest Christmas I've ever spent, because I didn't hear from you. I raised you better than that. You could at least have called to say 'Merry Christmas' and 'Thank you.' The presents aren't the important thing. Responding to the people who loved you enough to send them is the important thing."

Then I made the biggest mistake I ever made. Out of my hurt, out of my confusion about what I wanted and why I was living as I was, I said something I didn't mean and couldn't take back.

"You know where I am. If you ever need me, just pick up the phone and call me because I'll never call you again."

After I hung up the phone, I lay on the bed and cried for a long time. When Marty came in, he asked what was wrong.

"I just talked to Patty. We had a terrible conversation," I said.

He said, "Forget it. You don't need that problem."

I wanted to call her back, but Marty felt that we didn't need her between us, causing tension. Now I realize how absurd it was for him to suggest that my daughter could cause tension when he kept me trapped in the nightmare of his family.

After that conversation, it would be nearly ten years before I heard Patty's voice again. I began to block out everything about my life with her. It was too painful to remember, and I had no choice, I thought. I had created this situation. It was my choice, and now I had to find a way to live with it. The isolation from my daughter probably intensified my feelings for Marty. He was all I had now, and we had to make things work. It was a hard, dark time in many ways.

Hindsight allows us to see all sorts of ironies. I lost my daughter because I thought I had to respect her desire for independence. Yet here I was, bound to a man who couldn't love me as he wanted to because his family refused to allow him any independence. They could not let him be an individual. We finally got away from Marty's family long enough to take a two-week trip to Hawaii, one of two vacations alone we enjoyed in ten years together.

Never had Marty been so relaxed, so jovial, so loving. I wanted it to last forever, but all too soon we were back in the zoo. I had little choice but to tolerate it. Of course, I could have left him, but my love was much too strong to do that. The intensity and sweetness of the times when we could reach out across all the turmoil and hostility were so powerful that they kept me going, they held me there, through the bad times. I kept believing we could get to the place where all the times would be like those wonderful days in Maui.

In 1978, I gave up my apartment and moved in with Marty. All my friends questioned this decision. They knew what a negative situation it would be for me, confined to the same quarters as whatever members of the menagerie were around. They didn't want me to give up my only haven from the tension. It was a last shred of my own independence. But I saw the move as a positive one for my relationship with Marty. I felt that he was at last totally committed to our love. I felt he was making a statement to both the family and me. He wanted what I wanted.

All during our relationship, I was still performing at the top clubs and the demand for my act was greater than ever, but I started taking more and more time away from my career to be with Marty. Soon after I moved in with him, I left for an engagement at the Twentieth Century Hotel in Las Vegas. While I was there, we began having problems concerning other women. People in Las Vegas kept coming up to chat with me and talking about how surprised they were that Marty and I had broken up. I didn't know why they would be thinking that, since I had thought we were getting along better than ever, that our living together was a big step forward in our commitment to each other. Then they told me about seeing Marty out with other women. When I confronted him, we had an ugly scene and stopped talking for a while. He reacted in a way I'd never expected. He held a garage sale and sold all of the clothes and personal belongings I'd left behind in his home. When he told me what he'd done, I was finally mad enough to break up with him. I decided to get even: if he could have other women, I could have other men.

Clearly, my emotional health was in a precarious condition. It's not surprising, I guess, that I had an affair with a Las Vegas hotel owner who put me up in a penthouse at the Regency Towers during my stay there. When he heard about Marty's selling my clothes, he refurbished my wardrobe with designer clothes. He said a man should know a woman's needs without her having to ask. I appreciate a man who thinks that way, who has the sensitivity to be gracious. This relationship was never for a minute love in my mind. I knew it for what it was, good times but clearly a rebound from the breakup with Marty. I knew I was still in love with him, but I also knew that love was dangerous.

In August of 1979, Marty and I got back together. I was appearing in San Francisco under a good contract with the Mitchell Brothers Theater. It was a wise career move for me, and Art and Jim Mitchell treated me like royalty, providing every possible support for me. They furnished me with first-class accommodations at the Mark Hopkins Hotel, limo service, and a live drummer, Mark Rosengarten, who once played with Bette Midler. As the contract was extended from two weeks to five, then to an agreement for regular performances for a year, I moved into a lovely Knob Hill condominium. Marty called me while I was staying at the Beverly Wilshire Hotel in Los Angeles, and I agreed to have dinner with him and talk. He said he felt terrible about selling my belongings. To make it up to me, he flew back to San Francisco with me and took me shopping in some of the finest boutiques there. The spending spree may have been spurred by his trying to win me away from Engelbert, whom I had been seeing again, but at the time I took it as an expression of love and apology.

Working for the Mitchells and living in San Francisco had given me a new lease on life. I was happy, content, busy fixing up my condominium—I felt reborn, good about myself and my life. I began to be glad about my break-up from Marty; it was good riddance. To make the sense of finality clear to myself and to Marty, I wrote him a letter, explaining how I felt and enclosing a photograph of myself and Engelbert. I figured that woud be the end for sure.

But the picture didn't make Marty angry. It made him determined to get me back. Thus, his phone call, our meeting in L.A., and the return to San Francisco, complete with shopping spree. He swore to me that selling my clothes had been all his family's idea, which I could believe. But I told him that he should have stopped them. He agreed and apologized, and he asked me why I would have sent him such a cruel letter. I asked what he expected, how he would have felt in my position. He understood, and I believed yet again that we were finally on the right track.

Our relationship became more stable after that reconciliation, and I tried to spend more time with him. In 1980 I gave up my San Francisco apartment and moved back in with him, but I was already under contract with "Burlesque U.S.A.," which turned into a seven-month run.

Then, in December of 1981, Marty broke some news to me that was to alter our lives dramatically. We were walking along the beach, one of our favorite pastimes and one of the few opportunities for privacy that we had, when he said he wanted to tell me something, but he made me promise not to get upset.

I agreed, but panic was already seizing me. He said that he had discovered two lumps on his neck. He assured me that it was probably nothing, but he thought he should check it out to be sure. He also made it very clear that he did not want the family to know about this. I was not to discuss it with them at all, nor was I to behave in any way that would suggest the slightest thing out of the ordinary. I agreed because so much of what involved the family was stranger than this request, but I now realize that this was my first indication that the entire group, Marty included, had some very bizarre attitudes about sickness and death.

It turned out that Marty had cancer of the lymph nodes. He never used the word "cancer" around me, another sign of the strange phobia, but he became very ill. He kept going from doctor to doctor. He could afford the best when it came to medical care, and he spared no expense. His sister always went with him. I wanted to be the one to accompany him to the doctor, but he wouldn't hear of it. He was an extremely proud man. I know it was awful for him to have to depend on anyone, but he was adamant that I wouldn't see him in circumstances that might make him appear weak or inadequate. He would not have the woman he loved be a part of the disease that had taken control of him. He put up a good front, and I never told him that I knew he was dying. I thought that was the least I could do for him, but it meant that I had to suffer alone. I had no one to confide in, to share my fears and grief with. Marty's sister-in-law Jan was a sympathetic ally in the midst of all the trouble, but she, like me, was always an outsider. She suffered some of the same problems I did at the hands of the family.

The entire period of his illness was filled with secrecy and denial. He underwent his first surgery for cancer in April of 1982, and not until September of 1984 would he agree to undergo chemotherapy. One reason for his going to so many different doctors and hospitals was his constant belief that the ones who told him bad news must be wrong. He kept looking for the one who would tell him what he wanted to hear.

In 1982 Bob Feldman, Marty's doctor in New York, came to visit Marty and me at the apartment Marty had asked me to have Mitchell Brothers arrange for us instead of the suite where I had been staying. The visit was pleasant, and I didn't feel any particular concern about Marty's illness. He had told me after his surgery that the tumor was benign, and I had no reason to doubt that.

When Dr. Feldman returned to New York, he phoned me and told me he thought there were some things I should know. He told me about the malignancy, and he said that Marty must have chemotherapy if he was to survive. I found myself in the terrible position of being unable to confront this horrible truth. I couldn't confide in Marty. With him, I had to pretend I knew nothing. Although Jan Caplan knew what I was going through and was always willing to listen, I found myself slipping into the same pattern of denial Marty persisted in.

In 1984, he bought a new house in Hallandale, Florida, just before the family's annual spring trek to the Catskills. My concern for him was mounting daily, and I wondered why he was buying a new house if he was dying. But that too was probably part of his denial. He said he wanted me to stay in Florida while he went to the Catskills. He wanted me to help decorate the new house. At this point I was willing to do anything that would make him happy and encourage him to keep battling.

I threw myself into the task of making the house absolutely beautiful, especially the master suite for us, and that helped take my mind off Marty's condition. I turned down all engagements to make that house a special place for him, a place that I hoped would make him happy. I'm sure that my urgency about the decorating was my own way of denying what was really happening. I certainly gave no thought to what my abandoning my regular performance schedule might mean to my own future. I was living for Marty, and he was living for this house. That's the way I thought about it, and I could think of nothing else.

I stayed busy picking out the materials for the drapes in the master suite and selecting furniture. When Marty and his family came down for the Jewish holidays in September, they were able to walk in and live there. Everything was perfect.

By then, Marty was very sick. He told me in the bedroom one night that he was going to Pittsburgh to a special doctor.

"I'm going with you," I said.

He was a dying man, but he still couldn't admit that to me.

"No, you're not," he said firmly.

"Marty, I'm going."

"You're not going to Pittsburgh with me," he said. I could see he was getting upset.

"Why?"

"Just because, by God, I said so."

"I love you so much, and I want to be with you, especially when you're seeing these doctors. Please let me go."

His stubborn pride would not let him accept my help or my comfort. I didn't want to upset him, so I gave up on my going with him and suggested that he take his sister

"She's not going, either. No one is going with me. Can't you understand that? No one!"

He left the next morning for Pittsburgh. I stayed at home and waited for him. I tried to carry on as usual, but I had no one to turn to, I couldn't talk to Marty about what was really happening, I wasn't working, in short, I had no way to be myself. I was getting swallowed up in this nightmare of Marty's illness. The situation inevitably began to take its toll on me. I became nervous and depressed and went to a doctor myself. He listened to my story. Then he told me that if I didn't make a dramatic change in my lifestyle that I was going to be a very sick girl. He was convinced that my physical and emotional problems were directly related to stress. But I could see no way to reduce that stress. The tension was only going to get worse because Marty was only going to get sicker.

Marty decided to fly from Pittsburgh to Los Angeles to see another cancer specialist. I stayed in Hallandale. We talked every day, but I was miserable being in the same house with his family without Marty. He understood what was happening to me. At one point, he said, "I just don't know whether you can take my illness and the way my family treats you. That's what I'm worried about. I don't want anything to happen to you."

"I love you and want to be with you. It's as simple as that. If you want me out of your life, I'll pack my things and leave right now, and you'll never hear from me again. But it will have to be because you want it. I'm where I want to be, and I'm staying till you tell me to go."

"No, honey, that's not what I mean. Don't do that, don't leave me. I love you, and you're my only inspiration. I just don't want you to suffer or be unhappy."

At that moment, he sounded very tired, like a little boy who was lost and lonely. I couldn't keep the tears from my eyes as I told him that I loved him and wanted to be with him. I knew we couldn't be together forever, but I wanted to be at his side and live every day that he had left to the fullest.

On a Thanksgiving trip to California in 1984, I noticed that Marty's hair was coming out when he brushed it, but he denied this. I woke up one morning to find him trying to sweep it under his pillow with the hairbrush. In less than a week, all of his hair was gone. I still played his game, pretending that I didn't know that he was taking chemotherapy.

When all of his hair was gone, he didn't want to go downstairs where the others were. I knew this galled them. There was nothing they wanted more than to see me gone. Instead, I had their "godfather" all to myself in our bedroom. And, despite the circumstances, I liked doing things for Marty so much that I wouldn't even let the maid assist me in caring for him.

I tried to cheer him up in every way I could. I'd put a rose on his breakfast tray to get him to smile, and I told him that the sexiest men I knew were bald. He started putting on a hat to go downstairs. In fact, he became so attached to the hat that he'd put it on first thing in the morning and sometimes he'd fall asleep at night with it still on his head.

His family was heavily into their own denial game. They swore that Marty's hair loss was the result of a bad dye job he'd had. But whatever the explanation for the loss, they weren't willing to accept a bald brother or to make him feel good about himself. One of his sisters went out and bought him a cheap hairpiece for fifty dollars. God, it looked awful!

I could tell that he felt self-conscious and uncomfortable, so I tried to make him more secure. I suggested that we go see a friend of mine who could make him a really beautiful hairpiece, one that would make him feel like his old self again. But Marty took my remarks the wrong way, thinking I wouldn't like him without a fancy hairpiece. He forgot I was the one who had said bald men were sexy. He just said he didn't want to waste the kind of money I was talking about.

I stayed with Marty through the holidays. Just before Christmas, my agent called.

"Tempest, I've got you a marvelous engagement at the Reno Hilton," he said.

"Listen, I'm not interested. Marty is really sick, and I want to stay with him."

"You need to get back in the business," he said. "People really want to see you. Do you know how much you've worked this year?"

I thought about 1984. "Not much," I said.

"That's right. Exactly three weeks. Come on, Tempest, take this job. It's a great opportunity, and it's only four weeks."

I turned him down and hung up the phone. Marty had been listening.

"What are you thinking, honey?" I asked.

"If it's only four weeks, why don't you take it?"

"I want to be with you. I'm staying with you because you need me."

A week passed, and the agent kept calling. Marty encouraged me to take the contract. Finally, on the Saturday night before the show was to open on Tuesday, I agreed to return to the stage at the Reno Hilton in January of 1985. I kissed Marty good-bye and told him I'd see him in four weeks. My heart was breaking because I so wanted to be with him, but I hoped my doing as he asked and taking the engagement would let him know that I believed in our future, had confidence the he would get well.

Something really magical happened in Reno. The Rainbow Cabaret was a perfect setting for me. I was a instant success, and all my love for dancing and for entertaining people

surged forward from those dark recesses where I'd been
surpressing it. The devoted attention I was receiving there
contrasted sharply with the hate and distrust Marty's family
had shown me. The pleasures of success washed away the
unpleasantness of the rejection by Marty's family.

But I missed Marty. We talked just about every day, and he
came to Reno to see me on February 23. But, as always, he
was accompanied by two of his brothers. The only privacy
we had during his visit was while we were in bed.

Marty had gained some weight, and he put up a good
front. But I could tell that his energy level was low, so low
that I was frightened. He did enjoy the show, and he was
proud of me and the wonderful response I got from the
audience. Still, I ached inside when I imagined the pain he
must be in.

"Darling," I said, "I'm going to go home with you."

"No, baby, I don't want you to do that," he argued.
"You're doing fantastic here. They love you, and I think this
is the best place for you while I'm getting well. Don't worry.
I'll be all right."

"But I've told you a thousand times . . ."

"No, no. I insist. You stay here. I'll be all right."

I knew him too well to argue with him, and I certainly
didn't want to create any additional stress.

We reminisced about a 1983 trip to Hawaii, our one other
solo vacation, and Marty promised that we would build a
home on Maui, a real home, for just the two of us, no family,
nothing. That way, he said, we could have what we wanted.
We could live quietly and well, travel, do whatever we
wanted. And we could always be together. We made plans to
be married.

Even as I listened to his dreams, I felt a bitter sense of
irony. He was saying all the things that I had felt for so long,
and now it was probably too late for us to realize our
dreams. Just when we both knew exactly what we wanted,
the time for us to enjoy it was running out. I was afraid.

I knew that Marty loved me and that he understood what I had sacrificed for us to be together. I had given up my family, my precious daughter, for him, and now, at last, he was ready to make that same sacrifice. I knew this was a huge step for him. His overwhelming and, I think, finally destructive sense of obligation to his family came from a promise he made to his mother on her deathbed. For him to be ready to leave them behind and marry me was a hard decision for him to make. But he had made it.

I had also sacrificed much of my career to our relationship. Even though my current appearance proved that I could still draw and please crowds, there was no way to calculate the financial effects of all the time I spent away from performing. For Marty to move to Hawaii with me, it would be necessary that he give over much of the control of the family's business to others, another hard decision that he had already made. It did my heart good to see that the commitment I'd longed for had finally come. Of course, if Marty didn't get well and we didn't marry, I was pretty sure his family wouldn't remember any of the signs that he had made these decisions. I was in a vunerable position, and I knew it. But I could only trust in the power of our love. The two of us understood everything.

I held tightly to him and prayed that what he was dreaming would really happen. I said, "Oh, please, don't let anything happen to you. What would happen to me? What would I do?"

He placed a finger over my lips. "Haven't I always told you that I'd take care of you?"

I could only trust in that.

We stood there in a close embrace for a long time. I felt his weakened body and wished I could pass some of my strength to him. But that was impossible, of course. Then again, he was down to the point that only the impossible, only a miracle, could save him.

The Hilton picked up option after option. The four-week engagement stretched into months.

In April of 1985, Marty returned to Hallandale and doctors there immediately sent him to Dana Farber Cancer Institute in Boston. When he called and told me about his hasty trip to Boston, I figured the end for him was near. And I felt like I was dying, too.

I canceled reservation after reservation to go see Marty in Boston on my day off. That I would be with him for only a few hours didn't matter to me, but he was still putting up the front, still insisting he'd be well, and I felt I had no choice except to go along with him. He absolutely forbid me to come every time I suggested it during our telephone conversations. He said that my coming there and seeing him would only make him feel less of a man. He had never wanted those close to him to see him down, and he wasn't about to change now. When all other arguments failed, he'd insist that he was going to be all right and accused me of overreacting. I tried to understand his mood, even though I longed to be at his side.

In his calmer moments, he talked again and again about buying that condominium in Maui, about our marriage and our finally being alone together. He said we could find peace and privacy in Hawaii. He promised over and over that everything would be all right, that he would take care of me, of everything. And I closed my eyes and prayed to God that he would.

My own health grew progressively worse as uncertainty about Marty's condition and my own future, should he really die, weighed upon me. The man I loved was dying. He wouldn't admit that to me, his family hated me, I was thousands of miles away and he forbade me to come to him—I couldn't handle the stress. On two occasions my doctor hospitalized me for treatment, and it was my own fragile condition that made me postpone having Patty visit after that joyous phone call in April. She kept insisting that I should let her come, and I kept saying that she should wait until I was feeling better. I didn't want her first image of me in ten years to be a negative one. I was at an all-time low, and I didn't want her to know.

Thank goodness I had raised an independent child. She came anyway, saying that I needed her and that was when she should come, not when everything was perfect. When I first saw her come through the door, I beamed. She was a beautiful woman of twenty-one. But then I broke down. The sight of her brought back the image of that ten-year-old who had pleaded for assurance that her mother would not leave her. All the guilt and agony of my separation from her, all the emotions I had denied for ten years, flooded into my heart, and I could not face myself or her.

She cried with me, we held onto each other, and for the first time in ten years, I felt that I had a real ally, a friend who could share my burdens. She was the thing that saved my life.

During Patty's visit, I called Boston shortly before Marty's sixtieth birthday. I asked to speak to Marty, but his sister said he didn't feel like talking. She knew that I always sent flowers to him on special occasions, but she told me not to bother wiring them to Boston for the birthday because they were moving Marty to a hospital in Canada. I checked on the Canadian hospital she'd named and found out there was no such hospital and no such doctor as the one she had mentioned.

Meanwhile, Marty's son, Larry, who had just returned from Europe, called me to find out where his father was. I gave him the number of the Boston hospital. When he called, the family told him that his father was much worse and that they were taking him to Pittsburgh. When Larry phoned back and told me that he had found out that they had never been going to Canada at all, Patty and I began talking and she suddenly said, "You don't think he might already be dead, do you?" Of course, she hated to say anything so harsh and shocking, but I understood immediately what she was thinking. Marty's family was so obsessed with my not knowing about his condition that they were willing to lie to anyone, even his own son. Larry didn't find out until he reached Pittsburgh that his father was already dead.

I was sure that Patty's suspicions were a real possibility, so I had my psychologist in Reno, Dr. Jerry May, call the Boston hospital. He was told that Marty was dead. Then I found out how truly cruel his family could be. They barred me from the funeral and refused the flowers I sent. Only because the florist checked back with me and let me know that the bouquet couldn't be delivered did I know that they had been so hateful. On the phone his sister had raved about how beautiful the arrangement had been and how much they all appreciated it and the long letter I'd sent along with it. I didn't even know where he was buried until my attorney obtained a copy of the death certificate.

I wound up in a hospital on three different occasions as I tried to cope with the loss of my lover and the cruel refusal of his family to acknowledge my right to mourn him and to be considered one of his survivors. Only Patty's love and her brave statement that I had her to live for pulled me through.

Marty's family stooped to one more sorry act. They boxed up some of my things from both homes and shipped them to me. The items weren't packed. They were thrown together like garbage. And they never allowed me back into either house to pick up anything, even though there were some personal items that were missing. The contents of those crudely packed boxes are all that I have left from the ten years of devotion and love that I put into my relationship with Marty Caplan. When I was well enough to return to the Hilton after three weeks, I was starting out again with little more than I had had when I walked into Lillian Hunt's office all those years ago. Somehow it didn't seem fair.

In the months that followed, I never used the word "comeback" to describe my performances onstage or coping with my emotional problems offstage. More than a comeback, it was survival, pure and simple. I put my heart and soul into my work, which had always been the best cure for me, and I spent a lot of time—and money—with my psychologist, Dr. William Danton, to whom Dr. May referred me. I'm convinced that he and Patty are responsible for saving my life. I remember Patty's saying, "It is better to give one smile for the living than fountains of tears for the dead," and I guess I've taken that as my motto for my future.

After playing to packed houses, we closed the long-running "Sugar Daddies" in April 1986, and I took two and a half months off while producers built another show around me. It was called "Hot and Stormy," and it played before packed houses until November 15, 1986.

I shall never forget the staff and management at the Hilton. They treated me like the star I was and like a friend. They knew I was going through one of the most difficult times in my life, and they did everything they could to ease my pain. I learned that I had a large, extended family who were more than happy to open their hearts to me.

As we closed that show, I marked my thirty-sixth anniversary in burlesque. I was miles away from my beginnings, yet I felt good enough to believe that there were other days ahead, happier days. I felt that I might still realize all of the dreams I started out with.

# Epilogue

In March of 1987 I went home to Georgia. It was the first time I'd been in the state since 1971 and the first time I'd visited Eastman in thirty years. I walked around town in amazement at how small everything looked, as if the whole town were shrunk down to fit in a picture book. When I went there as an child, I truly believed that Eastman was a city. Everything seemed huge, larger than life, intimidating to a young girl off the farm. Now, as an adult who had seen much of the world, everywhere I turned, I saw a landmark of my childhood, and I would have sworn they were all less than half their original size.

All the years of blocking out my life in Eastman seemed to disappear. I was reminded of my roots, and I took stock of the things that had happened in the passing years. I'm convinced that many of the insecurities I've felt during my life began in Eastman, and those insecurities directly contributed to the failed marriages and the other problems in my relationships with men. Growing up afraid, ashamed, and unable to confide in anyone may also have contributed to my satisfaction in playing the part of the vamp. After all, the vamp never gets hurt; she doesn't take that chance. Instead, she controls others and their reactions, and she can always call a halt to the game when it suits her.

In 1973, when my stepfather died, I finally told my mother about the events that led up to my running away all those years ago. When I visited her in Eastman in 1987, I realized that she had always been a beautiful woman, that she liked makeup and pretty clothes as much as I did, and that she would have understood my dreams and frustrations better than I gave her credit for when I was growing up. I also realized that she, too, had been a victim of my stepfather's abuse and that she had had no escape from the violence and the psychological cruelty that I had been able to leave behind.

Talking with her, I felt like the child in the old story. That child leaves home at fourteen, say, as I did, convinced that his parents are the dumbest people on earth. When he returns home, after having experienced the outside world, he finds that the parents have somehow miraculously acquired all the wisdom they were lacking before his departure. I see now that my mother was a much wiser and much stronger woman than I gave her credit for years ago, and I'm sure that I could have benefited from that wisdom. She might have surprised the young Annie Blanche Banks. She might have taken my side and consoled and protected me.

There's no way to know such things, of course. But it is possible to remember such lost chances and to take advantage of advice and concern in the future. It is also possible to use patience and understanding ourselves and to share with our children what we have learned so that our mistakes and unhappiness do not repeat themselves in the lives of the ones we love most.

Returning to Eastman also brought back memories of my early marriages. They were, I'm certain, the product of my immaturity and my desperate desire to escape my stepfather and the harsh realities of my home life. The problem in my marriages to Rural Giddens and Jack Locke was that I didn't really want to be married to them or to live the life they offered me. I was too busy dreaming of the life I had created for myself out of movies and magazines. I wanted romance, but it had to be Romance, with a capital *R*, Hollywood romance. Rural and Jack both had better attitudes and intentions about marriage than I did at the time. Their only mistake was not recognizing the dangers of marrying a teenager with stars in her eyes, stars put there not by them, but by a world they had no access to or desire for.

I now know that those dreams that led me away from Eastman and away from those two decent men come equipped with all sorts of pitfalls and treacheries that the young Annie Blanche Banks never imagined. When I attained fame and fortune, when I became a star of burlesque and traveled the world, loving wonderful, famous men and seeing sights that truly were the oversized, mythic visions that I'd so foolishly thought Eastman to be, I also soon found myself a victim of my own success.

Once I'd worn minks and diamonds, once I'd sailed on luxury liners, attended glamorous parties and dined in the world's finest restaurants, once I'd worn the most beautiful creations of the world's designers, I found it impossible to turn away from those things. Burlesque gave me what I'd dreamed of having, but it didn't give me the deep, lasting satisfaction that I guess I had assumed would come along with the things.

I wish I had been able to break away. I wish I had been willing to risk everything—money, glamor, cars, travel— everything, to gamble on the move into acting or singing. But, somehow, I didn't have the drive it took to persist, to follow up on the smallest opportunity, the slimmest lead. I could not be a starving actress, a poverty-bound aspiring singer. Then, too, fairly quickly after I became financially successful in burlesque, I was married, with bills to pay. I had to work to keep up the lifestyle my work had given me, and I always seemed to wind up in marriages or love affairs that drained my finances as well as my emotions.

When I look back on the money I have earned and spent, on the gifts that have been lavished on me by men who looked for every way they could to spend their money on me, I am amazed. I certainly don't mean to suggest that I have lived in poverty since leaving Eastman. I know what poverty is. What I am saying is that the truly amazing thing is how ephemeral wealth and possessions turn out to be. They *are* dreams, in that you always wake up, and if you haven't been careful, if you haven't prepared and saved against that awakening, you have to begin your pursuit of the dream all over again. It is a vicious cycle.

Another thing that amazes me as I look back is my belief in romantic love, the real thing, the right man. I still believe that he's out there for me. I still believe that true romance is possible. My faith in this idea just won't die. I don't know why. I've certainly experienced evidence to the contrary.

My experience with Frank Engle is typical of my problems in attaining the love I believe in. Frank was involved with the Bryan and Engle burlesque circuit. In 1956, we met, and he treated me wonderfully, showering me with beautiful gifts, culminating in the seven-carat, emerald-cut diamond that he gave me when he proposed. He sent me to Priscilla of Boston to have my wedding gown designed, and we planned a huge country club ceremony.

My New York agent Dave Cohen was not enthusiastic about the match. He warned me that Frank was not divorced from his wife. When I confronted him, he showed me what he said were divorce papers. I was in love with him, the papers looked official enough, and we went ahead with our plans, despite my advisor's doubts.

I should have been suspicious when Frank refused to show me his home in Newton, Massachusetts, but I wanted so badly to believe in the relationship and in my chance for happiness that I refused to doubt him, no matter what the evidence to the contrary. Ed DeVere, my press agent, drew up a press release on our engagement and wedding plans, and when he sent it to Frank so that he could check it for accuracy, Frank gave his okay to the announcement and to the press conference that Ed wanted to call.

Imagine my humiliation and disappointment when Frank, who had agreed to be at the press conference, failed to appear. When he told me that his parents were ill, I tried to be sympathetic, but it was hard. After all, I had been the one to face the reporters and photographers alone. Still, I persisted in my optimism.

All my hopes and dreams came crashing down around me when his wife came into town. All the rumors had been true. He had never obtained a divorce. So, instead of a wedding, I found myself involved in a lawsuit for breach of promise and damages for loss of work. Crushed once again, still I remained a believer. When I walked along Eastman's streets thirty years later, several broken hearts later, I was still a believer.

I continue to have hopes of finding the right man, of having the kind of relationship that means love and security that will last a lifetime. My relationship with Marty Caplan taught me that even the strongest and most devoted love cannot flourish if there is not security also, both emotional and financial. I also know that real love, the kind of love I'm looking for, would not separate me from my daughter.

I know that my relationship with Marty damaged my relationship with Patty, just as I know that my being in show business made it more difficult for me to be the kind of mother I would like to have been. My own stubborn pride also got in the way of repairing the damages that my love and my career caused. But, as the old saying goes, your daughter is your daughter for life. Patty and I are closer than we've ever been, and I am blessed by a future that will allow us to make up for the hard years, the years apart. Seeing my own mother again and realizing how much I had missed with her, largely without cause, made me even more determined that Patty and I will do better. We will know and love each other. We will not be separated again.

My trip back to Eastman also renewed my sense of family responsibility in another way. For the first time, I learned, from my brother, of the sometimes frightening impact my life and my career had had on those I left behind. I had never considered that what I did in Los Angeles or San Francisco or Las Vegas would create trouble for anyone in Eastman.

As we drove around town on my visit, my brother Leonard told me about the town's reaction to the *National Enquirer* story about my marriage to Herb. He said they did everything except burn crosses in our front yards. Whether or not the stories were true was immaterial to the citizens of South Georgia. All that mattered was that somebody had said that Annie Blanche Banks had married a black man, and her family was sure going to know what people thought of that news.

Nobody deserves that kind of grief. My family may not have been the richest or the most influential in Dodge County and Eastman, but they were and are good, decent people. They should not be held accountable for my life. My brothers are strong and handsome and gainfully employed. They are going about the business of making lives for themselves. My sister Gloria carries on the beauty and dignity I saw in our mother, and my niece and namesake, Tempest Greer, is a beautiful young woman that anyone would be proud to call family.

I regret that my career has caused my family in Eastman or Patty any pain or embarrassment, but I could never regret that career. Being in Eastman again, seeing those shrunken buildings and those tiny streets, made me understand all over again what it was I was running from. I wanted to leave behind a world of small possibilities and fading hopes. I

wanted to find a world of sweeping probabilities and dazzling fortunes.

Burlesque put me into that world. It gave me money, and
no one can make it in this world without those all-important
financial resources. I'm a pragmatist rather than a romantic
in this area. When I entered burlesque in 1950, where else
could a woman earn the kind of money I earned? As a singer
or an actress maybe, but certainly not in the business world.
There just weren't female corporate executives in 1950. And,
if there had been, they wouldn't have been large busted and
poorly educated girls from Eastman, Georgia, with crooked
teeth and serious emotional scars.

By the mid-1950s I was making $3,500 a week. That kept
me in elegant furs and dazzling burlesque costumes. A
$1,000 negligee, a $500 rhinestone-studded G-string were
nothing to me; I bought such things without batting an eye.
But I also managed from time to time to send money back
home to Eastman. When Leonard and I were driving around
Eastman, he pointed out a house and said, "We lived in that
house for a while, and it was really nice after living in those
old houses out in the country. But we couldn't have afforded
it if you hadn't sent us money."

My money also helped educate Patty at good schools, the
best. Any time that I look back and wonder where all the
money went, I can think of Leonard's comment about the
first nice house he'd lived in and I can remember my bright,
gifted daughter, and I'll know that some of it went for things
that will last.

I also believe I have made contributions to my profession
that will endure. I have always held myself to the most exact-
ing professional standards. I have rehearsed, I have surrounded myself with top-notch choreographers and
musicians, I have never allowed my personal struggles and
my private life to detract from the fantasy and illusion that
people want to see acted out when they watch me dance. I
have always worked to provide a touch of class in my per-

formances, whether the stage was in Carnegie Hall or in a small club. Many burlesque dancers burn out quickly and resort to vulgarity that leads to a second-class act. I have refused to do that. Instead, I am constantly using my imagination and creativity to develop an act that is both first-class and original. Maybe this is where the romantic and the pragmatist in me meet; maybe this is the key to my longevity in a business noted for quick flashes of notoriety and fast-forgotten faces and faster-forgotten names.

The great names of burlesque still endure. Gypsy Rose Lee. Sally Rand. Lilly St. Cyr. I'm proud that mine will be added to that list of enduring legends, that Tempest Storm will be remembered as a true superstar of burlesque.

I'm equally proud that I still believe in the future. My life is far from over. When I look ahead, I see the possibilities of other accomplishments, new relationships, and deepening ties with the people I love. I am wiser now, I have lived many of my childhood dreams, I have learned from the mistakes of my past. But I am still a dreamer, still a believer in the potential of the person I am. I can't know what the future will bring, but I do know that the future can be a place of sweeping probabilities and dazzling fortunes. It can also be, I hope, a place of deep contentment and lasting happiness. I'm certainly willing to take the chance.

# Acknowledgments

I would like to thank the following people for their help and support:

Herb Jeffries, who has become my special and dear friend after all these years; Jack Rosenbaum, Herb Caen, Ralph Pearl, Joe Delaney, Forrest Duke, and all the other people in the press who helped make me a star; Morey and Kay Amsterdam, dear friends who helped me through the loss of Marty Caplan; Dr. William Danton, who brought me back from the twilight zone, and Dr. Jerry May, who helped show me the way back to reality; Dr. Stanley Thompson, my cardiologist and dear friend; George and Patty Soares; Larry Lewin; Henri Lewin; Bob and Pat Dee; Bob Sheldon; Barron Hilton; the staff of the Reno Hilton, for their crucial support; Richard J. Moore; Tom and Pat Edwards; Terry Burden; Bradley Edwards; Dalton and Inez Gautreaux; my dear friend Audry Pinto; Lue Thompson; Jess and Dorothy Mack, my agents who have booked me all these years; LeRoy Griffith, a good friend who was always there in times of need; Art and Jim Mitchell; Phil and Lorraine Olsson; Gene and Darlene Pond; Anthony and Olga Fernicola; Woody Woodbury; and Nathan Cohn. To my family, I extend my deepest thanks and love. And I want to acknowledge Marty Caplan, whose memory is with me still.

I would also like to thank the staff at Peachtree Publishers, Ltd., for their confidence and support.